One For the Earth:
Journal of a Sierra Club President

————————— ❧ —————————

Susan D. Merrow
and
Wanda A. Rickerby

SAGAMORE PUBLISHING CO., INC.
Champaign, Illinois

Printed on 100% recycled paper.

We have made every effort to appropriately acknowledge ownership of all copyrighted photos. We will be pleased to make any necessary changes in future printings.

Production supervision
   and interior design: Susan M. Williams
Production Assistant: Brian J. Moore
Cover and photo insert design: Michelle R. Dressen
Editor: Sara Chilton
Marketing Coordinator: Katherine K. Dressel
Proofreader: Phyllis L. Bannon

Printed in the United States of America.

Library of Congress Catalog Card Number: 91-98423
ISBN:0-915611-52-x

To all the volunteers, who sacrifice their time, energy, social lives, job advancement opportunities, dining room tables, and family harmony to work for a clean, sustainable environment in which nature and humans live in peace; to the paid, unpaid, and poorly paid staffs of tireless organizations, who go into the fray time and time again against the big guns, armed only with the strength of their convictions; to anyone who ever loved a special wild place and pledged to save it from harm—we salute you, and we thank you for the privilege of counting ourselves among you.

———————————————— ❧ ————————————————

Contents

Acknowledgments

We would like to thank our families, friends, and the patient, helpful staff of the Sierra Club in San Francisco and Washington, D.C., for bearing with us during the writing of this book. Special thanks to Bob Howard, Annie Merrow, Arthur Merrow, Mike McCloskey, David Rickerby, Sarah Wade, and Kayden Will, each of whom pitched in when we needed it most.

S.D.M.
W.A.R.

Preface

─────────── ❧ ───────────

This grand show is eternal. It is always sunrise somewhere; the dew is never dried at once; a shower is forever falling; vapor is ever rising. Eternal sunrise, eternal sunset, eternal dawn and gloaming, on sea and continents and islands, each in its turn, as the round earth rolls.

— John Muir

By his word and example, John Muir did as much to keep the round earth rolling—and its natural systems intact—as any environmentalist in history. When he wrote these words, however, he probably could not have foreseen that the sun would never set on the organization he created.

But then, that band of a little over one hundred people who were the first members of the Sierra Club thought they were coming together to protect and preserve just one spectacular mountain range, the Sierra Nevada. What they began that May 24 of 1892, however, would live to reach a hundred years in age, and count over 600,000 people in its ranks. The Sierra Club today numbers its accomplishments not only in terms of landmark laws passed, but most especially in wild places saved and resources protected. Our predecessors would recognize those victories right away, for they were savvy lobbyists as well as ardent outdoors people.

For one remarkable year, I had the chance to serve as the fortieth successor to John Muir, as President of the Sierra Club. This honor did not come to me like a bolt from the blue. It was the culmination of years of grassroots service to the environment and unstinting labor in the trenches of the organization, starting at its most fundamental local level.

As it happened, that year that I was President, May of 1990 to May of 1991, was one of the most exciting and one of the most alarming in environmental history. The threats to our fragile earth—global warming, ozone depletion, deforestation, species annihilation, overpopulation, air and water pollution—had reached proportions that worried people from all walks of life.

On top of all this came a war and all its attendant environmental calamities. Perhaps as a result, the peoples of the world began to realize that the natural systems on which all life depends are indeed hostage to human behavior. Renewed levels of activism turned the quest for natural resource protection into a potent political force.

During that exciting time, I became the engineer who drove the powerful engine of a huge and complex organization. It was my job to scout down the track, to watch the gauges, to stoke the fires when necessary—and sometimes to let off the steam. It was the most demanding, exasperating, exhilarating, and stimulating experience I ever expect to have, but it didn't come without a cost. I had to put the rest of my life on hold and ask my family to take second place to the needs of a much larger and sprawling family of environmentalists. A noisy, quarrelsome, hyperactive family they could be, too.

It was not a small price to pay, but one I would have paid again in a minute if the bylaws allowed me the chance to continue. It kept me going to know that all over the country there were people—selfless, tireless people—giving their time, their social lives, their souls for a cause we shared. I kept faith with them and still do.

Some years ago, I was asked to speak at a symposium about what it takes to be an environmental activist. I polled my friends about the criteria. One of my dearest friends said, "That's easy. You just can't be a self-centered, comfort-loving introvert."

That was certainly true. Yet during my year as President, I saw expressions of environmental concern from all sorts of personality types. There are few people left who don't take global warming, destruction of the ozone layer, fouled drinking water, smog, and oil-covered beaches personally.

Environmental damage has caught the attention of the self-centered because it is, in fact, already decreasing our quality of life—our "comfort" levels—and even the most self-effacing have been moved to speak out. I took one year of my life and made it "one for the earth." The rewards I reaped were enormous. This book is the story of that year.

Susan Merrow
East Haddam, Connecticut

Introduction

———————— ❧ ————————

I have been an environmentalist all my life, but when I worked at it full time—as Administrator of the United States Environmental Protection Agency under President Jimmy Carter and, earlier, as Commissioner of the Connecticut Department of Environmental Protection—I worked from inside the government. It was my job to push the buttons of bureaucracy so that government responded to the incredible things we were learning about mankind's destruction of the ecosystem, the very same ecosystem upon which our existence depends.

In that capacity I was able to observe the process by which human beings have become aware of the threats posed to our earth, have organized themselves to change basic behaviors, and have institutionalized those changes in all branches of government, including the courts. I know a good many people who wring their hands and prophesy doom. They do not believe our species has the intelligence or the self-control, or the gumption to do what is necessary to sustain human life on this planet. I am not one of those people.

It was my good fortune to meet Susan Merrow and Wanda Rickerby early in my career. I served as Commissioner of Connecticut's practically brand new Department of Environmental Protection in the 1970s. Citizen activists in Connecticut had convinced lawmakers to create the department. Now they were demanding laws for the department to enforce. One of the country's first bottle-return bills was enacted after two years of strategy sessions in the offices Sue and Wanda shared near the Capitol. A model clean water act, coastal management, inland wetlands protection, preservation of agricultural lands, solid-waste planning: they fought for them all. And won.

Later, as a member of the Carter Cabinet, it was my pleasure to meet and work with dozens of other citizen activists who were almost as enthusiastic, charming, and savvy—and almost as stubborn—as these two women. Now, all over the world, human beings are uniting to demand clean water, pure air, rational energy policies, open space, the protection of pristine lands. Their enormous successes come as no surprise to me. I knew from my encounters with Susan Merrow, Wanda Rickerby, and their many friends in Connecticut how powerful the voice of the people can be. Nor was I surprised when mutual friends told me that Susan had gone on to one of the highest offices an environmentalist can achieve. "Of course," I thought. "Who else?"

Just how does the human race go about saving itself from its own suicidal tendencies? From what I have observed, the process works something like this. First, scientists point out a specific weak point in the ecosystem. A recent example of this is the warning from the National Aeronautics and Space Administration that we are on the verge of creating another big hole in the ozone layer, this time over New England. Similarly, twenty years ago, scientists described the beginnings of our food chain in salt water marshes and called for an end to the filling-in of those lands for the sake of high-priced seaside resorts.

In both those cases, and thousands of others, educators and the media then spread the word until enough citizens heard and began to voice their concerns. Elected officials in the legislative and executive branches of government will almost always respond when the people who vote for them become agitated about a problem. In the early years of the environmental movement, when the lawmakers didn't respond, citizens went on to seek protection in the courts—and a whole new branch of law was created.

The critical link between knowledge and action is public concern, effectively expressed. There are plenty of environmental heroes in state and federal legislatures these days—but I wonder how heroic they would be without the knowledge that the Sierra Club, the Audubon Society, Greenpeace, the League of Conservation Voters, and dozens of others like them are out there watching? More than watching: writing newsletters, making phone calls, circulating petitions, testifying at hearings, marching in protest. If we are, indeed, going to preserve our fragile planet, it is to these stalwart souls that the credit must go.

In *One for the Earth*, Susan Merrow tells the story of how she, as one person, dedicated one year of her life to the proposition that mankind can create a natural environment that will sustain life for generations to come. Her book is an exciting history of a year that, because of the Gulf War, was pivotal in the environmental movement. It also tells us a good deal about the life styles, values, and ethics of the women and men who are leading that movement.

What I most enjoyed in this book, however, were its descriptions of the professional and technological heights that the "tree-huggers" have achieved. As President of the Sierra Club, Susan Merrow was at all times hooked up electronically with 250 other leaders across the nation. Whether in San Francisco or Connecticut, she knew within moments what was happening in Congress. She gave interviews that were made available, via satellite, to every major television network. She brought Indians from the Amazon jungle to compare experiences with Indians in the Arctic wilderness. She staged press conferences in the heart of an international summit meeting. She consulted with experts in marketing, public relations, demographics and opinion polling, all so that the Sierra Club might remain honed and in tune with changing trends.

By herself, Susan Merrow cannot save the Earth. But acting in concert with the 620,000 other members of the Sierra Club, the millions of organized environmentalists in the United States, and the vocal "green" movements that have sprung up on every continent, she certainly can. With their leadership, and their example, I firmly believe that our planet will be preserved.

Douglas M. Costle
Woodstock, Vermont

Foreword

────────────── ૨**&** ──────────────

We face a time of unparalleled challenge and rare opportunity. Through our own neighborhoods to remote villages, across continents and seas, the global environment is virtually screaming for attention, providing startling signals of disaster and devastation. Scientific findings of an ozone "hole" opening over our heads in North America— bringing massive increases in dangerous ultraviolet radiation for the first time over heavily populated areas—is only the latest in an increasingly long list of environmental warnings the Earth itself is providing.

- Increased emissions of carbon dioxide and other greenhouse gases are fueling increases in the Earth's temperature, which foreshadow catastrophic consequences.
- Forests are being destroyed at one and a half acres per second, and with them thousands of species that can never be replaced.
- Each day, almost 40,000 children under the age of five are dying from hunger and malnutrition caused in significant part by environmental devastation.
- We continue to generate waste in the United States at a daily rate more than twice the average body weight of every American.
- Dead dolphins wash up along the Mediterranean coast, their immune systems weakened by too much pollution. Within the last few years, several million starfish washed up over miles of the White Sea, thousands of seals washed up on the shores of the North Sea, and our own children dodged hypodermic needles washing in with Atlantic waves.

It's beginning to resemble what the comedian A. Whitney Brown called, "A nature hike through the Book of Revelations."

It's past time we paid attention and took action—as individuals, as families and communities, as states, and as nations. Just as the first Earth Day did in 1970, two years ago Earth Day 20 focused the world on this environmental challenge. From our homes to our schools and businesses, from state houses to national capitols, the world seemed poised, eager to act.

This year, as world leaders prepare to gather at the first-ever Earth Summit (the United Nations Conference on Environment and Development) in Brazil, we are once again reminded of not only how far we have come, but how much farther we must go to ensure the protection and survival of the world's environment.

In this historic time, Susan Merrow has provided leadership, vision, commitment, and courage. The victories we can celebrate in protecting the Earth's environment are her victories, the result of tireless energy, selfless dedication, and tenacity. *One for the Earth: Journal of a Sierra Club President* offers a thoughtful, insightful, and inspiring view of just how difficult this challenge is to all who step forward to meet it. Moreover, it provides a rare glimpse behind the headlines of the people who move policy, and of one extraordinary woman who is a leader in this fight. Susan Merrow's story reminds us all that we can make a difference; that a problem that seems too large to even be understood, can be solved.

I have come to believe we must take bold and unequivocal action: We must make the rescue of the environment the central organizing principle for civilization. Whether we realize it or not, we are now engaged in an epic battle to right the balance of our Earth, and the tide of this battle will turn only when the majority of people in the world become sufficiently aroused by a shared sense of urgent danger.

Adopting a central organizing principle—one agreed to voluntarily—means embarking on an all-out effort to use every policy and program, every law and institution, every treaty and alliance, every tactic and strategy, every plan and course of action—to use, in short, every means to halt the destruction of the environment and to preserve our planet.

The ecological perspective begins with a view of the whole, an understanding of how the various parts of nature interact in patterns that tend toward balance and persist over time. But this perspective cannot treat the Earth as something separate from human civilization. We are part of the whole, too, and looking at it ultimately means also looking at ourselves. And if we do not see that the human part of nature has an increasingly powerful influence over the whole of nature —that we are, in effect, a natural force just like the winds and the tides—then we will not be able to see how dangerously we are threatening to push the Earth out of balance.

Senator Al Gore
Washington, D.C.

May 1990

In May 1990, government officials, businessmen, and ordinary citizens all over the world were still trying to evaluate the meaning of the outpouring of concern for Mother Nature that they had witnessed the month before — April 22, 1990, the twentieth anniversary of the first Earth Day.

On that date, 326 million people in eighty-two different nations had participated in concerts, teach-ins, festivals, and cleanups — all designed to draw attention to the need for environmental protection.

"Never in the history of this globe has there been such a crescendo of concern for its well-being," said Denis Hayes, one of the principal organizers in the United States. Earth Day 1990 had indeed signalled a new and worldwide recognition of the need for conservation of natural resources and the abatement of pollution.

Events in the preceding year had brought vividly home the need for environmental protection. In March 1989, the tanker Exxon Valdez had run aground off the Alaskan coast, spilling more than 10 million gallons of crude oil into Prince William Sound. The resultant enormous destruction of wildlife habitat had angered citizens the world over, yet the legal battle over who would pay for the damage threatened to last for decades.

In the Soviet Ukraine, frightening new statistics were emerging from the city of Pripyat about the after-effects of the April 1986 nuclear disaster at Chernobyl. More than 600,000 people, including 250,000 children, were now acknowledged to have received high doses of radiation. They would need periodic check-ups for the rest of their lives. A two percent increase in cancer rates was predicted for the group.

Perhaps worst of all, in November 1989 at a seventy-nation conference in the Netherlands, atmospheric scientists declared that the threat of global warming was not only valid, but fast approaching. Despite international support for the group's conclusions, the United States refused to support reduction measures and called for further study. Subsequently the Bush administration was successful in keeping Congress from linking foreign aid to reductions in the use of chemicals that contribute to the so-called greenhouse effect. On May 1, 1990 in a speech at Harvard University, Budget Director Richard G. Darman declared that the United States should not abandon economic growth to clean up the environment, saying, "Americans did not fight and win the wars of the twentieth century to make the world safe for green vegetables."

Legislative leaders were more protective of natural resources. In a proposal hailed as "the single biggest step Congress can take to curb global warming," the U.S. Senate in April introduced the so-called Bryan Bill. Sponsored in the Commerce Committee by Senator Richard Bryan (D-NV), it required car manufacturers to increase the average miles per gallon achieved by their new cars from the 27.5 mpg currently required to 40 mpg by the year 2000. Backers of the bill estimated that this would cut in half the amount of carbon dioxide emitted in the lifetime of each car on the road. Carbon dioxide, the most prevalent greenhouse gas, backers said, accounts for 49 percent of global warming.

In the House of Representatives, the battle over clean air legislation reached a fever pitch. The Bush administration's bill, HR3030, actually weakened existing law by crippling enforcement and citizen-suit provisions. Environmentalists were determined to see the bill's provisions strengthened before it came to a vote at the end of May.

ॐ

I suppose there may still be people who think that environmentalists are a bunch of little old ladies in tennis shoes. They would quickly lose that notion if they watched a national Sierra Club election. With a total budget of over $50 million, and a lobbying network that ties in 620,000 members in every part of the country, the Sierra Club wields enormous power, and the election of its leadership is taken very seriously.

I had been elected to the Board of Directors of the Sierra Club by popular vote of the entire membership, nationwide — but officers of the Board are selected by its fifteen members, campaigning and voting among themselves. I had worked my way up through the Board leadership, becoming the so-called fifth officer, then the Vice-President; now, in 1990, I was running for President. My opponent, Freeman Allen, was a chemistry professor from Pomona College in California. He had a formidable record as an environmental activist, and he was campaigning hard against me for a seat we both were determined to win.

If I won, I would be — out of the forty-one Presidents in Sierra Club history — only the third woman and the first person from the Northeast (I'm from Connecticut) to attain that honor. While I was well liked by the board members, I lacked the direct, forceful style of a man, and I knew some people were saying I was "too nice." How do you fight that kind of allegation, by demonstrating your nasty side?

Also, I was known to be very concerned with process. *How* we would get where we were going was my specialty, not *what* we were getting to. Sierra's history is full of leaders who gave their lives to a particular issue. Their passion and their zeal carried the day, saved the mountain, stopped the dam, and so forth. These days, issues are more complex, less amenable to a bluff, single-minded approach.

Anyway, the truth is, I *am* nice. But I am also tough — and in twenty years of Connecticut politicking I've gained enough savvy to know how to deal with whisper campaigns, even when they appear benign. I spent most of April making long-distance calls, having heart-to-heart talks with members of the Board, urging key Board members to support me and to campaign on my behalf.

I never said a word against Freeman. I stood on my record of twenty years of service, with more than a few wins in hard-fought environmental battles — and I urged them to give me their votes because I was uniquely suited to pull our club's stragglers together and to light a fire under them. The election was scheduled for the evening of May 3, 1990, as the culmination of a two-day retreat. The retreat was held at a rustic nature center, on a ranch on the Pacific coast, about an hour north of San Francisco, in Bolinas, California.

The fourteen other Directors checked in at various times on Wednesday and I tried to greet them all. I wanted a personal, eye-to-eye moment with each. My chances seemed good, but these people are enormously proud of Sierra's volunteer system. They demand top quality from anyone who aspires to be the top volunteer, and they like to test the mettle of their candidates. I moved my gear into the bunkhouse, stubbornly determined to pass any tests they might present.

The ranch was secluded, set in the far end of a box canyon, and the scenery was lush. In New England, our green hills have an immediacy, an almost intimate quality. Here, great vistas of distant mountains and nearer rangelands blended into a checkerboard plaid of tans and dark greens. The strange shapes of eucalyptus trees dominated the horizon, with the purple blossoms of ceanothis accenting the landscape's peaceful beauty.

I had been allotted time after dinner Wednesday night to explain why I should become Sierra's President. I prepared to play my cards boldly. I knew that these "friends" were probably the toughest audience I would ever face. Friendship and shared goals would count for little as they measured me against the job I sought.

The Sierra Club is an action-oriented environmental organization, with an annual budget for central operations exceeding $35 million. When chapter monies are included, the total budget tops $50 million. The Club hires qualified professionals and maintains busy offices in both San Francisco and Washington, D.C. — but its strength is in its volunteer members. Fifty-seven chapters nationwide, many with their own paid staff, work on local problems and form a vigorous grassroots lobby. There are also seventy-four national level committees, working on specific concerns. The national organization provides coordination, and tries to give the grassroots the up-to-date information they need. It is one of the most effective environmental groups in the world.

I was asking to sit on top of the pyramid for a year, to be at the place where the buck would stop. It was an awesome responsibility, not only from the inside — keeping everyone marching in the same direction — but from the outside, as the living symbol of one of the country's oldest environmental organizations. I would have to learn to talk in sound-bites, be ever concerned with image, and still retain the kind of sincerity that would elicit the faith and trust of the membership — a membership whose life philosophy might well be summed up in the two-word bumper sticker: Question Authority.

I remember the scent of dusty air, the faintly medicinal odor of eucalyptus, that filled the room as I stood up to make my case that night. I told them I respected the job, I respected our members and our staff, and I respected my own ability. I promised I would put in all the time and travel the job needed (knowing that few women — or, for that matter, men — could make a similar pledge). Then I asked for their votes. When I sat down, I felt I had given a good speech. When my opponent spoke, I noted with satisfaction that they gave him no more applause than they did me.

The next day I tried to put the election out of my mind. We were getting ready for the big annual Board meeting, to be held in San Francisco on May 5-6. The Board meets six times a year, but the May meeting always has hundreds of members in attendance. I was too busy ironing out kinks in the agenda to worry very much about my personal popularity.

Two items were high priorities for me at the San Francisco meeting, and I wanted to "prepare the soil" for them while we were still in Bolinas. The first was the commitment of nearly a quarter of a million dollars in support of state-level lobbying (i.e., getting good environmental laws passed at the state level, not just at the federal level). Lobbying was the way I earned my living. I had seen first hand the need to "raise the floor" under federal law — by toughening up state law — so that the men and women of the U.S. Congress would know their constituents were behind them when they voted for tougher environmental regulation.

Consider, for example, the California tailpipe emissions standards. Far more stringent than federal law, these state regulations resulted from California's terrible smog problem. And they stood alone, a standard for the rest of the country, until 1988, when the Governors of nine northeastern states signed an agreement to begin raising their tailpipe standards too. Now the pressure from western and eastern states was squeezing federal decision makers, and we were starting to see action in Washington.

If such pressure worked on tailpipe standards, I reasoned, it would also work to protect wetlands, to eliminate combined storm and sewer systems, and in dozens of other ways. I chaired the committee that nurtured the proposal for two kinds of grants to state chapters, and a new central office coordinator to keep the program moving. It offered more carrots than sticks — because I believe that is the best policy when dealing with Sierrans — and it was the biggest new program the Club had considered in some time. It was coming up for a vote that weekend in San Francisco, and I was working hard to guarantee its passage.

I lobbied less for the second item on my private agenda, but it too was based on personal experience. In twenty years I have traced many a natural resource disaster back to its roots. They are almost always found coiled around dollars, embedded in the economy, and fertilized by those whose investments depend on maintaining the status quo.

A multitude of environmental resources are vulnerable to development interests, especially wilderness (be it tropical rainforest or ancient temperate growth), wildlife habitat, wetlands, and endangered species. The Sierra Club's International Committee, protesting the loss of Brazil's rainforest, had not failed to note that the World Bank was about to loan $167 million for a project in Rondonia (a section of Brazil about the size of Oregon), where earlier road building had already caused deforestation, mercury contamination, illegal logging, and violent conflicts among colonists, indigenous people, and large landowners.

The arguments that our internationalists put forth first educated and then convinced me of the global ramifications of international development finance. Also, I have to admit, it pleased me to see concerned citizens look beyond local problems and commence a sophisticated campaign that confronted big-money interests in their private preserves. I was determined to see that Sierra gave this effort a high priority.

For the most part, my fellow Board members agreed with the items on my agenda, but that agreement was not something I would ever take for granted. Environmentalists are mavericks. If they didn't take such delight in thinking for themselves, they probably would be somewhere else, making more money and having less fun. Sometimes, though, some of them make being a maverick into an art form. Tedious as this may be in an individual, it can be a rich source of strength for the movement; I try to cherish it.

On this occasion, though, there was agreement. At 8:00 p.m. on Thursday, May 3, 1990, voting in secret ballot, my fellow directors chose me as their new President, for a term of one year. When the vote was announced, I found myself feeling not smug or satisfied, but very humble.

As soon as I could get away from the well-wishers, I found a secluded telephone and called my husband. He and my daughter had flown to San Francisco that day and were waiting for me at the Richelieu Hotel. We had talked about this eventuality a thousand times, but it was a reality now and I wondered how Arthur would take it. I was about to become a half-time marriage partner. Would he really go along with it?

I certainly didn't find out from that phone call. Arthur was deep in the throes of jet lag.

"You're talking to the President of the Sierra Club!" I told him. "I won!"

"Ummmph," he grunted, and lapsed back into sleep.

The next day the entire Board of Directors drove down to San Francisco. I was still hoping to get a few quiet moments with Arthur — for my own peace of mind as much as for his — but, throughout that busy day, there simply wasn't time.

The Sierra Club's national headquarters in San Francisco is located in a roomy old rehabilitated brick warehouse on Polk Street. The four-story building has a slightly battered air and, come to think of it, so does the neighborhood. If that building could talk, I think she would tell us, in a whisky contralto, that she has seen it all, but has come through the experience with her jauntiness, if not her innocence, intact.

I had been in the President's office on the top floor hundreds of times, but now it was mine. I was about to begin an existence where I would live in a farmhouse in Connecticut and work in an office in downtown San Francisco. Awed by that thought, I went to look at the corner room with its bare brick walls and waist-to-ceiling multipaned windows.

What I saw was familiar: beige industrial-grade carpeting, a loving cup with antlers for handles, dated 1909, a sofa, an easy chair, and an imposing walnut desk. I looked out the windows at the back side of the Mitchell Brothers Theater, a local strip joint, made more famous by the colorful murals that cover its outer walls — murals that have nothing to do with what goes on inside. Whales, dolphins, and porpoises had been recently painted over with elaborate tropical forest scenes. I took that, not as a specific message to the Sierra Club, but as a reflection of popular concern to which I had better be sensitive in the year to come.

I walked over to stand in front of my desk — my desk — and studied the five-foot, gold-framed oil portrait of John Muir that would be looking over my shoulder now whenever I worked. On the other, nonwindow wall, forty identically framed photographs of previous Presidents also seemed to stare at me. I gulped and closed my eyes briefly — and in that split second, I swear it, one of those portraits whispered, "Don't blow it, Susan." When I opened my eyes, however, Muir returned my gaze stonily, without the least hint of concern.

John Muir, who founded the Sierra Club in 1892, always got out of San Francisco and into the mountains as fast as he could. He would be surprised, I thought, to find himself in such an ornate frame, and so permanently fixed in an urban spot. Since I, too, was going to be fixed here for much of the next year, I vowed to hold myself open to any advice or encouragement he — or any of the others — might offer me from those walls.

How I got to this place was a story in itself. I grew up in Massachusetts and spent many of my summers on the Maine coast — a very magical place. There was a wildness there of great importance that I hoped would never change. My sense of this made me ripe for the plucking by the environmental movement.

Arthur and I are veterans of the first Earth Day back in 1970. We know that the natural beauty we value is finite. I guess what motivated me to get involved in the Sierra Club was the feeling that not only the natural beauty, but the world's essential resources were being destroyed, and that somebody had to do something about it.

I had no notion of getting as involved as I now found myself. I didn't think I had that much to offer. We received a notice about a local group meeting, and we decided to go and see what it was about.

After that meeting, I think we volunteered to bring cookies to the next meeting. Then we volunteered a little more. Pretty soon, I began to keep the group records.

By 1979 I was involved in state committees, and was elected to the National Club Council. In 1984 I was asked to run for the Board. It was a classic case of if you never say no, there's no limit to where you can go. I kept accepting offers and requests as they came up.

Now here I was, President of the entire Sierra Club — and it was not the only part of my life that had gotten both richer and more complex. Thirteen years previously, to the day, I had given birth to my only child, Annie Merrow. She is willowy, wise beyond her years, and the delight of my heart. I often tell people that she is the product of a lifetime of benign neglect, but the truth is that Annie and her father are the center of my image of myself.

Now Annie was waiting for me downstairs — and I took her birthday as a challenge. Since the Board's annual meetings always come on the same date, I had missed being home with her on this important date for ten years straight. Arthur claims that, as soon as she was able to reach above the counter, she began making her own birthday cakes. Now I was determined that I would have a wonderful first day as President and that she would, by God, have a wonderful birthday.

I was very lucky throughout my term as President. All the people in the Sierra Club always wanted me to succeed (even Freeman Allen, my opponent for the presidency, eventually became a good friend) — and so, it seems, did Arthur and Annie. At any rate, that first day, hectic as it was, gratified everyone. It ended at a small private dinner, an annual event for Trustees of the Sierra Club Foundation and Directors of the Club. The dinner, unlike most Sierra events, is rather elegant, held in a fine hotel. I guess that is because it includes the Foundation Trustees. They are a dignified lot — bankers, publishers, and successful business people. Dessert that night was chocolate cake, accompanied by a thirty-voice choir singing, "Happy Birthday, dear Annie."

"That was scrumptious cake," Annie whispered sleepily to me in the cab going back to our hotel, and then, "Who needs candles?" Was there a wistful note in her voice? Damn these maternal guilt trips; would they never end?

The annual meeting of the Sierra Club is one big wing-ding. In 1990, when I first took charge, it was held in the Ballroom of the Marines' Memorial. The huge room — decorated with highly un-Sierra-like heraldic devices — contained nearly two hundred people. The Board of Directors sat at the front, at tables organized into a hollow square. Microphones made it possible for the members to hear the decisions being made.

I suppose I have attended five dozen of these meetings over the years. However, I had never been in charge. I always had the time, while others were speaking, to think of what I would say next. This was a luxury no longer available to me. It was as if I had been handed the controls of a 747, or thrust in front of a symphony orchestra. I had no flight plan. I didn't know the score. Everybody wanted to speak. Everybody played to the audience. It was my responsibility to keep things moving, to be fair to all, but to quash frivolous debate, and bring action items to a vote.

I began seeing things in vivid new ways. One discussion seemed to me about to drag us all down an open elevator shaft. I tried to slam the doors. I saw signs that a Director was getting ready to throw a verbal hand grenade. I managed not to call on him by never looking in his direction. Later, one of our more outspoken members released a barrage of complaints and accusations. I remembered another officer saying, on another occasion, "She just wanted to let loose a bunch of mice and watch us scramble to catch them." Smiling broadly, I managed to throw a net over her "mice" before the others took offense. When it came time to debate the state lobbying proposal, I handed the gavel over to my recent opponent, Freeman Allen. I had no intention of being neutral on this one.

Freeman did a great job. If he was disappointed with the election, he was far too much of a gentleman to let it cloud an important issue. The Club passed the resolution handily, and I resumed the chair. The weekend was a blur of meetings, executive sessions, and a huge banquet. Eventually it was done. Evidently I landed the 747 neatly; everyone seemed pleased.

Arthur and Annie had left for home on Sunday afternoon. She had school and he had work the next day, and a country to cross to get to them. Bleary-eyed, desperately tired, I caught the cursed midnight "redeye" — with its changeover in Chicago so that no real sleep is possible — back to Hartford. That entire weekend Arthur and I had exchanged perhaps six sentences, all in front of dozens of other people.

In my East Coast incarnation, I earned money by lobbying at the Connecticut state capitol for two clients, Common Cause and the Connecticut Clean Water Coalition. On May 7, the General Assembly was in its final frenzy. A proposed law that would fund our state Department of Environmental Protection by allowing it to keep part of the fees it collected was still to be passed. Afraid to miss any opportunity to persuade lawmakers of the desperate need to pass that bill, I went straight from the airport to the State House. It was 9:30 a.m. when my plane touched down, 11:30 p.m. when I finally headed for home and family.

The rest of that week is blurred in my memory, but three things stand out. First, a *Hartford Courant* photographer tracked me down in the state capitol and took me outdoors to pose. When he first appeared, I assumed he wanted the Senator I was talking to — but he ignored the politician. My picture and a teaser about the story of my election was on the front page Tuesday morning, with a more detailed story inside. What a kick!

Second, in both the state Senate and House of Representatives, they halted the proceedings while — to my complete surprise — two of my favorite legislators called for a "point of personal privilege." Each of them then made a charming little speech about all my good works in Connecticut and "now, the nation," and introduced me as if I were a celebrity. The lawmakers — those men and women I had spent my life persuading — all rose and applauded me. I had come back from California feeling like royalty, but the instant immersion in state environmental struggles let me know I was still just Sue to the folks back home. Now for a brief moment, they let me be royalty again. Double kick!

The third thing I remember clearly is that on Thursday night, after a very simple supper, I finally got to talk to my husband. Sure enough, he was having some misgivings. But they were not along the lines I expected. Rather than pound his chest and demand his share of my time, Arthur seemed genuinely proud of me.

"You know me," he said. "I don't have the time or the inclination to do what you do. I wouldn't want to be President of the Sierra Club for any amount of money — but I do get a lot of pleasure out of hearing you talk about the places you go and the politics involved. Your job adds a dimension to my life that I value."

What was bothering him was money. The presidency is not a paid position and, because it is so time-consuming, it precludes any other paid job. In theory, all expenses are reimbursed — but the previous weekend had convinced Arthur, a hard-working United Technologies engineer, that we could be swamped by the little extras that go with traveling — a paperback here, an expensive snack there, taxicabs and tips at every turn. I made a vow of frugality; swore that every expense would be recorded and turned in to my new secretary; reminded him that, while there was no salary, there was a provision for limited replacement of lost income.

"I don't know, Susan," he said. "It's a great opportunity, but it's going to be tough on all of us, especially you. Where does it take us as a family? Is there a goal — and is the goal worth all the aggravation?"

"*Now* you ask me?" I wanted to shout back at him, but that is not the way our marriage works. I kept my voice level and tried to be honest.

"It means constant travel, which I will enjoy," I said. "It means having a staff to help write my speeches and type my letters, which, after years of licking stamps at mailing parties, I will love. But most of all it means I can accomplish something worthwhile. I did a good job as Vice-President, and I want the chance to be in charge.

"I run around," I added, "giving speeches that end, 'There is a planet at stake.' I really mean that, and this is my big chance to see what I can do to help save it."

Arthur's sigh spoke volumes. I knew he agreed with every word I said. I knew that I was asking him to take on responsibilities that should be shared: the home fires, care of the animals, and, most of all, helping Annie through her first year of high school. I also knew that he saw himself as carrying a very big financial burden, especially with Annie's education stretching ahead of us, and that he feared losing control of it.

I moved over to the arm of his chair. "Give me a year," I said, "and I'll come home and get such a high-powered job you'll be embarrassed by our riches." Arthur's body relaxed. He laughed. "As if I had a choice," he said.

What a week that was! Flowers, telegrams, calls of congratulations from all over the country. I loved it. One of the best parts was hearing from so many old friends in the Connecticut environmental movement.

I had been feeling guilty about them since Earth Day. The Advisory Committee to the state Department of Environmental Protection had instituted a separate, tax-exempt Earth Day Twenty Committee to organize a statewide celebration. I was a member but, because I was busy campaigning for the Sierra Club election, I had not worked as hard as I felt I should have for them.

Nevertheless, I had found time to criticize them publicly about taking corporate money gifts.

Our statewide committee had been a bit too willing, in my opinion, to accept funds from corporate polluters. On the national level, with my support, the Sierra Club had set up a special committee to screen potential donors. Perhaps we were not 100 percent accurate, but we tried hard not to accept help that could give aid and comfort to blatant polluters or scofflaws.

Actually, on that score, the big industries were wary. They saw the flaw more clearly than the Connecticut committee leaders. Thus, when the *Hartford Courant* ran an exposé, there were relatively few companies trapped in the newspaper's net. I felt I had been proved right—but that's not always where you want to be when your best friends are on the other side.

I felt very strongly that the recent Earth Day 1990 hoopla— unless we kept our heads on straight—could make us overconfident. Also, I believed the Earth Day emphasis had been too much on personal life styles and how they had to change. Important as that is, it is not enough. There is danger in allowing "kitchen solutions" to soften the pressure for citizen action at the policy-making level.

Public policy is made in Mayors' offices, and state legislatures, and Senate Committees. If such people don't hear from their constituents — loudly and clearly — then all the recycling and ride-sharing and pesticide-limiting in the world will not be enough.

Not that I spent Earth Day disapproving of what others were doing. Far from it. I served on the Connecticut Earth Day Twenty Committee, and wrote a mission statement for them that was widely reprinted. It said, in part:

> "While victories alone would be cause enough to celebrate the twentieth anniversary of Earth Day, there's a much more compelling reason. The next twenty years will bring us face to face with environmental problems so far reaching and so challenging that we could hardly have imagined them twenty years ago. Unless we act now to reverse the trend toward the rapid depletion of resources, we will cause life-threatening social and climatic changes on a global scale. Our children will inherit a hostile and alien environment.

"We must galvanize the next generation, not just in this country but around the world. We cannot just pass a torch; rather, we must light millions more. The spirit of Earth Day, the feeling that together we can make a difference, must continue. . . ."

At the national level, the Sierra Club launched Earth Day Twenty with new public service announcements on global warming, via the network news and on "Entertainment Tonight." The 800 telephone number we included in the PSAs received 8,500 calls in the first week. We also joined the national Public Interest Research Group (PIRG) in gathering hundreds of thousands of signatures on cards that demanded a strong Clean Air Act, to be sent to the U.S. Congress. As a result of these responses, we believed that we had lighted a substantial number of new torches.

Nevertheless, I continued to harbor the fear that the very popularity of the environmental cause would lull people into inaction — an unthinkable turn of events when we had a Clean Air bill to push, and an occupant of the White House whose campaign promise to be the "environmental President" had yet to materialize.

As Sierra Club President, I would be deeply enmeshed in making the whole sprawling mechanism that is the Sierra Club function smoothly. I would have to find a way to keep the excitement of Earth Day alive throughout the year.

I wanted the same for my Connecticut peers. It felt especially good, therefore, when these cherished colleagues called. One of them put it bluntly: "Sue, in bad times we fight with our enemies; in good times, we fight with our friends. Let's rejoice that these are good times!"

On May 13, having buttoned up the state legislature and spent nearly forty-eight hours catching up on home laundry and other domestic duties, I returned to San Francisco. In my years as a member of the Board of Directors, I had formed the habit of staying at an inexpensive but very commodious hotel, the Richelieu, not too far from the Sierra office. It doesn't have spectacular architecture, or room service — but neither does a wakeup call there mean that it's time to feed the livestock and bring in the eggs, as it does at home. I have no responsibility for the clean sheets on my bed, and I'm provided with an unending supply of dry towels.

I returned to it now — thinking that possibly this was the way swallows feel on first picking out the familiar steeples of Capistrano — and then checked in with Michael Fischer, Sierra's Executive Director.

Without the furor of an annual meeting, without the fuss of an election, I hoped to pick up the reins quietly and try out my new relationship with Michael. We were now the twin heads of the Sierra Club, and it was vital that we work well together. Technically the President outranks the Executive Director. In reality, however, if they don't combine into one chief executive officer, then the functions they represent — professional staff and dedicated volunteer — may become dangerously divergent.

Michael had arranged for the two of us to attend a seminar put on by the American Society of Association Executives. Serendipitously, it dealt with elected volunteers and paid staff and how they best work together. The two days we spent at that seminar helped me from then on to picture us as two equally essential halves of one complex unit. Michael might be a paid professional, but I represented the consensus of our members, expressed through a series of elections, and we both wanted to work out a responsible way to share the power we held jointly.

I stayed in San Francisco for about a week. My new staff helped me clear an in-box that was choked with administrative problems. What a luxury to have a secretary, a speech writer, people to fold and stuff mailings, somebody else to edit the newsletter. Someone complimented me by saying that few Sierra Presidents take so quickly to letting themselves be staffed. I laughed. "I have been waiting all my life," I said, "for this kind of help!"

On May 20, I flew home. I had been teaching a series of adult education classes at an adult learning center outside Hartford, and I still had two to go. Also, I was the chair of a political action committee, ELECT, and a meeting was coming up. ELECT works to get state legislators with a demonstrated environmental commitment elected. We raise money though an annual "goods and services" auction. This year I had bought a hand-painted T-shirt and a hayride for eighteen people. I had donated three pounds of homemade candy and a truckload of horse manure (always a popular item at these auctions). I needed to make arrangements for delivering the manure and to invite some friends to the hayride, so there was a good deal of telephoning to do.

I have to admit, though, that most of that week, my heart and head were in Washington, where The Clean Air Act was on the front burner.

People get excited about wild animals. They quickly see the need to save a tree, a forest, a river, a bay, even a swamp. They get angry when they come upon land defiled by waste. But it's hard to get them stirred up about clean air. I guess that's because the effects on human health build so slowly and because, no matter how much smog clouds our skies, we continue to hope for a stiff breeze, a weather change that will blow it all away. Or perhaps it is just that the scientists and physicians who know the dangers of air pollution don't translate the complex chemistry into terms an ordinary citizen can grasp.

Ninety-six major United States cities still have not attained the national standard for ozone, which is the primary ingredient in smog, even though smog is known to increase human risk for cancer, lung disease, heart ailments, and reproductive problems. Smog comes from the volatile organic compounds and nitrogen oxides produced by gasoline engines, as well as from industrial smoke stacks. It is particularly virulent for those urban populations — and that's six out of every ten Americans — who often can least afford to move or vacation where the air is clean.

The American Lung Association estimates the annual health cost of air pollution at $50 billion. Unhealthy air affects the physical well-being of millions, and shortens the lives of tens of thousands. The number of deaths from air pollution is in the same range as those from breast cancer or auto accidents.

Nor is smog the only form of air pollution. The sulfur dioxides and nitrogen oxides that spew from coal-burning power plants combine with rain as it is formed in the atmosphere, and then fall on the eastern United States and Canada as a mild acid. A recent national study found that 4 percent of American lakes bigger than ten acres and 8 percent of our streams are now acidic (the percentage is higher for smaller lakes). Canada reports some 31,000 total lakes acidified in the eastern half of the country. As a result, much aquatic life is killed off. Also, there seems to be a high correlation between acid rain and dangerously high mercury content in otherwise edible fish.

As if that isn't enough, we know acid rain corrodes buildings and seriously impairs visibility. By-products of sulfur dioxide are recognized as major contributors to a regional haze that clouds the eastern United States. And now, to top it all off, the Harvard School of Public Health has warned us that acid aerosols, formed from acid rain precursors, may pose significant public health risks.

In addition to smog and acid rain, there are hundreds of airborne chemical compounds that are hazardous to human health. Benzene causes leukemia. Arsenic causes cancer. Beryllium affects the liver, spleen, and kidneys. Lead causes brain damage. Carbon monoxide impedes the blood's ability to carry oxygen. Asbestos causes lung cancer. The list goes on and on.

In the year ending July 1987, according to the U. S. Environmental Protection Agency, 2.7 billion pounds of toxic emissions were released, mostly from commercial and industrial sources. Because the issue is so critical, and yet stirs so few people spontaneously, the Sierra Club has made atmospheric pollution a top priority. With 620,000 members, we have substantial political clout. The trick is to keep those members informed about the issue as well as about the current state of affairs in Washington — and then to get them to act in a timely fashion by contacting the lawmakers who represent them and expressing an informed opinion.

How do we do that? First of all, we have paid staff in both San Francisco and Washington, as well as in many field offices. They do the research, the inside lobbying, and a great deal of the networking. Policy is decided by the Board of Directors, but staff and volunteers have great flexibility and must judge how to carry out policy as the legislative situation develops.

Second, we have conservation chairpersons in each chapter who are responsible for activating their members and adjusting our action agenda so that there is a good local fit. We also have the usual newsletters, white papers, and telephone trees. And we have e-mail! Our Washington and San Francisco offices, as well as personal computers in the homes of three hundred of our volunteer officers, are linked through an electronic mail system. Thus word on how a particular Congressman or -woman is behaving can go from our Washington lobbyists to the lawmaker's own constituents in an hour or so, minutes if it's really critical. Or sticky situations having to do with other environmental groups, friendly politicians, labor unions, etc., can be explained to San Francisco personnel and anyone else who needs to know, then decisions made rapidly by an informed and appropriate set of leaders. The computer and modem in the den of the Merrows' circa-1813 white clapboard farmhouse may seem an anachronism, but often they are the heartbeat of our home. They certainly were as the Clean Air Act Amendments were debated later that month.

Better than my own words, the actual mail I received on May 23 and 24 convey the excitement of that very important week in America's environmental history, so I am including them here. I've left in the technical and political jargon, and the wisecracks, because all are essential components of the Sierra spirit.

Remember, I had been getting messages off and on for several days, describing the behind-the-scenes maneuvering for the House vote on the new Clean Air Act. On May 23, at 5:30 p.m., Heidi Halik of our Washington staff sent this out:

SUBJECT: AIR NEWS!
TO: FIELD AIR MANAGE
FR: CLEAN AIR MANIACS . . . 5:10

THE SIKORSKI-GREEN EXTENDED WARRANTIES AMENDMENT PASSED IN A 239-180 VOTE. THIS MAY BE OUR ONLY VOTE TO WIN AS IT LOOKS LIKE A WAXMAN-LEWIS DEAL IS ABOUT TO OCCUR. WE'LL KEEP YOU POSTED.

Two hours later, there was news about strategy:

SUBJECT: AIR NEWS!
TO: BOARD, FIELD, CLEAN AIR VOLUNTEER LEADERS
FR: BRUCE HAMILTON
RE: LATEST NEWS ON CLEAN AIR AS OF 4:20 PACIFIC TIME

WE WON THE SIKORSKI AMENDMENT ON WARRANTIES BY ABOUT 70 VOTES. ALL DAY LONG THEY HAVE BEEN TRYING TO CUT A DEAL ON WAXMAN-LEWIS MANDATED PRODUCTION OF CLEAN CARS. MADIGAN JUST BLEW UP THE DEAL. WAXMAN'S STAFF WORRIES THAT WE COULD LOSE WAXMAN-LEWIS IF IT IS BROUGHT TO A VOTE GIVEN THE NUMBER AND TYPE OF DEFECTIONS WE HAVE SEEN. BLAKE, DOUG, CARL, AND I JUST HELD A CONFERENCE CALL, AND OUR RECOMMENDATION IS TO URGE WAXMAN TO OFFER THE AMENDMENT ANYWAY. WHAT IF WE LOSE? IT WILL GIVE US A

CLEAR VOTE COUNT ON A TOUGH VOTE THAT WASN'T PART OF A COMPROMISE DEAL. IT WILL TELL US WHO HOUSE TARGETS ARE IF A CARBON DIOXIDE AUTO CAFE STANDARD BILL COMES TO THE FLOOR. LOSING, EVEN LOSING BY A WIDE MARGIN, DOESN'T WEAKEN OUR HAND IN CONFERENCE BECAUSE THERE IS NO PROVISION IN THE SENATE BILL. SO, NOW WE'LL SEE IF WAXMAN IS WILLING TO GO TO THE MAT. IN THE MEANTIME, WE CONTINUE A FULL COURT PRESS. . . LOBBYING IN ANTICIPATION OF THIS BIG VOTE. THANKS FOR ALL YOUR HELP.

Biting my nails, I hovered over the machine in my den. By 9:00 p.m., Connecticut time the good news was official:

SUBJECT: CONGRATS AIR RATS!

THESE VICTORIES WOULD NOT HAVE BEEN POSSIBLE WITHOUT YOUR HARD WORK OVER THE YEARS. I'M REAL PROUD OF THE ROLE WE PLAYED AND THE EFFORT EACH OF YOU PUT IN. TAKE A DEEP BREATH. CHEERS. BRUCE.

At a few minutes past 11:00 p.m., Doug Scott sent this:

SUBJECT: VICTORY. . . THANKS TO YOU (AND A LOT OF JOHN MUIRS LIKE YOU)!!!
TO: EVERYONE
FROM: A VERY HAPPY CROWD OF PEOPLE IN WASHINGTON

TONIGHT, THE HOUSE OF REPRESENTATIVES PASSED — 13 YEARS LATER — THE CLEAN AIR ACT AMENDMENTS OF 1990. WE SET OUT, SO MANY YEARS AGO, TO MAKE THIS HAPPEN. WE HAVE REFINED OUR MESSAGE INTO A FIVE-PART CLEAN AIR PROGRAM — URBAN SMOG, ACID RAIN, AIR TOXICS, CFCs, AND PARK VISIBILITY.

TONIGHT THE HOUSE PASSED A BILL THAT ADDRESSES EVERY ONE OF THOSE ISSUES. IT IS NOT PERFECT. . . NOT BY A LONG SHOT. BUT IN THIS BILL, AND IN THE SENATE BILL, ARE THE ELEMENTS THAT COULD BE PUT TOGETHER TO MAKE A REALLY REMARKABLE CLEAN AIR ACT!

WE HAVE A JOB AHEAD OF US TO BRING THIS TO FRUITION IN CONFERENCE. . . THE "LONG HOT SUMMER." BUT BEFORE WE WORRY MUCH ABOUT THAT, WE ARE CELEBRATING! AND WHAT WE ARE CELEBRATING IS NOT THE WORK OF THE SMALL CREW HERE THESE PAST FEW DAYS (OR THE CREW THAT WAS HERE LAST WEEK, OR THE WEEK BEFORE). . . BUT THE WORK THAT LITERALLY THOUSANDS UPON THOUSANDS OF SIERRA CLUB PEOPLE

HAVE DONE FOR MORE THAN A DECADE — WHEN THE CHIPS WERE DOWN — BUILDING, BUILDING, BUILDING THE PRESSURE AND THE MOMENTUM THAT DELIVERED TODAY'S RESULT.

THE HOUSE DID NOT VOTE ON ALMOST ALL OF THESE ISSUES. THEY WERE COMPROMISED OUT BEFOREHAND, BECAUSE THE DINGELL/WHITE HOUSE/CLEAN AIR WORKING GROUP CROWD KNEW THEY HAD TO GIVE. THAT IN ITSELF IS A HUGE ACCOMPLISHMENT. YOU WILL ALL JOIN US IN THE PRIDE WE FEEL TONIGHT IN WHAT YOU — AND THE THOUSAND "UNSUNG HEROES" IN CHAPTERS AND GROUPS EVERYWHERE — DID OVER THE PAST DECADE TO MAKE THIS HAPPY OUTCOME POSSIBLE. A COHERENT (MAYBE) ANALYSIS OF THE BILL WILL FOLLOW WHEN DAN AND BLAKE SOBER UP, AND WHEN MEL COMES DOWN OFF THE CEILING, AND WHEN HEIDI GETS US ORGANIZED.

MEANWHILE, OUR HATS ARE OFF TO EACH OF YOU WHO MADE THIS MOMENT POSSIBLE. THIS TRULY WAS THE SIERRA CLUB'S DOING (AND OUR VERY GOOD FRIENDS AT U.S. PIRG).

HOORAY!!!!

AND PASS THE CHAMPAGNE.

Before noon the next day, May 24, I had received a memo comparing the provisions of the newly passed House bill with the one President Bush favored. I was also subjected to some well-deserved bragging about instances where our lobbyists knew about individual Congressmen's votes even before their staffs did. We all knew that this was only Round One, the House vote. Still to come was the Senate vote, the Conference Committee, the President's signature. It was, however, a big win, and we were ecstatic.

That afternoon, Richard Cellarius, our immediate past President, and his wife, Doris, sent out a message that summed up the whole event in true Sierra style:

TO: DC-AIR AND ALL THE HELPERS
SUBJECT: CONGRATULATIONS!

. . . THE CELEBRATION IS WELL DESERVED. YOU FOLKS HAVE PUT IN YEOPERSON SERVICE ON THIS FOR YEARS BEYOND COUNTING. YES, THERE IS WORK AHEAD, BUT RELAX AND ENJOY THE SATISFACTION OF A JOB WELL DONE. AS A RECIPIENT OF MANY, ALMOST DAILY UPDATES AND REQUESTS

FOR HELP, I KNOW FULL WELL THE EFFORT THAT OUR ENTIRE CONSERVATION "STAFF" — DC, FIELD, AND VOLUNTEER HAVE PUT IN TO GET TO THIS DAY.

Richard then quoted Sierra's founder and favorite prophet, using what might be considered the Sierra mantra:

"GO TO THE MOUNTAINS AND GET THEIR GOOD TIDINGS," MUIR SAID. YOU SHOULD DO SO AT THE EARLIEST POSSIBLE TIME, BOTH FOR YOUR GOOD HEALTH BECAUSE "NATURE'S PEACE WILL FLOW INTO YOU AS SUNSHINE FLOWS INTO TREES. THE WINDS WILL BLOW THEIR FRESHNESS INTO YOU AND THE STORMS THEIR ENERGY, WHILE CARES DROP OFF LIKE AUTUMN LEAVES," AND ALSO SO THE MOUNTAINS CAN THEN SHARE THEIR JOY WITH YOU OVER YOUR GOOD WORK FOR THE EARTH. THANKS!!!

So, there I was, twenty days into my presidency, with a historic victory to tell my grandchildren about!

Did I deserve to brag to them? You bet I did! I had been working on clean air issues since the early 1970s. I had done fun things — like helping my colleagues at the Connecticut Citizen Action Group wheel a typewriter table down the street, on which stood an ugly, brown cardboard construction labeled "smog cake." We presented the cake to a Commissioner who was vacillating on dirty air sanctions.

I had done challenging things — like forcing myself to learn the heavy-duty chemistry involved in almost any air issue. I had done the personal, practical things — like banning spray deodorants in my home, and driving a small car. And I had done some things that I remember with great pride — like organizing a Clean Air train from Hartford to Washington in 1976, and packing it with citizen-lobbyists who deluged our state's federal lawmakers for two days, and I like to believe, convinced them of the need for the amendments of 1977.

I had carried Annie in a backpack so that I could demonstrate against new highways that would encourage auto pollution, and I had written thoughtful letters to editors describing the horrors of lung diseases brought on by air toxics. Yes, this was my victory too.

You can imagine the excitement the following day, May 25, when I met more than fifty conservation chairpeople from across the country on a long-planned training weekend held at a ranch near San Antonio. Since volunteers are the backbone of Club activism, the organization puts significant resources into training them. This particular session had been planned for months. It included workshops on organizing skills, on issues, and on finding and using Club resources. The camaraderie that develops at such an event is as valuable as the substance of the workshops.

These were the people whose grassroots work had won the Clean Air victory. We were all burbling with excitement, hugging and slapping each others' backs, as we assembled at the San Antonio airport.

We rode in vans supplied by our Alamo group for more than an hour and a half out to the ranch of fried chicken entrepreneur David Bamburger. It was a magical journey. As the roads grew progressively narrower, we passed hedges of juniper and low, spreading oaks, interspersed with clumps of prickly-pear cactus. The land felt arid to me at first, but the last ten miles, over a dirt road that seemed to branch endlessly, included a couple of stream crossings. We drove across the dams, under arches of graceful green willows, our tires making a merry splashing sound.

Mr. Bamburger is a gentleman with a very original mind, and (fortunately) the money to implement his ideas. He has, for instance, built a comfortable bunkhouse-cum-meetingroom out of local stone. With its huge fireplace, mounted animal heads, and banners emblazoned with the words of famous naturalists — including John Muir's "Whenever I try to pick out anything by itself, I find it hitched to everything else in the universe" — it makes a wonderful setting for weekend meetings. Not every group can use the place; you have to be, by Mr. Bamburger's standards, politically correct. Happily, Sierra passes that test.

Mr. Bamburger not only plays host to worthy groups, he puts his money where his mouth is when it comes to ranching. His cattle are bred to live more gently on the land. He calls the breed "grassmasters" and tries to develop stock whose life style will ease some of the damage that ranching can inflict on the ecosystem.

He also breeds a curious animal called the oryx, an antelope from the Middle East, in a serious scientific attempt to preserve its depleted gene pool. We went out at dusk on the second evening we were there to view the oryx herd. They are lovely animals, white with tan markings and long, nearly straight antlers that stretch back almost the length of their bodies. I watched a couple of bucks conduct a playful but speedy race. Exhilarated, I breathed in the dry night air of Texas and gave my wrist a little pinch. But I wasn't dreaming. I really was in Texas watching exotic antelopes and celebrating events in Washington, D.C. What's more, I had eleven months of such adventures stretching before me. With a contented sigh I leaned against some bales of hay and gave myself over to the wide Texas sky. They have a special kind of cloud in Texas — a thunderhead shaped like a giant anvil — and these were silhouetted against the sunset glow. It was a magic moment— but only a moment.

A man from Oklahoma walked over to me. "Redwood Summer sure got off with a bang!" he said and laughed, but without true mirth. I knew that Redwood Summer was an initiative being put together by a group called Earth First! I knew that they shared our concerns about the ancient forests of the American northwest and about the importance of maintaining wildlife habitat. But I also knew they were far more radical than we were, with less (indeed, almost no) control over what was done in the name of the group — and that included some nonviolent and maybe even some violent protest. What I did not know was what my Oklahoma colleague was talking about. When he saw my puzzled expression, he put his arm around my shoulder. "Bomb," he said. "Somebody blew up a car while Darryl Cherney and Judi Bari [two Earth First! leaders] were in it. Damn near killed them!"

One thing more I know: the Sierra Club's membership was already deeply divided with regard to timber interests vs. endangered wildlife. Members of the Redwood Chapter, I was told, had come close to blows over this issue, and Sierrans across the country held strong views as well. Clear-cutting and absolute prohibition of activity in the ancient forests were the two extremes. It was my job to ease tensions and bring the two factions together, or at least into peaceful coexistence.

This violent act was going to make that job triply difficult— if not impossible.

June 1990

ૠ

Biodiversity — the preservation of many kinds of life — was a
major issue in June of 1990, and the Mount Graham red squirrel, an
endangered Arizona rodent, was for a time at the very center of the
hubbub. A proposal to build a $200 million Mount Graham Interna-
tional Observatory was vehemently opposed by citizens who feared it
would mean the end for this particular squirrel species — and the
beginning of the end for the Endangered Species Act.

While arguments about gene pools, the interdependence of all
living things, and the folly of poking holes in an ecosystem raged in the
U.S. District Court in Tucson, the Science Committee of the U.S. House
of Representatives quietly set a new bill on the legislative track.
H.R.1268, the National Biological Diversity Conservation and Research Act, called for a federal strategy to preserve diversity and
established a National Center for Biological Diversity and Conservation Research within the Smithsonian Institution. The two incidents
were not directly linked, but they both reflected a concern that seemed
to have taken center stage in the environmental movement.

And not just in the United States. Death threats dominated the
environmental news in Brazil, where the accused killers of a humble
worker in the rubber forests, Chico Mendes, were coming to trial.
Mendes' murder two years earlier had riveted global attention on the
rapidly disappearing tropical rain forests. Although more than a thousand people have been killed in Brazil alone in rainforest land disputes,
Mendes' whistle-blowing made him an internationally respected mar-
tyr. Now the judge in the case had become the target of terrorist threats
— and of a letter-writing campaign sponsored by many of the United
States' environmental organizations.

In a related development, environmentalists launched a full-scale attack on the Tropical Forestry Action Plan (TFAP) endorsed by the World Bank and the United Nations Food and Agriculture Organization (FAO). Although the $8 billion plan is supposed to halt deforestation and promote sustainable development, a report by the World Rainforest Movement claimed that TFAP had resulted in national plans that promote logging. The invasion of the rainforest by landless settlers, commercial logging and logging roads, cattle ranching, conversion of forests for agriculture, and internationally financed projects such as oil drilling, dams, and power projects, are the main causes of deforestation.

Oil drilling was also named as the culprit in Ecuador, where Conoco, a wholly owned subsidiary of E. I. duPont de Nemours & Co., announced plans to drill within and adjacent to the 6,797-square-kilometer Yasuni National Park. Designated a UNESCO biosphere reserve, Yasuni contains 4,000 flowering plants, more than 600 species of birds, 500 species of fish, and 120 species of mammals, including jaguars, fresh-water dolphins, and giant armadillos. The park also includes some of the dwindling territory of the Huaorani people, native hunter-gatherers whose numbers have been reduced from 20,000 to about 1,500 over the last 20 years.

Wilderness violence also continued to make headlines in the United States in connection with the bombing of a Subaru owned by activist Judi Bari, while she and a friend, Darryl Cherney, were riding in it. All through June, charges and countercharges were hurled. HE had done it to get her. THEY had done it to get publicity. Rival radicals had done it to get even. Foresters had done it to silence them forever. With so many possibilities, and little hard evidence, the Alameda County District Attorney's Office declined to press charges against anyone.

The young couple were both highly controversial leaders of a group that called itself Earth First! They led wild, unpredictable protest actions on the streets and in the woods. A few months previously, Bari had announced a new protest initiative, "Redwood Summer." Earth First! would use college students from across the nation, she said, to participate in mass nonviolent disobedience in the mode of the civil rights movement of the 1960s. But Redwood Summer had begun with more excitement than even Bari had expected.

&

I was back home in East Haddam, Connecticut, by June 1, but thanks to modern communications, the problem of Sierra's relationship with Earth First! came with me. Things were worse than I had feared. I learned now that our Redwood Chapter shared the rent on a suite of offices in Santa Rosa, California, with Earth First! If the bombing was truly part of an environmental backlash, our people were in danger. What's more, because our Sierra Club chapter in Northern California called itself "Redwood," there was sure to be confusion over our role in "Redwood Summer," which was purely an Earth First! initiative. What a mess!

Michael and I agreed to ask for legal advice before we moved ahead. In the meantime, I tried to immerse myself in the things that needed care in the east.

I went to an Aquifer Task Force Meeting outside Hartford. The Metropolitan District Commission, a Hartford area water and waste utility, which has elegant meeting rooms in a downtown office building, chose to host us all at its sewage treatment plant. You knew where you were every time you drew a breath. I closed my eyes, called back that Texas sunset, and told myself that one day of bad odor was a small price for the life I lead.

While I was busy on the east coast, my staff in California ghosted a letter to the *New York Times* correcting mistakes the paper had made in an editorial about the Mount Graham squirrel. This animal was believed extinct until it was rediscovered in a 424-acre tract on top of Mount Graham in 1987. In addition to the squirrel, several other plants and animals that exist nowhere else in this world were also found there.

"Mount Graham's biological uniqueness," we told the *Times*, "has been compared to that of the Galapagos Islands. The top of Mount Graham is an endangered ecosystem unique on this globe ... and there are many other places to put a telescope."

On Tuesday, June 5, while I was standing at my back door chatting with the horse vet, a telephone operator interrupted to arrange a conference call that evening among the five members of the Board's Executive Committee. Our lawyers were insisting that we move the Sierra Club's Redwood Chapter to new office space immediately. They argued that, should any violence result in injury to our members, we would be liable by virtue of the fact that we knew a dangerous situation existed. The chair of the Redwood Chapter had been contacted and seemed willing to comply. Sierra's national office had agreed to defray the costs of the move.

But it was by no means that simple. Redwood Summer, as staged by Earth First! was getting intensive media coverage. It was an apple-pie issue at first glance, but peel off the top crust and the pie was found to contain more than a few creepy-crawlies. As a result, some serious chasms were starting to divide our own memberships.

We were all united, 100 percent, on the importance of saving the ancient forests of the northwestern United States. Besides our concern for the redwoods, Sierra was considering filing *amicus curiae* briefs in two lawsuits to halt timber sales in the Sequoia National Forest. Timber may be a renewable resource, but America's last remaining primeval wilderness cannot be dismissed as mere "timber." We are talking here about trees that are hundreds of years old, cedars with trunks up to 12 feet in diameter, fir more than 250 feet tall, disappearing under the lumber industry's mechanized assault. Gone, never to exist again. Yes, I come from Connecticut; all the more reason to mourn the loss of these magnificent wild places. They are not regional resources, they are national treasures.

Still, the Sierra members closest to the scene understood the emotions of neighbors who made a living from lumber. They sought a way to compromise, while more purist members — usually from farther away — demanded an absolute end to the "chainsaw massacre of the ancient forests."

Further complicating the matter were the civil disobedience tactics of Earth First! activists. The Sierra Club wants to preserve the redwoods, but only by reasonable and lawful means. Some members of our Redwood Chapter, caught up in the excitement all around them, were demanding that Sierra take a more visible posture. Others were calling for us to distance ourselves from Earth First! — and the farther, the better. My job, as President, was to knit all these frayed ends back into a coherent and effective strategy.

During the conference call that night, we set up a meeting for both sides within Sierra, complete with facilitator, in northern California for the weekend. It was our hope that if all parties came together, they might be able to iron things out. I asked Carl Pope, our chief national staffperson for conservation, to be present and to make it clear that the Sierra Club does not and will not participate in unlawful activities. I myself flew to the west coast on Thursday, but I had other matters to handle, including an inbox that had filled to overflowing in my eighteen-day absence.

The Sierra Club will be one hundred years old in May 1992, and you can bet that we are proud of that fact. As in most Sierra undertakings, however, we don't intend to just sit there beaming. Our anniversary will be used to collect money — lots of money — and new members — many, many new members — so that we can grow in vigor and effectiveness. It will take all the dollars and all the individuals we can muster to win the battle for a healthy global environment. The Centennial Campaign Planning Committee meeting on Friday, June 19, was important enough for me to fly across the country. Happily that put me on the right coast to attend an impressive luncheon sponsored by the Sierra Club Legal Defense Fund (which is of, but not legally joined to, the just plain Sierra Club). Mike Traynor, the SCLDF President, was presenting awards to various attorneys who had volunteered their expertise in the massive legal tangles that resulted from the *Valdez* oil spill. It was a high-spirited, high-calorie meal, and I left to catch my plane to Eugene, Oregon, in great good humor.

Why was I flying to Eugene when I had barely arrived in San Francisco? To attend a meeting of the club's Committee on Committees (ComCom for short). This is no joke. As the Sierra Club grew, it spawned a committee on conservation, and a committee on water quality, and a committee on toxic air pollutants, and a committee on membership, and committees on this and committees on that: seventy-four in all! It became impossible for the Board of Directors to keep track of them all. And budgeting for their needs would have boggled King Solomon. Hence the very necessary, and hard-working, Committee on Committees.

We met all day Saturday at the home of Sandy Tepfer, one of my fellow directors, and his wife. We slept in sleeping bags scattered around their house that night. Sunday morning I woke with a real case of the blues. It was my birthday and somehow, since I was due to leave soon to fly to Washington, D.C., it seemed inappropriate to mention it as the ComCom members assembled.

No flowers from Arthur; no phone call from Annie. If there was a card from my father, it was three thousand miles away. Oh well, *noblesse oblige* called for a cheerful smile as I said good-bye to the Tepfers and boarded the puddle-jumper plane that would take me from Eugene to Seattle.

I have flown a great deal. I have never been afraid of cracking up, but I do worry about throwing up. That flight justified my anxiety. As we circled the Seattle airport, delayed by air traffic controllers, buffeted by choppy winds, my heart yearning for a birthday hug, my stomach churning, tears ran down my cheeks and I wondered what ever made me want to be President of the Sierra Club. Happily the flight from Seattle to Dulles Airport was smooth—and by now anticipation of the party I was going to attend in Washington was cheering me up.

I want to stop here and put in a pure, unabashed plug for the Bellevue Hotel, near Union Station, in our nation's capital. It's the kind of funky, old-fashioned place that has all but vanished from the American scene. It has been my home in Washington throughout my membership on the Sierra Club's Board of Directors. Cross the worn marble floors in the lobby, nod pleasantly to the elevator operator (a vanishing breed), and you will be whisked to a pink and black Art Deco room exactly like every other room in this six-floor establishment. I went there first because the Bellevue charges less than $70 per night and is located only three blocks from Sierra's capitol office. I went back again and again for its unobtrusive friendliness and homespun but reliable service.

But I digress. To properly describe the events of June 11 and 12, I must take you back several weeks, to a phone call I received while I was washing pots and pans in my Connecticut kitchen.

"Hello," a voice said, "this is Jason Isaacson. I'm an aide to Senator Chris Dodd. We'd like to congratulate you on your election as Sierra Club President." As I sought for an appropriate reply, he added, "There's someone here who would like to speak with you." Senator Dodd himself came on the line and I hastily dried my hands. One does not do the dishes while one is talking to a U.S. Senator.

Chris Dodd lives in East Haddam, my home town. He has restored an old schoolhouse on the main street and is as active as he can be (given his busy schedule) in community affairs. I have talked to him many times over the years about environmental matters. We share a love for the country town we both call home.

Even so, I turned from the sink and came to full attention when I heard his voice.

I could scarcely credit what came next. Chris was inviting me to a reception in my honor at the U.S. Capitol Building on June 12. Me! I thanked him profusely and hung up the phone. "Arthur, you won't believe this one," I shouted. "Get your suit pressed!"

Needless to say, the staff in Sierra's D.C. office was excited. Having the undivided attention of a Senator is a dream come true for most lobbyists. When they learned from Dodd's staff that the invitation list would include the entire U.S. Senate, selected Congresspeople, and members of the environmental community, they were struck dumb.

I was supplied with extra invitations — a beautifully engraved note card embossed with the seal of the Senate — and told to invite my family and friends. The only requirement was that I supply a social security number for each guest to Capitol security.

I wanted my father to be there, along with Arthur and Annie, and I pressed some of my frequent flyer miles into service for plane tickets for all three. Arthur's folks said they would drive down from Buffalo. THIS was an occasion!

On the appointed day, we walked over in a group from the Sierra offices. It was perfect June weather. The flags on the mall were dancing on their staves and it seemed to me that every face I saw was smiling broadly. I suppose the brightness outside lent a special aura to the darkly handsome Mansfield Room, with its panelled walls, brocade chairs, and soft lighting.

I felt instantly at home. This was my party, after all. (How quickly we acclimate ourselves to privilege!) A bar was set up in one corner, and a central, circular table held a handsome floral arrangement and trays of hors d'oeuvres. Senator Dodd arrived and began introducing me to his colleagues. I met lawmakers in whose outer offices I would normally have cooled my heels. Teddy Kennedy even tried to lobby me about one of his pet projects!

Chris Dodd was graciousness personified to my family (especially my father, who was wearing a name tag that read "Susan's Dad"). When the party was at its height, the Senator called his guests to attention and introduced me as his neighbor and a powerful advocate for our country's natural resources. I had planned to talk about the outpouring of environmental concern since Earth Day, about stewardship and focus, and what was still to be done. Maybe I did. I have absolutely no idea.

It was over too soon. A Sierra lobbyist had counted the attendees. Twenty Senators and eighteen Representatives had turned out to meet me. It was an enormous compliment to Senator Dodd, to the Club, and to me. My Sierra colleagues were acting as if they had won the lottery. Meanwhile, the guest of honor and her family — six of us in all — crowded into a friend's Toyota for the ride to Dulles Airport.

The next morning Arthur got up and went to work. Annie hurried off to take a final exam, and I went out to feed the horses, sheep, and chickens. Working in the barn, with a shovel in my hands, I was grinning from ear to ear. I knew I would never be quite the same person again. As I left the barn, I saw my father staking some hollyhocks in our back yard. He looked happier at that job than he had yesterday shaking hands with power brokers. As a matter of fact, yesterday he had looked a little dazed. I knew he could tell people what I did, clearly enough, in a few short sentences — but I wondered how much he really comprehended.

I wished fervently that my mother could be here too. We had been a classic middle-class family. She taught fourth grade; he ran a flower shop; I did my best to make them proud of me. I didn't always succeed, and now I regretted that she had died before I had this one great chance to win her approval. Then, for a brief moment, I was a little girl again, watching my father putter in the garden in Brockton, Massachusetts. I remembered my mother scolding him because he would be late for some meeting. And then I remembered something I had not thought of in years: my dad, in his role as civic activist.

It came as a surprise, although I don't know why. I remembered his deciding that the Brockton Youth Symphony (in which I played the violin) should have a parents' auxiliary — and then organizing one. I remembered his deciding that handicapped children should have special buddies among their non-handicapped peers — and arranging the whole thing, through the sheer force of his conviction. I remembered the good times I enjoyed with Janice, who had cerebral palsy, and I wondered how many other adults, both handicapped and not, look back with pleasure on some relationship my father pushed them into.

I had never before realized how much my impulses toward public service were rooted in his example. I thought of him as a florist, a businessman, a loving grandfather, the kind man who nursed my mother through her terminal cancer. He was all of these. He was also the genesis of some of the parts of me I most valued. I walked across the yard and began working next to him, tying the plants as he set the stakes. He didn't comment, but I could tell he was pleased.

There are supposed to be about ten days between my horse vet's spring visits. When I saw his truck pull into the driveway on June 14, I was dumbfounded. Wasn't he here just yesterday? I checked the calendar, and got a clear picture of just how fast my life was leaping along.

Arthur and I chose this old house to fix up and love because we value its connection to a more peaceful, harmonious age. We purposely have no heating on the second floor, no television, no dishwasher, only one bathroom, a wood stove, and a fireplace, in an effort to turn back the tide of twentieth- century freneticism in our personal lives. Now it seemed that I was losing that cherished country simplicity. Ironically, I had adopted a jet-set lifestyle in order to wage a nationwide fight for preservation. I might help to save my country's quality of life, but at what damage to my own?

That afternoon, instead of my going to the Sierra Club, it was coming to me, in the persons of the immediate past President, Richard Cellarius, and Marianne Briscoe, whom we had hired to head up the Centennial Campaign. They were traveling around the country, calling personally on potential large donors and on each member of the Board of Directors, in order to ask for what is known in fund-raising lingo as a "stretch" pledge, so called, I guess, because the donor gives more than he thinks he can afford.

I knew it was necessary, if we were going to raise money, for the Board of Directors to donate generously. "Don't expect others to give if you haven't done so yourself," the rule goes. I have to admit, however, as I polished the bathroom sink and dusted the dining room mantle, getting ready for our callers, I experienced just the tiniest trace of resentment. I had already pledged Sierra my life. Now, not only did they also want money, they were making me clean house!

Arthur drove us to the airport, where we picked up a rental car for Dick's use during the week. Then we split up, with me driving the rental back to East Haddam, Annie and Marianne as my passengers. Unfortunately, on the highway home, the car blew a tire. I pulled over and found the spare. Because of the darkness and the strange car, I decided the wisest course was to climb the fence, scramble up the embankment, knock on the nearest lighted window, and try to call the car rental agency for help.

When I was halfway up the hill, I heard Annie get out of the car. She was shouting something about "the phone number." Then there was the sound of her falling over the fence and into the ditch I had managed to jump. "Mom," she cried out, "Mom, I'm bleeding and you need the phone number." I raised my eyes to the heavens. "Oh, come on," I cried. "Isn't it enough that I dusted?"

That night and the next day, a curious thing happened. I saw myself, my home, and my family through the eyes of my visitors. Perhaps because I have stayed in so many Sierra homes, helped dry dishes, examined their books and paintings, slept on the couch, made judgments about their values and life styles, I was keenly aware that Dick was doubtless doing the same to me.

What I saw him seeing pleased me very much. My husband is not handsome, not rich, not especially outgoing, but he cares deeply about his family, his hometown, and his country. He is well informed (don't ever play Trivial Pursuit with him unless you are on his team), slow to anger, dogged about issues once he makes up his mind.

My only child, Annie, is tall for her age and beginning, at thirteen, to acquire the form and grace of womanliness. Because of my frequent absences, she is required to do more than her share of whatever homemaking happens around our house, and as a result she has acquired a "can do" attitude that I like to call maturity. Annie is just beginning to explore the teenage sulks, but she keeps them within the family. When company comes, she is poised, affectionate, and a joy to be with.

Our home, as I have said, is a nice old farmhouse. It is set on the upper level of two grassy meadows that descend gradually to a distant brook. Out back, the old farm buildings house some elderly horses, a handful of chickens, two sheep, and a crowd of barn cats. The house lot comprises ten acres; across the narrow country road, we own another thirteen acres of woodland, acquired in bits and pieces, so as to keep it wild (land is what we buy instead of dishwashers and television sets).

I have visited homes that are very different, that I liked very much; but those homes were in California or Texas or Minnesota or Tennessee. Mine is, in my opinion, exactly what a Connecticut home should be: a main course of country, seasoned with history, and garnished with horses and chickens.

Leslie Carothers, a former Connecticut environmental commissioner, once told me that Montana, to her, was Beethoven. If that's true, then Connecticut is certainly Mozart.

Perhaps I was appreciating Connecticut more because I was so often away, but my chauvinism continued the next day when I took my guest sightseeing. As we rode the funny little car ferry across the Connecticut River, I truly believed that Dick was not likely to see anything more beautiful in all his travels.

We toured the antique shops and craft boutiques that have multiplied as my section of Connecticut grew chic, and ended at Gillette Castle State Park. We have some wonderful parks in Connecticut—parks commemorating Revolutionary War battles, parks with lovely waterfalls, parks where you can ride on old steam engines, even one park that has a geodesic dome built over dinosaur tracks that are aeons old — but, for my money, Gillette Castle is the gem. It was erected in 1919 by William Gillette, the actor who brought Sherlock Holmes to life on the stage. He built his castle high above the Connecticut River, with a patio from which you can see for many miles. The view there is more peaceful than Hong Kong harbor, less cluttered than the Rhine, gentler than the Irish coast. But, then, maybe I'm prejudiced.

I spent the next six days in Connecticut. Two of my environmental colleagues gave a garden party in my honor; there was a meeting of ELECT, a Clean Water Coalition picnic, and a fundraiser at the Hartford Carousel for Joe Grabarz, a state legislator with a strong environmental record. All these local affairs claimed me during the day, but at home, at night, my computer kept me tied to the rest of the country.

Carl Pope had achieved at least a temporary ceasefire in the redwoods. We had publicly disavowed violence, and even civil disobedience, but we had also gone on record asserting that the physical safety and civil rights of the Earth Firsters must be protected. Best of all, we had agreed to sound off at the lumber companies, not at each other, from then on.

The annual G-7 gathering, a summit meeting of world powers, was scheduled in Houston in July and we were deep into preparing for it. This would be the sixteenth gathering of the seven most industrialized nations in the world. Dedicated to "economic growth and international stability," G-7 meetings had become forums for policies that had direct impact on the global environment. We were urging all members to write to their local papers, demanding that the meeting accomplish two things: a pledge for a 20 percent reduction in the emission of carbon dioxide, the principal greenhouse gas, by the year 2000; and a retraction of G-7's earlier support for the disastrous Tropical Forest Action Plan.

Our press people sent out, over my name, an op ed article about global warming entitled "Turning Up the Heat in Houston." It appeared, I am told, in more than fifty daily newspapers. Localized versions, signed by other club members, were also blossoming in papers across the nation. In addition, a blizzard of letters and phone calls were being directed to the White House. We wanted President Bush and his cronies to heed our message when they gathered with other world leaders in July.

On June 22 I flew back to San Francisco. That date happens to be my wedding anniversary, and I was experiencing a mild reprise of my birthday blues. "Sue," I scolded myself, "you're not too nice to be President. You're too silly!" Still the melancholy wrapped itself around me. I seem to be especially vulnerable to depression when I am flying. On land I always know exactly who I am and what I am about, but while I am up in the air, my emotions tend to be helter-skelter.

I sit by a window, not to admire the clouds, but so that my seat mate won't notice if I sniffle as I turn magazine pages, or let out heartfelt sighs during in-flight movies — even when I have not purchased headphones. I don't think you need a doctorate in psychology to figure out that the stress of being Sierra Club President and my own self-doubts caught up with me in those long interims when I was between the two halves of my life. It's as if the sky were my therapist, my safety valve in a pressure cooker life.

That day, I felt anonymous, depersonalized — until I arrived at the office. There, my workaday walnut desk was bedecked with a splendid basket of yellow flowers — all the blooms that symbolize, for me, renewal and continuance — flowers from my faraway husband. It turned out to be a great day. That is, if you can have a great day talking about garbage—which is why I had returned to California.

Shortly before our May meeting, the Sierra Club had polled its chapters to find out what issues were of concern to them. We wanted to make sure we were on target in serving their needs. The results showed a wide range of concerns. One issue, however, was listed in every response: municipal refuse, solid waste, garbage.

The Chair of our Committee on Hazardous Waste had prophesied this result; she received, she said, countless queries on the subject and was frustrated because she could be of little help. In all our vast committee structure, we had no group directly responsible for formulating Sierra policy on solid waste disposal.

Our hazardous waste chair knew who the most interested activists were, and with her guidance, we called them together for a weekend brainstorming session in San Francisco. These sessions run to a pattern: arrival on Friday afternoon, dinner together while we all measure each other; full-day session Saturday; time allowed on Sunday to settle the things we needed to "sleep on." We finish up around noon on Sunday so that participants — no matter where they come from on the continent — can sleep in their own beds that night.

The need for a national committee that would help the locals swap information on solid waste disposal methods was obvious. Also, the federal Resource Conservation and Recovery Act (RCRA) was soon due for reauthorization, and would probably be amended to include some solid waste issues. Sierra would need a team of experts when that happened.

The real answer to our country's garbage woes is to throw away less. Too often, the things we buy — razors, paper plates, pens, diapers — are meant to be used one time, then thrown away. Clothes get tossed out as fashion changes. Durable goods now have built-in obsolescence (so we will be sure to buy another whatever-it-is sooner). Our grandmothers' advice — "use it up, wear it out" — is alien to our life styles. To make matters worse, the modern self-service market makes it necessary to put things in packages that are too big to steal easily. The result is a sinful waste of cardboard, paper, and plastic.

Some of these materials are toxic and harmful to human health, especially if they are burned in an incinerator. All of them contribute to water pollution when they decay and their juices mingle together in landfill leachate. In Connecticut, we ran out of landfill space years ago. We turned to resource recovery systems, where garbage is burned to create energy. Properly equipped and maintained, they cause little air pollution, but you still need landfill space for the potentially toxic ash residue, and for bulky, nonburnable waste. If incineration becomes an easy, readily available alternative, it will take away the incentive to produce less garbage in the first place.

Generally, when it comes to solid waste, Sierra Club favors a series of rules that can be adjusted to suit the local situation.

Rule # 1, reduce at the source—make less garbage. Refill-able bottles of household cleaning agents, yes. Items wrapped in paper, inside cardboard, covered with plastic, no. Dehydrated products that can be mixed with water at home, yes. Individual servings, separately wrapped, then bonded together in shrink wrap, absolutely no.

Rule #2, recycle. That means tag sales, and returning cans and bottles to the store, and giving to charities that rehabilitate secondhand furniture, and cutting Nancy's dress down to fit Sarah, and fixing things that break instead of throwing them away. It also means buying things that are made from recycled materials.

Rule #3, compost. Keep organic waste out of the ground or incinerator.

Finally, rule #4, when you have cut the waste stream as much as possible, try to reclaim the energy in what's left. And if you must make the odious choice, try to pollute the air instead of the groundwater, because when water is poisoned, it stays poisoned for a long, long time.

By Sunday noon, we had established a national committee on solid waste, given them a budget of a few thousand dollars (out of my President's discretionary fund), and charged them with conducting ongoing policy discussions and starting a news-letter on the topic. All in all, a highly productive two days.

Sunday afternoon, on my own in San Francisco, I set out to see the sights. I ended up at the Gay Freedom Day Parade, a "must see" spectacle, if there ever was one. The things I saw — men with orange hair, men in black leather tights, transvestites dancing on floats, women hugging as they watched the parade, and Mayor Feinstein riding serene above it all, waving to her flock — gave me a whole new view of my home away from home.

Curiously, although you would certainly never see anything like this in East Haddam, Connecticut, there was a good-humored neighborliness that reminded me of home. This parade was part of the fabric of San Francisco life and the people parading, though they had chosen an alternative life style, were integral to the fabric. There was a lot of good feeling; it was a nice place to be.

The following Wednesday, Arthur and Annie flew cross-country again, and joined me at my office. The newly seated Board of Directors schedules a retreat one month after the election, and immediate families are invited. This year we were going to Yosemite National Park, the spiritual home of the Sierra Club. Our founder, John Muir, was the prime mover in saving this wilderness for mankind. It has become a symbol for me, this valley, its steep rock walls, the dramatic waterfalls, of what we — the Sierra Club and the people who belong to it — are all about.

Remember, the Sierra Club is a century old. A hundred years ago, who worried about sulfur dioxide or biodiversity? But even then a few wise men were beginning to understand the need for people to protect and preserve Nature, rather than conquer her.

The Sierra Club founder, John Muir, accomplished astounding feats in his life, guiding the national government into preserving millions of acres. When he tried to explain his passion, he said, "Thousands of tired, nerve-shaken, over-civilized people are beginning to find out that going to the mountains is going home; that wildness is a necessity; and that mountain parks and reservations are useful not only as fountains of timber and irrigating rivers, but as fountains of life."

Muir and others of his era believed that humans are kin to all living things, bound to them in a mutual dependency upon a finite pool of physical resources. In the century since, science has confirmed the essence of that message by recognizing that the inherent value of every lifeform is of practical importance to humans.

There is a mystical side to all this. I think it was best expressed by author Wallace Stegner: "Something will have gone out of us as a people if we ever let the remaining wilderness be destroyed; if we permit the last virgin forests to be turned into comic books and plastic cigarette cases; if we pollute the last clean air and dirty the last clean streams and push our paved roads through the last of the silence, so that never again will Americans be free in their own country from the noise, the exhausts, the stinks of human and automotive wastes. And so that never again can we have the chance to see ourselves single, separate, vertical and individual in the world, part of the environment of trees and rocks and soil, brother to the other animals, part of the natural world and competent to belong in it."

Competent to belong in it! Stegner knew how to get to the bottom line. We destroy what we fear. And we fear the wildness of storms, the wildness of fire and drought — as well as the wildness inside our own hearts. In short, wilderness allows us to maintain our connection with the wildness of nature, an essential element of ourselves that is all too easily lost.

Wilderness has a spiritual side too, which we should not be embarassed to acknowledge. Nancy Newhall said it beautifully in *This is the American Earth*: "Were all learning lost, all music stilled; man, if those resources still remain to him, could again hear singing in himself and rebuild anew the habitations of his thought."

The wilderness ethic is father to our more recent concerns about endangered species. When scientists talk about biodiversity, when rubber tappers give their lives to preserve a few acres of rainforest, when car bombs explode in Oakland, when a tiny squirrel can bring a giant observatory to a halt, when garden clubbers picket on behalf of a spotted owl they never expect to see, I understand at a basic, intuitive level, because I remember what my heart feels at Yosemite.

It is important, of course, also to understand with your head. Sometimes I feel as if there must be more jokes about the snail darter and the furbish lousewort than about mothers-in-law and farmers' daughters combined. When I try to help people understand why we work to protect even the most insignificant species, I tell them about a television commercial I once saw in Boston.

As the television spot opens, the viewer sees an American eagle in flight, wings fully extended— a stirring sight. But what the viewer hears is the steady thrum of an airplane engine, and a voice says, "Think of Creation as if it were a Boeing 707, made up of thousands upon thousands of tiny parts. You can lose a bolt here or there without effect, but every loss weakens the overall structure — and you never know when one more tiny loss will be the last one." With those words, we hear a terrible crash, the eagle fades from the screen, and a print message entreats us to protect endangered species.

There are countless examples of how human tampering has led to unfortunate results that could not have been foreseen: for instance, the farmer who destroys all the hawks in the area (because they have killed a few of his chickens), and then sees a surge in the rodent population that seriously cuts into his grain supply.

Or the alligator hunters who sought hides for shoes and handbags in the Everglades. When the alligators' numbers diminished, so did the special holes and nests they created — and that changed the hydrology of the entire area. One obvious and economically important loss to humans were the bass and other sport fish. They were being eaten by the spotted garfish — which had been held in check by the alligators.

A truly dramatic example involves domesticated corn, a major cash crop in the United States. Most of the corn our farmers grow is one of six in-bred lines. All of them are annuals — that is, they complete their growth cycle in one year, then have to be cut down, the land replowed and reseeded. Because we depend on so few varieties, we run the constant risk of having a major harvest wiped out by a blight or viral disease.

Recently Mexican agricultural scientists rediscovered what had been considered extinct — a tall, unprepossessing species that is probably a primitive antecedent of the corn we eat today. They found that this corn is resistant to several varieties of the viruses that plague domestic corn. Even more exciting, it is a perennial! The infusion of this genetic material into standard strains may eventually mean that corn would come up by itself, year after year, just like daffodils. The amount of diesel fuel saved would be at least two and one-quarter gallons per acre — worth hundreds of millions of dollars to American farmers in fuel costs alone, and a godsend from the global warming point of view.

I don't mean to say that America's vast cornfields will eventually depend on the preservation of the rare, wild Mexican species — but it will be one factor, one of many natural ones that include the acidity of rainfall, the prevailing temperatures (which may change with global warming), and the purity of the available water supply. Each of these in subtle ways will help to determine the prosperity of our agricultural industry.

So when you hear about environmentalists out fighting for the bog turtle and the short-nosed sturgeon and the Mount Graham squirrel — or the snail darter and the furbish lousewort — don't think they are defending just one kind of life form. What they are actually defending is species diversity. They are defending millions of years of genetic history that have resulted in complex interrelationships — many of them unknown and, at this point, probably unknowable. They are demanding respect for the web of life.

If, at times, their demands seem strident, remember that, because the rate of exinction has increased so dramatically, we are losing not just single species but entire ecosystems — the nurseries of new life forms. One scientist calls such losses, "the greatest single setback to life's abundance and diversity since the first flickering of life almost four billion years ago," and one of the world's leading experts on biodiversity, Harvard biologist E. O. Wilson — a man definitely not given to hyperbole — has coined the phrase, "the death of birth."

When I look around a wilderness, I see it as a vast library of untapped knowledge, of usefulness stored for the future. For example: a brief item in a recent issue of the *New York Times* describes the use of a component of rattlesnake venom to stop the growth of cancer cells; another potential cancer-fighting drug, taxol, has just been discovered in the same habitat as the controversial spotted owl (it comes from the bark of the Pacific yew, a tree that loggers usually burn along with other underbrush); or consider the $100 million in annual sales of a drug for Hodgkin's disease, a drug extracted from a tiny purple periwinkle that grows in Madagascar; and don't forget the fungus that produces ergot, a medicine long used to aid mothers in labor.

What other wonders exist in nature and are yet to be analyzed? And are perhaps soon to be extinct? We don't know.

But it seems to me that allowing the loss of a species before we learn its value is about the same as burning a book before it's been read.

Species preservation is inextricably linked to saving forests and wetlands. You can't preserve a species outside of nature except by the most extreme methods — usually involving zoos, laboratories, and very large dollar amounts. No, what we must do is preserve habitat, the space where a species thrives, especially because the interactions within the habitat can be even more important than the individual species involved.

A popular concept these days is the theory that if you protect the habitat of, let's say, the bobolink, then you will also protect all the life that thrives in the same habitat: lichens, apple trees, ladybugs, sumac, earthworms, chipmunks, monarch butterflies, white birches, wild blueberry bushes, goldenrod, red foxes — even humans.

In short, we protect one species, any species, because of its connection to all others. And we protect areas in which many species flourish — such as tropical rainforests, swamps, virgin woods, or the top of Mount Graham, because that is the cheapest, most efficient way to slow the current rate of extinction, which scientists fear could lead to terrible changes in life as we know it. These are awesome thoughts, but it's hard not to think them in the grandeur of Yosemite.

Because of John Muir's role in creating this park, the Sierra Club has always kept a special eye on its management. When we decided to hold the 1990 retreat there, Dr. Edgar Wayburn — one of our other heroes (twice President of the Sierra Club, and currently its Vice-President, and universally regarded as the grand old man of national parks) — asked us not to use the facilities of the Curry Company, the Yosemite concessionaire, because of its poor environmental practices. Instead, we stayed in Oakhurst, at an Episcopalian conference center.

The purpose of the June retreat is to help the Board members do some bonding (they will be making important decisions later via telephones and computers; they need to know the person behind the technology to do so effectively) and also give them time to discuss some of the big issues, such as the Club's overall direction, its position vis-à-vis other national environmental groups, even the direction of the movement itself.

While we were at Yosemite, we also took part in the dedication of LeConte Memorial Lodge as a National Historic Landmark. This quaint stone building is not much more than an exhibit room and a turret, but it has been there since 1904 when it was built in memory of Dr. Joseph LeConte, a Sierra Director and geology professor who spent summers in the 1800s exploring the Sierra Nevada. The lodge is used now as a library and for interpretive nature programs.

I was especially pleased to be there with my fellow Director Sandy Tepfer and his wife, Bert — recently my hosts in Oregon. Sandy is a small, almost gnomish man, with abundant energy and an unending flow of enthusiasm. He and Bert tended LeConte Lodge back in the 1940s, sleeping on a tent platform behind the building. This dedication was part of their reward, their immortality, and well deserved.

On Friday, June 29, we all ate dinner together at the Wawona Hotel, a beautiful white frame building that was once a stagecoach stop. Arthur and I had spent the afternoon on the valley floor, seeking to reinvigorate the spark of John Muir's spirit that is in us all. Most of the others had done the same. Our gathering that night was colored by the knowledge that we must keep alive the flame Muir and his forty successors nurtured. There was some serious talk, but mostly there was singing, and laughter, and hope for the future.

By the time we packed up on Sunday night, I'm afraid I had lost some of that hopefulness. In a few days I would be in Houston, at the G-7 summit meeting. President Bush had just announced some new offshore oil and gas decisions that, on the surface, seemed to reverse James Watt's "full speed ahead" policies. But when you held Bush's decisions up to the light, their fabric was woven out of equivocation and politics. Many important oil-rich areas remained unprotected, and, worst of all, the President's proposals lacked any energy strategy for conservation or alternatives to our national dependence on petroleum.

I remembered Richard Darman's crack about making the world safe for green vegetables. I remembered John Sununu's opposition to joining other powers in trying to avert global warming by reducing greenhouse gases. And I wondered if we could expect any kind of environmental leadership at the summit from George Bush.

I knew no one would hold me accountable if the Sierra Club and the other environmental leaders failed to persuade our leaders to act responsibly. But here I was, right where I had wanted to be, at the top of the pyramid, and now I had to consider, carefully, how my presence at a world summit meeting might actually make a difference.

July 1990

___

ॐ

___

On July 9, 1990, leaders of the seven most powerful nations in the world convened in Houston, Texas, for the sixteenth annual economic summit meeting. Because decisions made at such a gathering will inevitably have a profound effect on the global environment, economic summits have in recent years become highly significant to environmentalists from every corner of the Earth.

At the Paris meeting held in July 1989, several environmental concerns were discussed and the Tropical Forest Action Plan adopted. In the year since, environmentalists had grown disillusioned with TFAP. They came to Houston determined to see that it was either amended or scrapped.

Fueling their concern was a brand new United Nations report authored by a distinguished panel of scientists. It concluded that global warming has begun, that temperatures will rise in the next century faster than they have in the last 10,000 years, and that urgent measures are needed to curb greenhouse gases. In a separate poll, 89 percent of the scientists responding said they believe that the nations of the world should act at once to reduce emissions of greenhouse gases, primarily carbon dioxide (CO_2) and chlorofluorocarbons (CFCs).

West Germany's Helmut Kohl and Britain's Margaret Thatcher both announced before the summit that they were prepared to commit their nations to substantial reductions in emissions. All signals from the Bush administration, however, indicated that the mounting scientific evidence of global warming would be ignored by the United States delegation.

A coalition of environmental groups, calling themselves the "Envirosummit," demanded that President Bush not only recognize global warming, but also support a 20 percent reduction in CO_2 emissions by the year 2000. They pointed out that the United States contributes the most to the problem, and argued that other countries would follow if the U.S. led the way.

Environmentalists saw tropical deforestation as a major contributor to global warming because it accounts for 18 percent of greenhouse gas emissions worldwide, mainly through the burning of vegetation. They also asserted that the G-7 nations consume 60 percent of the world's CFCs, produce 41 percent of the world's carbon dioxide emissions from fossil fuels (causing about half of the greenhouse effect), and are the source of 67 percent of the world's official development assistance funding, which is rarely restricted to projects that are environmentally benign.

Although George Bush made no comment, some observers noted that his decision in late June to limit offshore oil drilling showed that he understood the political popularity of environmental protection.

On July 1, writing in the New York Times, Daniel Yergin and Joseph Stanislaw of the Cambridge Energy Research Associates revealed a new survey of 1,250 Americans. They found that 74 percent of the people surveyed would select environmental cleanup and slower growth over unchecked economic growth. They also found a large majority who said they would reject political candidates who do not agree with the preference for environment over economics. In its headline, the Times hailed environmentalism as the new "litmus test for candidates."

If Bush administration officials truly underestimated the environmental crisis confronting the Earth, would they at least recognize the political clout environmental issues now enjoyed — and conduct themselves accordingly at the summit?

The answer was no. In Houston, West Germany's proposal to set limits on greenhouse gas emissions was defeated by U.S. opposition. Instead, in the final communique issued by the G-7 leaders, another German proposal to preserve tropical rainforests was the only environmental-protection measure taken. The proposal, citing the vast sections of rainforest that already had been destroyed, called on the World Bank to develop a pilot program in Brazil to ease the financial burden of restraining development activity there.

The Sierra Club, in an impromptu press conference, immediately accused President Bush of "hiding his inaction behind a scanty fig leaf." Infuriated, the President responded with a rare display of public anger.

"We cannot govern by listening to the loudest voice on the extreme of an environmental movement," he said. "I did not rely heavily on them for support in getting elected ... and I'm not going to be persuaded that I can get some brownie points by appealing to one of these groups or another."

Three days later, the New York Times *editorially chided the President, saying, "Americans had reason to be supremely disappointed at Mr. Bush's reluctance to embrace even a modest strategy for limiting emissions of carbon dioxide that could cause a catastrophic warming of the earth's climate." Calling the administration's view of global warming "cramped," the* Times *asked for "a maximum of care and a minimum of cant," and categorized Bush as "a petulant President who keeps threatening to pick up his bat and ball and go home."*

Meanwhile, in Congress, environmental matters were faring better. Senator George Mitchell warned opponents of the Bryan Bill, dropped during the Senate debate on the Clean Air Act, that they had three weeks to prepare for a possible floor debate. One of the most heavily lobbied bills of the session, the Bryan Bill was hailed by many as a major step toward reducing CO_2 emissions because it required more fuel-efficient new cars.

In the House of Representatives, a $55 million increase in the budget for international family planning remained despite an across-the-board cut for most foreign aid. The increase brought the total population assistance level to $325 million, a new record. Motivating the increase was a new United Nations Population Fund study reporting that the world's population will triple, to an astounding 14 billion, by the year 2050 if action to control population is not taken. Environmentalists were quick to point out that overpopulation exacerbated (if not caused) every other environmental concern, and called overpopulation "an environmental time bomb."

❧

Every summer, from the time I was seven until I was sixteen, my parents sent me to stay with my maternal grandmother in Tenants Harbor, Maine. In my memory, those months are perfection—perhaps even sacred is not too strong a word. My grandmother lived near the sea, in a tidy white house set on a rise. The view of the cove, stretching in the distance, was pure magic for a little girl from Brockton. We were remote, but not isolated. There was no television, but never mind; instead of making friends with Howdy Doody, I got acquainted with Heidi, and Ann of Green Gables, and Christopher Robin.

Best of all, we had each other. My grandmother managed to give me absolute love at the same time she freed me to explore tide pools and craggy woods and whatever else caught my fancy.

In those years, a friend of my grandmother's told me — to this day I have no idea whether this is true or not — that after a thunderstorm—when the air has been pierced by lightning—ordinary oxygen, O_2, turns into ozone, O_3, which gives people increased energy. It certainly is true that, after a storm, the air has a different smell. I can remember sitting on my grandmother's kitchen steps — a skinny ten-year-old in denim shorts and a yellow plaid halter — breathing in great lungfuls of the stuff.

Fifteen years later, ozone, as the chief component of smog, had been identified as a chemical villain. We learned that ozone is released by gas-burning automobiles. In the presence of sunlight, it combines with other chemicals to form deadly compounds. For people with allergies or breathing problems such as emphysema, ozone can cause great distress. Rather than gain increased energy, humans who breathe smog experience headache, fatigue, and, over enough time, serious respiratory illness, perhaps even cancer.

Now another fifteen years have gone by, and we have come to a new way of thinking about ozone. It seems that it was always there, as a layer at the outer edge of our atmosphere, protecting us from the harmful ultraviolet radiation of the sun.

Unfortunately, one component of several technologies, chlorofluorocarbon (CFC), reacts with and destroys this upper-level ozone, thus allowing more and more ultraviolet radiation to reach the Earth. This excess radiation has sent human skin cancer rates off the charts. It also causes cataracts and may suppress the human immune system. When we fully assess its effect on the vegetation in our ecosystem, however, human ailments may be the least of our worries. According to U.S. Senator John H. Chaffee, "All forms of life on land and in the sea may be at risk."

As President of an international conservation organization, it is my job to fight ozone at ground level and protect it in outer space. I blush as I tell you, however, that after a good thunderstorm, I still like to go out on the back porch and draw a few deep breaths.

Ozone depletion had been taken up by world leaders in Montreal. Overall, the United States has been diligent about complying with the Montreal protocols. In Houston, however, summit leaders would be considering another environmental problem with worldwide ramifications: global warming.

In this case, not only CFCs but also carbon dioxide and methane are the primary culprits. These gases, which mankind started releasing in large quantities during the Industrial Revolution (with its massive use of coal, gasoline engines, and oil-fired electric generating facilities), form a blanket that traps the Earth's heat and causes temperatures to rise. In simple terms, it works the way a greenhouse does — or your car's windshield when you park in the sun. Without this layer of greenhouse gases, the Earth would be too cold for us to inhabit. Subtle alterations in this layer, however, will have major effects on our environment.

As the Earth warms, the waters on it will expand. This, in addition to faster melting of the polar ice caps, will cause sea levels to rise. Scientists predict we will lose — as just two examples — one third of Florida and all of Bangladesh. Both violent tropical storms and droughts will increase, and the climatic conditions favorable to agriculture will shift far north, resulting in large scale migrations of plants and animals— those that can migrate, of course. The rest may vanish. Tidal marshes, the nurseries of marine life, will flood and shift locations, with drastic consequence to commerical fisheries.

1990 was the warmest year in recorded history. Many reputable scientists have declared that global warming is as real a threat, as "here and now" a catastrophe, as ozone depletion. Why, then, did I feel so negative about the way the upcoming Summit would deal with global warming? Because, although I am not a cynic, neither am I any longer an innocent.

There is money to be made in finding substitutes for CFCs, so our power brokers face up to ozone depletion. Global warming, on the other hand, is mainly the result of carbon dioxide. The only way we can get a handle on it is to reduce our use of fossil fuels. This is not a popular idea among oil barons, auto czars, and a wide array of others with economic ties to the use of coal, oil, and gas.

Leading the see-no-evil, hear-no-evil, speak-no-evil advocates for carbon-based power are George Bush, John Sununu, and, in Congress, Rep. John Dingel of Detroit. That's why I was feeling so negative.

On Sunday, July 1, Annie, Arthur, and I drove from Yosemite back to San Francisco with Doug Scott, the Club's Associate Executive Director, and fellow Director Dick Fiddler. One of my campaign promises had been that there would be more singing in the Sierra Club. On that particular ride we sang every song we ever knew and, among us, we knew quite a few: folk songs, protest songs, hymns, musical comedy hits, everything but operatic arias.

The Merrows, determined to have a few stolen days as a family, checked into the familiar Richelieu. In the next two days, I combined sightseeing (Point Reyes, Muir Woods, Bolinas) with time at the office. It was nice, but underneath I was worried. The Fourth of July was approaching and we would be in a strange land.

My New England chauvinism was asserting itself. How could we celebrate Independence Day in California, for heaven's sake? What did a Californian know about liberty, or Paul Revere, or even Bunker Hill? But of course I was wrong. Maybe they had a somewhat different slant on these subjects, but when Doug Scott insisted we spend the day with him in Berkeley, we met some people who really know how to celebrate a holiday.

Doug and his wife met while working on the Alaska Lands Bill in the late 1970s. They named their older daughter Kyana, after an Alaskan river. The Scotts lived in the kind of neighborhood where on a holiday you put up saw horses at each end of the street, and then fill the block with hamburger grills and volleyball nets and lawn chairs. And water balloons! I may spend every July 4 left to me in New England. If so, I shall certainly introduce my friends to that indispensable Californian accoutrement to patriotic frenzy: the water balloon.

Sonoma and a couple of winery tours filled Thursday. On Friday Arthur flew home. To comfort ourselves for his loss, Annie and I indulged in her favorite San Francisco outing: "walking the bridge." Starting at the city's end of the Golden Gate

Bridge, you walk across (sunlight, fleecy clouds, a view so vast and exotic it beggars description), and then down the back roads into Sausalito. You eat a rich ice cream treat, browse in the tourist shops, then take the ferry back across the Bay and a cable car back to the hotel. Believe it or not, that evening we still found the energy to go with friends to the San Francisco Zoo.

The next day Annie went off with some Sierrans to the Club's funky old ski lodge at Donner Pass. I did what any sensible woman left to herself in San Franciso would do — I went shopping for clothes. Of course, I felt I had good reason—I was on my way to the G-7 meeting in Houston. A wardrobe suitable for retreats at Yosemite and training sessions on a Texas ranch just wasn't going to make it for this big do. I went in search of a dress that packed well — and maybe a few accessories.

I know how to lobby in Connecticut. You wait outside the men's room door for Senator Gunther. When he emerges, you shout, "Doc! About that shellfish vote . . . ." Or you supply carefully crafted reports to House Speaker Balducci, hoping he'll read them and be persuaded. Or you spend twenty minutes playing with Representative Mushinsky's baby at a picnic, and then proceed to make your points with her. But how do you lobby the leaders of Germany, Japan, France, Canada, the United Kingdom, Italy, and the United States when they assemble?

By their actions, these men and women form de facto global environmental policies. Recognizing this, environmental groups spend a lot of time figuring out how to influence these summits. Michael Fischer and I flew into Houston, rented a car, and then checked into a far glitzier hotel than Sierra generally chooses (all the cheaper ones had been booked for months). As soon as we were settled in, we joined the rest of the Sierra Club staff in the lobby. Besides Michael and me, our team consisted of Dan Becker, our global warming lobbyist, Kathy Fogel, our tropical forest specialist, and Roni Lieberman, our press person. Together, we were about to begin our assault on G-7.

The secret to influencing a summit is influencing the press. It works this way:

1.   The world leaders hold ceremonial meetings and exchange documents and white papers (most of this has been choreographed in advance by their staffs).

2.   Thousands of press people observe them, read their re-
      leases, decide what their gestures mean, and report it in
      words and pictures.
3.   The staff people scour the news, and then whisper in the
      ears of the world leaders what people must be thinking.
4.   The world leaders in turn make subtle changes in the
      "spin" of their communications, and those subtle changes
      have profound effects on world policies.

Therefore: Forget about influencing the leaders; the key is to
influence the press.

The Sierra Club had declined to join the coalition of environmental groups attending the summit. We decided to go it alone,
partly because the cost of joining the coalition was high and
partly because we wanted to focus on a narrower range of issues,
two in fact: global warming and TFAP.

Each of the other six nations at the summit meeting had
made a promise to reduce emissions of CO_2. It was (and is) an
embarrassment to us that the chief CO_2-producing nation, our
own United States, was dragging its feet. Our main goal in
Houston was to get the Bush administration to acknowledge that
global warming exists and to adopt a policy that does something
about it. Secondarily, we wanted the Tropical Forest Action Plan
— the showpiece of the Paris summit — adapted so as to
eliminate some grim realities that had surfaced in the intervening
year.

Three of us had summit press credentials (representing
Sierra magazine) and so we set off to find press headquarters to
get two more sets. We found that it occupied three floors of
Houston's new glass-and-steel convention center—one floor for
print, one for radio, and the basement devoted to television, with
its vans and trailers and Action Eyes. We stopped at the credentials desk and soon we all possessed laminated press passes with
our pictures on them. Hung on a chain around our necks, they
opened the door to a whole new world of high-powered press.
First, though, they opened the door to all the freebies that
Houston and its businesses lavished on summit attendees. We
were given handsome tote bags with mugs, maps, snacks, scarves,
books, paperweights, and T-shirts. The city of Houston wanted
to be sure that at least *it* got good press.

We moved on upstairs where Roni had already set up our computer and printer in the print media operation — a ballroom, actually, with four enormous TV monitors in the center. While printers from all the summit nations were clattering out news, we would be clattering out press releases. We hoped to add fuel to their fires.

Houston's generosity to the press included all-you-can-eat food. A huge banquet hall was set up with six double buffet lines. There was a choice of Tex-Mex, health food, Japanese food (there being a large contingent of Japanese press in attendance), burgers, steaks, and much more, all day long. There were also tables set with linen cloths and napkins, and waiters to whisk away your plate. An ice cream stand dispensed cones all day; there was free wine and beer. Just outside the door to the banquet hall was a stand where they gave away toothpaste, toothbrushes, combs, aspirin, candy, and cigarettes.

It was dazzling, but we had work to do. We had to figure out the lay of the land, discover where the action was, and begin to make our presence felt. Our secret weapon was our global warming lobbyist, Dan Becker. The veteran of a previous summit, he is blessed with plenty of chutzpah and a real talent for the sound bite.

Dan informed us that the first act of the summit drama would be played out in the White House press headquarters, where John Sununu was to give a press briefing. Since "enviros" do not have favored status at the White House, we decided to attend but to try to be inconspicuous. However, if Sununu said anything about global warming, we would abandon that guise. Becker would jump up on a chair as the session ended and shout, "Sierra Club reaction outside in five minutes!"

There was a risk that we would be banned from future White House press briefings; but we would be almost certain of getting attention for our cause.

Sununu made no mention of global warming until a reporter asked if it would be part of the summit discussion. President Bush's Chief of Staff brushed off the question, saying that it was his opinion that global warming was not an issue. Carbon dioxide comes from plants, he said — a throwback to the old Reagan "killer trees" argument. I stared at him in amazement, shocked to the core by my first personal glimpse of power being so cynically abused.

As the conference ended, Becker leaped on a chair and did his thing. We then trooped out in the hall, followed by a bevy of reporters. I talked to the Fox network cameras. Michael Fischer had the *New York Times*. Becker zeroed in on the Associated Press. We expressed outrage at the lack of action—the backward action — on global warming, and most of the reporters gave us a sympathetic hearing.

We didn't endear ourselves to the other environmental groups who had come under a collective banner. They feared that our behavior would get them all thrown out. Ironically, when the press picked up these environment stories, several times they referred to "the Sierra Club and a coalition of other environmental groups." We chuckled — but we also blushed. There is room in the movement for many variations, and most of the time we work very well together.

Fortuitously, Becker seems to have more lives than a cat. No one was ever banned from the press briefings, but I think he had to promise not to stand on the furniture.

As the summit progressed, we fell into a pattern: Becker would cruise the hallways, listening for action about to happen; then he and Roni would set up interviews with various reporters for us. We also issued press releases about what the leaders were saying, and Roni would distribute them to the right people. Our names and ideas began appearing in the media. The press was receptive, even friendly. We were making news in a place where any scrap of information was apt to set off a media feeding frenzy.

The only unfriendly note was sounded by TV anchorman Brit Hume. When we dropped by the ABC press trailer, we were warmly welcomed by the rest of the crew. Hume, however, made it clear that, in his opinion, we weren't serious journalists and we didn't belong at the summit. He may have been right about our not being journalists, but oh, my, he was wrong about how serious we were.

Word came down that the summit leaders had agreed to make what appeared to be cosmetic changes in the TFAP. Becker, the sound bite king, issued a press release that said, in part: "The changes in the Tropical Forest Action Plan are just a fig leaf to cover the administration's lack of action on global warming." That made a big hit with the press.

We organized our own press conference out on the lawn of the convention center. Houston in July is a sauna. I hadn't realized how insulated we were from the real environment until we went outside into the dense, humid air.

Roni set up a podium and microphone, and the big, green Sierra Club banner that follows us to all our press events. Twenty reporters listened as we hammered on the administration for taking no action on global warming, energy efficiency, or auto fuel efficiency. Every other nation present has taken a stand. The U.S. is the leading producer of the gases that will alter the climate for all living things, yet, we said, we are dragging our feet.

After the press conference, Michael had to return to San Francisco. I stayed on to help with the wrap-up, including one final press release decrying Bush's lack of action.

The summit finale was a press conference with all the world leaders, followed by a question-and-answer session for the American press with George Bush. At that meeting, Bush was peppered with questions about all sorts of things, including his son Neil, who was in the midst of a savings and loan investigation. The president's response to the S&L question was measured and polite, but there was anger there just waiting to spill out.

The very next question went something like this: "How do you respond to the environmentalists who say that what you did on TFAP was just a fig leaf?" Bush seemed to go berserk, spluttering that he didn't have to listen to us because we didn't help him get elected. My disillusionment of the previous day was nothing compared to what I felt then. This man had campaigned as the "environmental President." He was supposed to be the President of all Americans, yet he stood there disavowing me (and all the millions like me) as his constituents. This was a view of Presidential obligation so distorted, so narrow, that I wanted to cry for him.

Later, in the press room, veteran *New York Times* correspondent R.W. Apple came up to us and said, "Wow. The big guy was mad!" Helen Thomas, "the first lady" of the White House press corps, also said, "The President's very mad at you!" We packed up and got out. Nobody would say that the Sierra Club was lily-livered, based on our summit behavior. We could be gutsy, though, because apparently, on this issue, we had nothing to lose

with Sununu, or even Bush. We had a message to get out, and
we had accomplished that goal.

I was dazzled by the high-powered world I had been
exposed to, but it was not until a few days later that I felt real
satisfaction. As I read the *New York Times* editorial castigating
President Bush for his global warming failure, I concluded that
my presence had, indeed, made a difference. When you are
upheld by the *New York Times*, well — how sweet it is!

The adrenaline was still pumping on Wednesday, July 11,
when, late at night, I arrived back in San Francisco. On Thursday
we were supposed to begin planning the 1991 Annual Dinner —
my swan song as President — but I found it hard to put Houston
out of my mind and concentrate on anything as far away and
mundane as an annual banquet nearly ten months off.

Traditionally, the outgoing President gets to choose the
main speaker for the event and controls most other details.
However, I had only two requests. I wanted a woman as speaker,
and I wanted a woman to receive the John Muir Award —the
highest award the club can give. It is awarded annually but had
been given only once to a female. The committee agreed without
hesitation with my feelings about a speaker. I knew they would.
I had covered all bases by lobbying each member ahead of time.
The system does work, but if you really want something out of it,
sometimes you have to oil it first. The Honors and Awards
Committee still had to be convinced about the John Muir Award,
however, so I had a good deal of lobbying ahead of me.

In the middle of the meeting, I was called to the telephone.
My secretary said it was long-distance — Massachusetts — and
urgent.

It was Tony Cortese, the Dean of Environmental Studies at
Tufts University outside of Boston. I am a Tufts graduate and it
happens that Tony Cortese was the President of my senior class.
Then he was Mr. Joe College, and I was a humble work-scholar-
ship student. After graduation, he became a power in the Massachusetts environmental structure; I became a drone in the Connecticut environmental movement.

Years passed, and eventually I was elected to the Sierra Club
presidency. I notified our alumni magazine. Tony read about me
and now (be still my heart), he was waiting for me on a telephone
across the continent!

Cucumber cool, as always, I asked what I could do for him. He wanted to know if I could fill in for Maurice Strong, of the United Nations environmental program, and deliver a lecture at the North Pacific International Forum in Sapporo, Japan, on August 2. Strong, he said, had been taken ill. I was to speak on ozone depletion and acid rain.

Did I say my adrenals were pumping as a result of Houston? That was a gentle stream compared to the Niagara of emotion coursing through me as I listened to Tony. I tried not to sound overly excited. We Sierra Presidents are very laid back. When he mentioned a first-class ticket for Arthur to go with me, I even had the sense to negotiate that into two business-class tickets so Annie could come too. All other expenses would be paid and an honorarium was involved. I made certain he understood that I was definitely saying yes.

The next day Michael and I drove to Lake Tahoe for a Centennial Campaign Planning Committee meeting. It was held in a cottage owned by the Director of the Sierra Club Foundation. I should have been enchanted with the surroundings, but it was getting to be like overdosing on fudge. Yosemite, Bolinas, Austin, Houston, Lake Tahoe, San Francisco: I was beginning to think this was true life.

A tiny voice was whispering in the back of my brain, "No, Sue. Stay in the real world." But then a louder voice answered back: "Next month, Japan!" and the tiny voice backed away. I watched a pair of sailboats dipping and gliding on Tahoe's shining waters, and I didn't even bother to pinch myself.

Annie's adventures were also beginning to pile up. While I was in Houston, she stayed at the Clair Tappan Lodge at Donner Pass. She was helping out as a day care counselor for the children of parents attending an environmental education workshop.

On Saturday, July 14, our Director of Finance and Administration collected Annie and brought her to Tahoe. Michael and I had to go back to the office that night, but Annie — who knows a good deal when she sees it — quickly made friends with the two daughters of the Club's Director of Development, who was staying in a nearby condo. They, of course, invited her to stay over. She was returned to San Francisco the next day by the Centennial Campaign Director. Annie appeared to have invented the Sierra Club's private underground railroad.

The reason Michael and I went back to San Francisco early had to do with another "discretionary fund" item I was backing. Three Sierra members, all marketing experts in their business lives, had volunteered to spend some time with me and our membership and public affairs directors to brainstorm about how to "bring Sierra marketing into the twentieth century."

We had dinner together that night and met all through the next day, talking about focus groups and data collection. It was a lovefest of marketers. They suggested fascinating strategies and one of them, telephone marketing expert Joe Buckley, volunteered to travel widely for us collecting "perception data."

On July 16 Annie and I flew back to Connecticut. I had been away since June 22. I tried to take up my old life — went to the dentist, taught an adult ed class, cleaned the refrigerator — but some gears were not quite in place. As I look back, those ten days were mostly spent marking time, waiting to go to Japan.

I came fully alive once, during a day trip to Manhattan. There I met with Bob Meyers — the father of a staff member and Executive Director of the Carnegie Council — who has travelled extensively in Japan. He gave me a quick course in geography and manners. If I did not disgrace my country while I was in Japan, the credit goes to him.

I also took time to buy a "credibility suit." You certainly do need more clothes as a Sierra Club President than as a Hartford lobbyist. Arthur was kind enough not to say, "I told you so." But then, he had a free trip to Sapporo to solace him.

On July 26 I returned to San Francisco for a Conservation Coordinating Committee (CCC) meeting at Dominican College in San Rafael. It also gave me time to work with the staff on my Japan escapade. My free hours were filled with briefings on Japan's environmental problems and our role in the north Pacific Rim. A Sierra Club member and professional speech writer who had written for Japanese audiences helped draft my speech.

Meanwhile the staff picked out books, calendars, and T-shirts appropriate for gifts to my hosts and arranged for business cards with my name in English on one side and Japanese on the other. Even the CCC members got into the act. They took me to dinner at a Japanese restaurant — another lesson in etiquette — and presented me with a phrase book.

Monday, July 30, began with a negotiating meeting: the Sierra Club vs. the Sierra Club Legal Defense Fund. I said earlier that they were "of" but not formally a subdivision of the regular Sierra Club. What the connection should be was the basis of the conflict we were attempting to negotiate.

Although tempers had sometimes flared at the top of our two organizations, workers in the field usually got along fine. Lately, however, volunteers for both sides were confused, management was embarrassed, and the conflict wasn't doing much for the environment either. In the meantime, the leaders of the two groups continued to circle each other, growing more wary as time went on. It had all begun with the spotted owl. SCLDF wanted stronger action, and they took some stands in the press that we disagreed with — totally.

We said, "You can't do that." They said, "Sure we can, we're completely separate from you." We said, "You have our name; we gave birth to you twenty years ago; we are eighty-eight years older than you; you have to listen to us."

They said, "Legally we are in no way beholden to you. If we want to take a different stand, we will." We said, "Not with our name you won't; you know perfectly well you raise millions of dollars because people confuse us; give us back our name." They said, "No!"

And so it went. Listening to the debate, I thought to myself, it sounds just like an adolescent impatient with his old-fashioned parents. Fortunately, in this family, there was also a good deal of love and respect. It was my hope that those feelings would serve as a foundation on which we could build a mutually agreeable ongoing structure.

At noon, a solicitous staff person hustled me off to the airport shuttle. There I met Annie and Arthur, who had gotten up at 4:00 a.m. to fly to San Francisco. How proud and happy I was to see them, not just because I love them so much but because this trip was something very special that I was able to give them.

This is a feeling too often reserved for men, this pride in doing something really terrific for your loved ones. It goes way beyond a special chocolate cake, or typing a report, the things to which circumstances limit so many women. This was a trip to Japan!

I closed my eyes, directed a brief thank you heavenward, and reaffirmed my commitment to the women's movement. More of us should experience this marvelous lift.

August 1990

· ·

The Cold War was over. Glasnost dominated Soviet-American relations. Autocratic regimes in Romania, East Germany, and Poland made way for new forms of democracy. As August 1990 began, peace prevailed.

Renewed communications between eastern Europe and the rest of the world brought horror stories about the deterioration of the environment under communism. High air-pollution levels, fouled waterways, and climbing disease rates all stood witness to the devastation that accompanied technology without regulation.

As spending on the weapons of war declined, the United States government earmarked billions of dollars for the cleanup of its own grave pollution problems at active and inactive nuclear weapons plants in more than thirty states. Observers noted that Department of Energy spending would soon be within a billion dollars of the total annual budget of the U.S. Environmental Protection Agency. One branch of the federal government, it appeared, was causing more pollution than all the others combined. Indeed, nearly as much as all other branches of government plus private industry.

On Capitol Hill, progress on the new Clean Air Act lagged as conference committee members went off on vacation. Early agreement on a CFC phase-out program, however, gave a promise of good things to come.

Then, on August 2, Iraqi troops stormed into the desert sheikdom of Kuwait, seizing its capital city and its rich oilfields. President Bush immediately accused Iraqi leader Saddam Hussein of "naked aggression" and, within days, began mounting a military response that soon included war ships and aircraft carriers in the Persian Gulf and troops on the Saudi Arabia border.

As Americans faced the possibility of war, oil and anti-oil interests struggled to make their views known. Environmentalists proclaimed that American military personnel must not be allowed to die for oil. In the U.S. Senate, in a midnight move just before the recess, Senator Frank Murkowski (R-AK) amended a Department of Defense appropriations bill with language that potentially opened coastlines and wilderness areas for oil exploration.

George Bush, however, in all his public statements, played on Hussein's aggression against the people of Kuwait. He seemed almost unaware of the threat to global security inherent in America's oil dependency.

੨ӑ

Japan is a lesson in elegance under duress. Japan is myth and ritual underpinning high-volume productivity. Japan is pragmatic, enigmatic, shiny as silk, shadowy, shrill. And it is nothing whatsoever like America.

Except for a week in Italy nearly twenty-four years ago, I had never left the continental United States. I wish now that I had taken more time to prepare myself for the enormity of the Japan adventure. Instead, I was racing through life right up to the moment when I literally ran — suitcase and briefcase flapping — to the departure area where I was to meet my husband and daughter.

The plane was a 747 and we were in business class, with larger seats and nicer food than usual, plus free movies. I am always amused by Annie when she has a chance to travel other than economy class. Her back straightens ever so slightly, and her smile becomes less saucy, more gentle. Patient and forbearing with the "servants," she assumes the air of a princess born to this kind of life.

I reviewed my speech — fine tuning, practicing the emphases — while Arthur and Annie watched the movies. The ten-hour flight passed easily. Then came the first challenge: coping with customs and baggage at the Tokyo airport, where we changed airlines for the journey to Sapporo, on the island of Hokkaido in northern Japan.

At the baggage claim area, we watched the people, and were fascinated, until we realized that they had all claimed their luggage and ours was nowhere to be seen. Annie began to lose her composure. After all, she had been up for twenty-two hours and the day wasn't over yet. Arthur made complicated gestures to the baggage handler and, perhaps stirred by Annie's tears, he soon reappeared with all that was missing.

We stumbled our way across the huge airport and, after a wrong turn or two, found our gate. There was no place to sit in the crowded waiting area, and our U.S. money wouldn't work to buy a cold drink. Annie continued to wear a very worried face.

When we finally boarded the plane to Sapporo, I found myself seated next to Earl Anthony, the Canadian Director General for conservation of the Yukon. He was to represent Canada on the panel I was keynoting the next day.

I was having a wonderful time, feasting on facts about the Arctic, as well as a beautifully presented plate of Japanese food — until I happened to glance over at Annie. Since she doesn't like many vegetables or any seafood, she was not charmed and was not being charming. I decided to ignore her. How many fussy American teenagers, I wondered, actually die of starvation in foreign lands?

At Chitose Airport in Sapporo, a lovely Japanese woman and her chauffeur were waiting for us. A representative of the Fletcher School of Law and Diplomacy (the Tufts school hosting the Forum), she spoke fluent English and smoothed our way with grace.

There was one awkward moment when the chauffeur gestured for Arthur to get into the left-hand front seat of the small black limo. Arthur balked, thinking he was being asked to drive to the hotel. Things calmed down when he realized that the steering wheel was on the right (like Annie, he had been up over twenty-four hours by then; we were all a little dazed).

Our hosts helped us check into the Sapporo Grand Hotel — very European, very posh — and asked me to stay in the lobby to straighten out payment for my reimbursement and honorarium. I was ushered into a sitting area where a gentleman soon arrived carrying a briefcase and a shopping bag. He gave me a receipt to sign, then turned over the shopping bag. In it was the equivalent of $13,000 — in yen! We carried this money, a thick wad of paper bills, with us wherever we went in Japan, since there seemed to be no other way to cope with it.

Arms full of yen, yawning, I made my way to our room, which was furnished with beautiful western-style furniture, including twin beds and a fold-out sofa for Annie. Arthur was already stretched out on one of the beds. Annie was busy exploring the contents of the desk, refrigerator, and bathroom cabinets. I dropped my loot at Arthur's feet and climbed into the other bed. Exhausted, we all fell asleep without delay.

Because of crossing the international dateline, we had lost a day. My speech was scheduled for 1:00 p.m. the following afternoon. Perhaps due to jet lag, it was impossible to sleep more than a few hours. We were up before dawn, Arthur reading about Hokkaido and studying maps, me practicing my speech.

The Sierra Club gifts had been sent ahead, but had ended up at the wrong hotel. Our walking trip to retrieve them revealed a handsome modern city with a beautiful town square. Back at the hotel, I had to leave my family for a prelunch speakers' meeting. As I turned my back and walked away from them, through the door of the meeting room, I felt as if I were diving into a murky pond.

Tony Cortese welcomed me, and hearing his familiar Massachusetts accent bucked me up. Then we all sat around a table and, through interpreters, introduced ourselves. I spoke of my role in the Sierra Club and of our mission to influence environmental policy through grassroots lobbying. There were nods and murmurs. We were ushered into a small dining room where an elegant western luncheon of salad, beef, tiny potatoes, pastry, and wine was served on delicate Japanese plates by a smiling, waistcoated waiter. My luncheon partner was a Russian (Alexy V. Yablokov, Vicechair for Ecology of the USSR Supreme Soviet) who seemed to be the most intrigued by the Sierra Club's work, and to have a better grasp of our potential than the others in the room. His first question, "Vat is dis e-mail business?" set us off on a vigorous discussion. *

---

*I often wondered what had become of Alexy during the subsequent turmoil in the Soviet Union. Months later, one December day in 1991, his voice boomed from my car radio—a familiar, heavily accented sound bite about an environmental issue. He was introduced as "environmental adviser to Boris Yeltsin."

I would have enjoyed our discussion enormously, except that I knew there were 400 people — Japanese environmental leaders, students of the Fletcher program, and the good people of Sapporo — assembling in a large hall nearby to hear the American woman speak. I wanted very much to convince them of the need for international cooperation and I wanted to speak out strongly, but without causing rancor about Japan's role in tropical deforestation. I knew I had a good speech. I knew that I was a veteran speech maker. Still my stomach was in knots.

Someone handed me a glossy, four-color, sixteen-page brochure that had my picture in it. It gave my name and Sierra Club affiliation in both English and Japanese characters and listed my credentials in a most impressive way. Best of all, I liked the photograph of me, in high-necked white blouse, flashing a Candice Bergen smile at the camera. Ranged alongside Kim Ryong-Un from North Korea and Li Jinchang from China, I must have been quite a surprise to many who examined that program. I was not your usual Japanese keynoter.

An annual event, the North Pacific International Forum is sponsored jointly by the University of Hokkaido and the Fletcher School of Law and Diplomacy at Tufts University. Graduate students from the two schools spend ten days discussing economic issues of the north Pacific Rim. A feature of the forum is a one-day seminar, open to the public, on a topic of special interest. This year it was the environment, specifically "Challenges of Managing the Global Environment: Implications for the Northern Rim."

Thanks to Mr. Yablokov's friendly questions, I began to relax. When it was time to take our places in the auditorium, I breathed deep and held my head high. However, when I saw the translation arrangements, I was momentarily baffled. Each member of the panel and of the audience had earphones that could be tuned to any one of five simultaneous translations: English, Russian, Korean, Japanese, and Chinese. Annie, whose generation appears to have innate comprehension of all things electronic, came up to explain it to me. I settled down, facing the audience. I was still nervous, but when I heard myself being introduced as "Susan Merro-san, Shierra Crub" — the sun came out.

I told the large audience that we came from many different countries, but that we are all citizens of the same planet and that our joint actions, as consumers of natural resources, are driving that planet toward environmental collapse. I tried to speak slowly and with as much passion as I could. Because they defy translation, I could use no idioms or figures of speech. I did, however, compare the Japanese practice of contracting hundred-year mortgages, thus passing debt to the next generation, to the exploitation by industrialized nations of resources that will be irreplaceable in our children's (and their children's) lifetimes.

Acid rain and ozone depletion were familiar subjects to my audience. I broadened my speech to include global warming, which has been of less concern in the Orient because it is not perceived as having a direct or immediate effect. When I spoke of grain belt drought and more violent typhoons, they nodded. When I spoke of sea-level rises that would destroy commercial fish habitats, remap coastal cities, and create as many as half a million "greenhouse refugees" from South Pacific islands, they grew even more intent. I had their full attention.

Among the countries represented at the seminar were the world's largest importer of tropical hardwoods (Japan), the biggest lender of money for international development (Japan), two major exporters of old growth forests (Canada, United States), and a major potential burner of high sulfur coal (China). I tried to help them see that destroying tropical forests — even apart from the destruction of habitat and extinction of species — is unacceptable twice over. First it removes nature's largest carbon-fixing mechanisms, trees, so that they can no longer convert carbon dioxide to life-giving oxygen. Second, by burning the brush, and sometimes the product itself, carbon dioxide is released in ever greater quantities into the global atmosphere.

I made it clear, I think, that when a nation supplies the money for development, it assumes a moral responsibility for the damage done; that all of us who burn coal, oil, or our own forests, and even those who grow rich as an indirect result of increasing the greenhouse effect, must share responsibility. The audience listened politely and clapped enthusiastically. I felt they were impressed. The dignified gentleman who had introduced me bowed as I walked down from the platform.

After a short break, all the panelists reassembled on stage. Dr. John Perry, a Tufts professor, gave each of the others a few minutes to make statements. Then we answered questions. The audience was friendly and polite, and far more patient than westerners would have been. By the end of the afternoon, they had been sitting for four hours. The most provocative comments came from my fellow panelists. Obviously I had pricked (if not gored) a few sacred cows by placing blame for global warming on some of the most profitable enterprises in all our countries. What I found most remarkable, however, was the rapport and the commonality of interest that developed among us.

While the hotel management transformed the auditorium into a reception hall, we panelists were taken to a nearby room for Japanese tea. I had done well, so far, with some sort of translator never too far away. Now I found myself seated on the sidelines, thoroughly enjoying the hubbub around me but understanding little of what was going on. I was in even deeper water when an excited Japanese gentleman approached me. He held out a newspaper with a headline that he seemed to think important, but it was all in Japanese. Speaking in machine-gun Japanese, he tried to tell me what it said, but the only word that I understood clearly was "Kuwait."

"That's nice," I said sweetly. "Thank you for telling me about it." An hour or so later, Arthur told me that Saddam Hussein had invaded Kuwait and now controlled that country's vast oil supplies. My reaction, aside from concern about the human suffering involved, was naive in the extreme. "Well," I said, "now Bush will have to give us some serious leadership toward energy conservation!"

When we returned to the assembly hall, it contained two long, intersecting tables, each groaning with platters of elegantly prepared Japanese food. Even Annie found things she could enjoy — especially the Japanese version of french fried potatoes. I was beginning to feel at home. The room was packed with men and women in western business clothes, all looking tense — a scene you can find most any day in Hartford. They were all talking in a language I couldn't follow — but that's true on a city bus in New Haven. At any rate, these were speeches by local politicians, and those are the same anywhere in the world. Only the toasts, the raised glasses, and the shouts of "Kampai!" seemed alien to me.

The Sapporo Women's Club, which tries to assist international visitors to the city, had assigned one of its members as our interpreter. She came up to me at the reception, leading a young man and two older gentlemen. She explained that they produced and marketed a special health elixir at a factory — described as a golden pyramid — on the outskirts of town. They very much wanted us to visit their plant and, after checking our schedules, we agreed to stop by on our way out to the airport at the end of our visit. The younger man, especially, won my heart by saying that my speech had affected him deeply and that he felt we had much in common.

By then it was well into the evening. As we left for our hotel, Dr. Perry asked me to join the other panelists for breakfast the next day. He said it was momentous that North Korea had sent a representative to such a gathering, and he wanted to take advantage of the opportunity to create an ongoing dialogue. I learned later that all previous efforts to discuss environmental affairs with North Korea had been fruitless.

Sure enough, twelve hours later, I sat between the representatives of the two Koreas, eating oatmeal and nodding sagely, as they agreed to continue the discussions that had started in Sapporo. What an enormous impact it would have on the entire family of nations if these two countries — out of mutual concern for the environment — could begin to function cooperatively. Maybe, I said to myself, the threat to the globe's natural resources will be the ultimate agent for world peace. The Koreans seemed eager (or at least as eager as you can seem through an interpreter) to work with the other nations, and I was so carried away by this groundswell of amity that I offered to draft a mission statement. We needed to put something on paper — something on which we could all agree — and get it signed in order to formalize this breakthrough and guarantee its continuing. I promised to have it ready for signing when we met a little later to participate in a panel for Fletcher students.

I distributed my Sierra gifts (which Annie, bless her, had neatly wrapped). We all smiled and bowed. Even small amounts of encouragement to foreign environmentalists, while their countries' environmental ethic is emerging, can yield significant benefits. The Sapporo meeting, by strengthening its participants' concern for the interrelatedness of all our environmental fates, had done something very important. I believed I had helped in this and I left the breakfast elated.

At the meeting with the students, I found myself sitting next to a young man who had grown up in Westbrook, Connecticut, and whose father was first selectman there. Small world. Afterwards, the panelists met, hemmed and hawed a bit over the mission statement I had drafted, but finally all signed it.

That evening we were invited to a traditional Japanese dinner at a restaurant that specializes in crab dishes. Annie was skeptical — but our hosts were the Fletcher program's Japanese representatives. This was a matter of diplomacy, I told her; no arguments. At what seemed to me to be a small, obscure restaurant, we were shown into a private room with straw mats on the floor and a low table surrounded by pillows. We removed our shoes and sat down. Eventually Japanese women in kimonos took pity on us and brought some back rests that looked like beach chairs.

Before the night was through, we had crab in every guise conceivable. But first, the hors d'ouevres: raw shrimp, heads still on, their black eyes gazing up from bowls of chipped ice, were set before us. I had been warned that the Japanese take a certain amount of pleasure in watching westerners cope with their food. I ate my shrimp gamely, but Annie drew the line. Instead she nibbled on some cracked crab legs. There followed crab custard, crab soup, crab casserole, and the pièce de résistance: a whole horsehair crab. The size of dinner plates, they were placed before us cracked and ready to eat. The horsehair name comes from the bristles on the shell. Our hosts were very gracious and patient with us. I think they thought we were good sports. Underneath, however, I was yearning for a bite of mom's good home cookin'.

We had agreed to join some of the students at a nearby disco for a final fling. We left the restaurant guided by our interpreter and soon were engulfed by a throng of religious celebrants. Men in traditional costume were carrying elaborate shrines on their shoulders and chanting. In the shadowy streets, with the sights and sounds and smells of an older Japan all about us, I had a sharp perception of a world very different from any I knew. It sent a chill up my spine.

Our guide led us on foot through the crowd. We turned a corner and came upon a special drum ceremony. Periodically, men dressed in loincloths would beat furiously on huge drums. The noise echoed off the tall buildings and nearly took our breath away. We held hands and snaked through the crowd. Arthur was still carrying about a zillion yen in a belly pack. I reassured myself that there was supposed to be very little street crime in Japan.

Our guide deposited us at the disco. When I thanked her, I handed her a small, wrapped gift, a Sierra Club T-shirt. She was by no means pleased, and became rather flustered. I was told later that I had violated the code by giving her a gift when she had nothing to give in return.

The disco had loud rock music and flashing strobe lights. Annie, soon to be a high school freshman, adored it. As she danced by, gyrating next to a Fletcher graduate student—a college man!—her smile told me that even a meal of sushi and seaweed would have been OK with her just then.

The next morning, promptly at 9 a.m., a red limo called for us. The woman from the Sapporo Women's Club had come to take us to the elixir factory and then to the airport. There really is a golden pyramid. You approach it via a long, tree-lined driveway. Truly impressive, about five stories high, it is sheathed in reflective gold glass and seems to be without windows or doors, except for one entrance, tucked under a corner, guarded by a uniformed doorman.

The Young Corporation boasts that it has only one product and that its final aim, "the science of gentleness," is to make full use of Mother Nature for the benefit of mankind, but only while paying full respect to nature, both on a "global scale" and in the home. The bilingual brochure they gave us explains that "this 30-meter pyramid, our ideal head office and factory, stands tall, surrounded by a serene forest of great trees. . . . This pyramid, constructed as a 'symbol of health,' represents the belief that health is the result of balancing four factors: good physical shape, nutrition, lifestyle, and the mind."

Evidently the Young elixir is a financial success. The doorman showed us into the atrium of the pyramid where men and women in uniforms and white gloves stood at attention, as we gazed up into the apex. The floors of the building were marble, the walls a subdued gray. Through great glass windows, we were able to watch the elixir being processed from fermented soy beans. It was like wine making, with aging casks and such.

We were told that the elixir "is a unique liquid produced from a symbiotic culture of living bacteria." Without promising anything explicit, the company states that good health is the result of the ability of one's body to resist illness and disease, the implication being that a dose of Young will enhance immunity.

In the President's office, we were served goblets of raw milk with ice cubes. It seems they had puzzled about what to offer visiting environmentalists, and the finest raw milk from the best Hokkaido dairy seemed just the ticket (Hokkaido is the Vermont of Japan). They spoke briefly about waste minimization in their production process (since nothing is thrown away, there is no pollution), and we thanked them profusely for the tour. Later on, after we got home, we began a correspondence with our hosts at the pyramid. They have all become members of the Sierra Club. We have a bottle of the elixir, which Arthur agreed to try. Funny, he hasn't done so yet.

As we continued to the airport, we marveled that we had seen both sides of Japan merged in one endeavor — the almost mystical concern for stability, balance, and beauty combined with mass production and high-powered direct-marketing techniques.

At the airport we boarded another 747 for the vacation part of our adventure — a day and a half in Kyoto and a half-day in Tokyo. As it turned out, this was ridiculous, not only because it was so short, but because it was so hot. Travelling in Japan in August is like sight-seeing Mississippi at the same time of year. However, it was the only time we had, and we tried to make the most of it.

We flew to Osaka and took a bus into Kyoto, checking into the Kyoto Hotel, right in the downtown shopping district. This was our first night on our own as a family. We strolled the streets, peering into shops and restaurants. When it came time for dinner, however, we really blew it. We were passing the Kyoto McDonald's and decided that we just were not ready for another gustatory adventure. We took some burgers and fries back to our hotel for supper, and spent the rest of the night glued to CNN, trying to catch up on the news from the Middle East.

The temples of Kyoto are lavish and delicate. The Buddhas of Kyoto are layered with gold. The bridges of Kyoto are arches of heart-stopping perfection. The murals of Kyoto rank among the best of the world's art treasures — but it was beastly hot and I was staggering through the low that always follows a high like an international speech.

I read once that General MacArthur had drawn an inviolable circle around Kyoto when U.S. bomber targets were discussed. For that alone, the man deserves his own Hall of Fame. I pray that beautiful city will always be so respectfully treated, because I intend to go back some day and see what I missed. We did take an all-day bus tour of the Shogun's Palace, the Golden Pavilion, temples, pagodas, etc., but mostly I yearned to get back on the air-cooled bus. We drank Coke after Coke; it was 97 degrees, and very humid.

We went back the following day to explore the emperor's palace and grounds on our own. Then we boarded the famous Bullet Train for a trip to Tokyo. With the help of a guide, we found our reserved spot at the railway terminal (it was marked by numbers on the platform). Sure enough, the train pulled in, right on time, and the door closest to our reserved seats opened directly in front of us. We rocketed along through the Japanese countryside, making the 320-mile trip to Tokyo in two hours and fifty-three minutes — with a minimal expenditure of energy, I am told.

We knew there was no way to take in Tokyo in one morning, so we settled for taking in one small part of Tokyo as thoroughly as possible. Using a city map, we set out to find a public garden that had been recommended to us as being especially beautiful. We had the garden almost to ourselves and spent several hours strolling along its meandering paths, admiring the patterns and careful color contrasts of the plantings, the economy of design in the rock and gravel portions, the placid beauty of the reflecting pools. The artful control of nature was, in Annie's word, awesome. We felt we were recapturing a serenity that the world, even here in Japan, has otherwise relinquished.

The bus to the airport brought us back to the twentieth century. By the time we had finished at the airport and boarded the plane, we were again the children of one world, going home to a nation which is, for better or for worse, far more pluralistic than any other on this earth.

In San Francisco, I left Arthur and Annie at the airport to fly home to Connecticut, while I went back to the Sierra Club office. I shall never forget the look on the face of our finance officer, Andrea Bonnette, when I dropped more than one million yen on her desk.

I don't know how Arthur got up and went to work the next day; it took me a full week to recover. It is not simple fatigue— you are really out of it. A friend had warned me not to make any important decisions the first week I was back. Alas, a Sierra Club President does not have the luxury of postponing decisions.

Michael Fischer and his energy troops were waiting for me with pronouncements, press releases, and pleas for a sane national energy policy. They believed the oil companies would use events in the Middle East to convince Congress to weaken the Clean Air Act about to be born. In point of fact, a number of provisions in the act would enhance energy security and we needed to make that clear at once.

I had a good many sensitive administrative matters piling up — not the least of which was the hospitalization of David Gardiner, the head of our Washington office, who had been struck by a car and seriously hurt while riding his bike to work — but we managed to find time, on August 9, to release a short statement. In it, I called on Congress to reconvene and pass the Bryan Bill at once, because of its huge potential for saving fuel.

In an act of high cynicism, Senator Frank Murkowski of Alaska had already used the Mideast crisis to justify an amendment to a defense appropriations bill that threatened oil drilling in heretofore forbidden areas. Our release slapped at him with the words, "The very same oil companies and auto makers that only four months ago were painting themselves green for Earth Day have used the Iraqi invasion to fill their coffers with something green."

The next day we sent a two-page letter to the nearly 5,000 names on our "leaders list." It said, in part:

"Even if we escape from immediate danger, there are vital long-term lessons to be learned from this current crisis. We have the opportunity to let Americans who have not learned from the past know that it is dangerous to our environment and to our security to be so dependent on oil — foreign and otherwise.

"Our leaders need to hear this loud and clear. The Sierra Club is doing everything it can this month to reach out to the general public and elected officials to repeat these basic points:

"1. Saddam Hussein gets his power because of short-sighted energy policies favoring excessive consumption of fossil fuels. If the American economy were as energy efficient as that of our most successful economic competitor, Japan, the world would have far less need for the oil from Iraq and Kuwait, and Hussein could not tamper with our fate.

"2. The same energy efficiency technologies that would break Hussein's power to blackmail the industrial world would also avert the looming danger of global warming. Energy efficiency, global climate stability, wilderness protection, and national security are linked in the simplest possible way: What helps one problem helps all four.

"3. Increases in energy efficiency would also reduce the U.S. trade deficit, generate a new wave of economic growth among American industries that produce energy-efficient technologies, and stimulate economic growth in the U.S. Our total GNP actually increased from the mid-70s to early 80s while our energy consumption decreased 3 percent per year."

In the following week, editorial pages across the country carried letters and op ed articles over my name, pushing the Bryan Bill and demanding energy conservation. The more Bush refused to admit the relationship between the invasion of Kuwait and the U.S. importation of oil, the madder I got. An article in *USA Today* on August 14, headlined, "Susan D. Merrow: An Opposing View," began, "Like an opportunistic vulture, the oil industry gorged on the fear created by Iraq's invasion of Kuwait to satiate its hunger for petrodollars. Now it expects the American people to feed it the environment as well."

The next week, the Sierra Club ran a full-page advertisement regarding the lack-of-an-energy-policy/drill-the-wilderness-and-oceans issue. It contained clipouts to return to Bush, Congress, and the Club.

During that time, aside from energy matters, I was busy with an array of Sierra issues. It was in this week, I think, that I finally comprehended how complex (and ornery) an animal I was trying to ride. There were nice moments, such as the ceremony recognizing twenty Sierra employees for long years of service. There were also frustrating moments.

The Sierra Club Legal Defense Fund had presented a totally unacceptable document to us. "No," we said, "We must have control of the use of our own name." "OK," the lawyers said, "put down on paper what you would accept." They were acting exactly like lawyers. The problem was that we had always assumed these particular lawyers were ours!

But never mind our lawyer cousins, there were also plenty of sibling problems to deal with.

Item. The Los Angeles Chapter decided to sponsor an outing in Hawaii and disagreements over arrangements quickly escalated to heated correspondence involving the Board, the two chapters, and the Council Outing Committee. Later the Hawaii Chapter decided to visit New Zealand and our National Outings Committee was irate at not being consulted. Outings are a major Sierra activity, with many dollars at stake. It was important to smooth these waters.

Item. David Gardiner, in Washington, was not doing well in the hospital. Repeated surgery led to calls for blood donations and then prayers. The outpouring of love and offers of help from fellow Sierrans was overwhelming. Proud as I was of our support network, worry about David colored everything I did.

Item. The North Carolina Chapter, some of whose members live near a proposed low-level radioactive waste disposal site, appealed on its own to the national Nuclear Regulatory Commission. Their concern was the so called "best management practice" for storing such waste. But never mind the pros and cons of the issue; procedurally the Sierra Club simply cannot allow local chapters to deal unilaterally with federal agencies. In fairness to all members, there has to be dispassionate review of the merits of the issue. This potentially embarassing incident could be ascribed to failures within the national policy system. We had no policy on low-level radioactive waste; our North Carolina members were out in front with no national consensus within the organization to give them direction.

Nevertheless, when you deal with the feds as the Sierra Club, people have a right to assume you speak for the entire Club. It is not fair to members in Nebraska to have policy made — without review — in North Carolina. Indeed, on both substantive and procedural grounds, the Ohio Chapter had already filed an objection to North Carolina's action. This was an especially tricky situation because of the hysteria that any mention of radioactive waste elicits.

I want to pause here and discuss the NIMBY syndrome, a much misunderstood environmental process. NIMBY is an acronym for "Not In My Backyard." It is most often used to describe environmentally illiterate landowners who scream in outrage when needed public facilities are proposed for their neighborhoods. It also encompasses what I think of as "born-again enviros," those whose passions often get the better of their common sense.

The pivotal word here is "needed." Often the facilities are not really needed or have been thoughtlessly placed. Objection to them can bring about a healthy reexamination of how the decision was made. Some, however, especially various waste-disposal facilities, must be built until we, as a society, substantially reduce our volume of waste.

Whether or not the need is real makes no difference to a NIMBY. He or she uses every tool available — including environmental law — to fight the proposed structure. In so doing, NIMBYs often give serious environmentalists a black eye. So you would think that environmental leaders would put down NIMBYs, wouldn't you? Unfortunately it's far more complex than that. For one thing, sometimes they're right. Indeed, usually there is merit to some part of their claims. Beyond that, once a person becomes a NIMBY, he cannot help opening his mind to basic environmental truths. I have seen it happen dozens of times. Today's haranguing NIMBY is tomorrow's informed activist.

There is a final, but extremely important issue here: the relationship between LULUs and NIMBYs. Silly as the acronyms sound, they reach into the very gut of America's classism and racism. LULU stands for Locally Unpopular Land Use, and, as planning jargon, seems to crop up in connection with ghettos and poor rural areas.

Studies show that NIMBYism most often occurs in poverty-level neighborhoods without political power. Why? It's certainly not because the people who live in such places complain more. No, the fact is, we tend to use those neighborhoods to deposit our waste, to site less desirable industry, or to pave over for a new superhighway. The most polluted zip codes in the United States are also the lowest in income levels.

OK. But what if you are President of the Sierra Club and it appears that NIMBYism has emerged in the North Carolina chapter? Even worse, that two chapters are in conflict because one has acted unilaterally?

First off, I refused to stereotype any subdivision of the Club. These were real people with a real problem. Our solution began with a heart-to-heart chat with Carolina leader Jesse Riley, a thoughtful man and an expert on radioactive waste issues; followed by a weekend workshop in Washington. Warren Liebold of our Energy Committee planned to do some heavyweight listening and educating on Saturday, followed, he wrote me, "by a mop-up session on Sunday after a night of meditation, deep reflection, and beer." Our goal was to reach a compromise — to get the North Carolina petition withdrawn until the national Club had time to chart its course.

Item. Money makers, always sought after, bring their own set of problems. Should we add children's books to our highly successful publications list? Should local chapters be able to sponsor retail outlets, as many nature centers do? Can we accept money from the sale of a New Age music tape without appearing to endorse all New Age music? All of these questions were on the table.

Item. Demographics, marketing techniques, improved electronic communications, all the problems of keeping up with the times were pushed by some members, while others demanded what seemed like everlasting debates on more philosophic topics such as: Who has a right to speak for the Club? How do we set priorities and then allot appropriate funding? What planning mechanisms guarantee the broadest member input? When is it OK for us to disagree publicly with another environmental group? Sometimes I wondered how we would ever be able to march at the head of the issues parade when our feet were so tangled in technology and red tape.

On August 13, after a hot and heavy two-day meeting of the Club's Finance Committee, I flew home. I had been away two and a half weeks and I was beginning to feel a lack of balance in my life.

Of course, being home offered no real surcease of responsibility. There were sixty-five messages waiting for me on e-mail — and that night a Planning Committee conference call lasted more than an hour. Nevertheless, on August 22, I e-mailed a letter to my fellow Directors concerning the agenda for our September Board meeting. As I reread it now, it sounds pretty jaunty: "Greetings from eastern Connecticut," I wrote, "where the late summer katydids are chirping and a few trees actually have a touch of fall color. I've been home for a bit more than a week, slept late (around here that's 8:30), saw a couple of movies, poked around in some shops with Annie, went to a pops concert in a state park by the sea. These are things that regular folks do all the time, but obsessive club activists feel *wicked*!"

In that week, I passed up our Sierra Training Summit. This confab of Club leaders working on training issues was holed up for two days at the Clair Tappaan Lodge near Donner Pass. Once I would have jumped at that chance, but now I needed home. To assuage my guilt — and because I admire him — I spent one day working at a phone bank for the election of Connecticut State Representative James O'Rourke. I also drove to Chester, Connecticut, to a quaint old seafood place, Fiddler's, to have lunch with Sierra's Northeast Centennial Campaign representative. But mostly I made soup, and walked among the sheep, and let Arthur fill me in on all the local gossip.

It was the first real peace I had known since Tony Cortese's invitation to Japan. Unfortunately, while I healed, my family seemed to be focusing on the pain of my next departure.

"Sometimes," Arthur lamented, seated on a kitchen chair watching me clean out the refrigerator, "I think it would be easier if you didn't come back for these visits."

"I made blueberry crisp for dessert," I countered. "Don't I get some points for that?"

"The point," he answered, "is that next week you'll be gone, and we'll miss you all the more."

"I'll bring you some Ghirardelli chocolate."

"Susan, it's not desserts we miss," my husband said, "It's you."

I decided to quit before I got too far behind. I handed him a wedge of cheddar cheese. There were no words. We were committed and I knew that neither of us really wanted to turn back.

September 1990

_____ ❧ _____

As America entered the autumn of 1990 — nerves rubbed raw by the rasping threat of war in the Mideast — its people were re-evaluating their leaders. Many who had dismissed George Bush as "that wimp in the White House" were reassured by the President's castigation of Saddam Hussein. A powerful national yearning for heroism, for bold leadership, even for a war that could be won, asserted itself and appeared to be met in the White House.

"We're not going to let that Iraqi bandit push us around," people told each other. There was, too, an outpouring of rhetoric about defense of the underdog and America's obligation to help the Kuwaiti people.

The American media, kept busy just covering military events, gave its headlines to estimates of weapon power and spent little print analyzing the economic background of the confrontation. In the press of war, the threat of a diminished oil supply did not seem to be closely linked, in the American consciousness, with Kuwait's distress.

When the U.S. Congress reconvened after Labor Day, Clean Air Act conferees went about their business with scarcely a nod to the fact that one of the shortest routes to clean air was by way of burning less fossil fuel.

However, in the U.S. Senate, recognition of the link between the Bryan Bill and energy savings caused a small groundswell of sentiment for the proposed law. Senate Majority Leader George J. Mitchell, scheduled a cloture vote on Friday, September 14. A cloture vote, which demonstrates that a bill has enough support to cut off a filibuster against it, is often a prerequisite to committee passage. Although the Bryan Bill was solidly opposed by the Bush administration, it easily passed its *cloture vote in committee. On the Senate floor, however, on September 24, Senator John C. Danforth (R-MO) succeeded in adding an amendment that destroyed the bill's ability to set fuel efficiency goals for auto makers.*

The following day, a second cloture vote came in 57 to 42, a positive majority, but not enough to cut off debate. Three powerful lobbies—oil, autos, and the White House—had persuaded eight Republican Senators to change their votes.

While Bryan Bill advocates and antagonists battled in the Senate, members of the Conference Committee on the Clean Air Act were also busy. Talk of industrial smog, permit exemptions for small businesses, cold start standards, and alternate fuels ricocheted in the Capitol hallways. In mid-month, the United States Environmental Protection Agency released a study that said that the combined oil savings from the alternative fuels, clean (reformulated) gasoline, and acid rain provisions in the proposed bill were estimated to be between 800,000 and 1,000,000 barrels of oil per day. The study was hailed by clean air advocates as a major plus for their bill.

In the media, the World Bank and other Multilateral Development Banks (MDBs) were being criticized for policies that resulted in tropical deforestation. During September 18 - 21, the PBS series "Frontline" devoted five hours of programming to the destruction of the Amazon rainforest. The series discussed the slash-and-burn tactics of forest settlers, the gold rush, and the "short-sighted World Bank policies which contributed to the destruction." The series concluded with the story of Chico Mendes, the Brazilian rubber tapper whose murder brought international attention to the loss of rainforests.

On September 23, at its annual meeting in Washington, the World Bank issued a report which said that environmental concerns are built into policies and projects for economic and social development in poor countries. "Sound environmental management has been recognized as fundamental to the development process," the report said. According to the New York Times, *however, environmentalists at the meeting said the bank's commitment represented more talk than substance. The* Times *quoted Peggy Hallward, director of forestry research for Probe International, as saying the bank was sponsoring "the same old projects with a few trees planted around the edges." The newspaper also reported that an attorney for the Environmental Defense Fund said "some new bank programs are just as destructive as the old."*

Increasing concern among world religious leaders about environmental problems was expressed in mid-September at a four-day confer-

ence on religion and the environment. Held at Middlebury College in Vermont, the conference attracted Christian, Jewish, Muslim, Buddhist, and Native American theologians. An estimated 5,000 people crowded into the Middlebury indoor hockey rink to hear the Dalai Lama — spiritual and political leader of Tibetan Buddhists and winner of the 1989 Nobel Peace Prize — tell them that "Mother planet is showing the red warning light" and urge them to curb their overuse of natural resources.

ᴥ

The Sierra Club Board of Directors had decided to hold its annual summer retreat on the Maine coast next June and — since I was planning to spend Labor Day there — I had been asked to scout a likely location. Ah, the onerous burdens of a Sierra executive! So the Merrows and two Connecticut Sierrans, Bob and Phillenore Howard, set off for Maine in quest of the perfect location. We stayed at the simple farmhouse my family jokingly calls "the Winter Palace." It is where my grandmother lived when she was in her eighties— and just up the street from "the Summer Palace," where I spent my childhood summers with her.

I showed the Howards all the places that are special to me: the rocky coves and salt-spattered fishing villages, even the hardware store full of objects inscrutable to landlubbers like us. There is no pleasure quite like sharing a place you love with good friends. We made several scouting trips to nearby resorts, but in the end came back to where my heart had always been, a lovely old inn in Tenants Harbor called the East Wind.

The man who owned the place was reluctant to take on a large group in the summer, when he never lacks business. I talked very sweet and very fast, promised this was a bunch of straitlaced neatness fanatics who would spend most of the day in meditation. The truth is the Sierra Club Board of Directors is a very congenial group; there is always singing, dancing, and horseplay. I left wondering if I would end up mediating between my Sierra colleagues and the natives of my "home town."

Over the past few years, the people of the Sierra Club had become my best friends. We shared commitment to a cause, and we shared memories of incredible places. It may not be scientifically documented, but I have seen the things John Muir said about renewing yourself in the wilderness borne out again and again. For some people it may come from walking on the beach, for others strolling through an urban park, but for all of us, contact with nature is an important experience.

The Club activists had been a part of my most memorable moments, and I of theirs. The bonds that formed were incredibly strong. I luxuriated in the comfort of this far-flung support group. I knew that my family and the friends of my youth would outlast this phase of my life, but I was so consumed with Sierra activities that there was little time to keep in touch with anyone else; and also, since I was consummately happy, I felt little need.

After Labor Day I found some time to spend on Connecticut's problems. The era that began with the Industrial Revolution has seen extraordinary damage to the environment. Cleaning it up, teaching people to do no more harm, monitoring polluters so that they obey clean air and clean water laws: these are jobs that can only be done by government. The people want them done, but very often they would prefer not to pay for them.

Connecticut started out in the 1970s paying for its Department of Environmental Protection from the General Fund, the pool of money the state takes in, mostly through sales taxes. As the cost of cleaning up mounted, and as the number of sites eligible for cleanup escalated, the tax burden grew in proportion. To this was added the cost of examining applications for use of natural resources (a business wanting to pipe its waste fluids into a nearby river, for example), and working with the applicant to protect the resource, as well as dozens of other necessary but financially burdensome conservation programs.

Everyone agreed that the need for these programs was pressing. However, in state government they had to be balanced against funds for housing the impoverished, feeding babies, sheltering the mentally ill, and educating children, to name just a few. The Department of Environmental Protection often came in far down the list. At the same time, however, the department brought considerable monies into state coffers: parking at state parks, fishing and hunting licenses, fines for polluters, permit application fees. All these went into the General Fund.

At least give them back what they bring in, environmentalists argued. And, after much debate, the state legislature agreed. A law, popularly known as the "fees bill" was passed, setting aside certain department income to be earmarked specifically for DEP's use, and setting up a Task Force to oversee implementation of the new arrangement. The President of the state Senate was supposed to name one member of the Task Force, and he chose me. I had fought for the bill, but I had considerable regard for the arguments against it. Taxpayers are a funny breed: they respect what they pay for. Environmental protection is a major public issue. It needs citizen respect and it deserves financial support. If we allowed DEP to get fees of its own, the department might have an even harder time getting a fair allocation in the General Fund—even though the fees they collected would never cover expenses. Even worse, we could turn DEP officials into entrepreneurs, more interested in the money they could bring in than the good they were doing. I set off for the first meeting of the Task Force on September 4 with more questions than answers. By the end of the afternoon, I had even more questions.

After the session in Hartford, I drove to New London and took the car ferry from there to Orient Point, Long Island. The Centennial Campaign Planning Committee (CCPC) was holding a joint meeting in East Norwich, with the Trustees of the Sierra Club Foundation. The CCPC is part of the regular Sierra Club committee structure, but the Sierra Club Foundation is a horse of a vastly different hue, since contributions to it are tax deductible.

Like most environmental groups, the Sierra Club started out under Section 501c(3) of the federal tax laws. The funds we collected could be listed as charitable contributions by our donors, so long as we did not (in the fuzzy terms of the IRS) "devote a substantial portion" of our efforts to lobbying. As the Club, its treasury, and its political activity grew, the IRS began to watch it closely. Then, in 1966, when two huge hydroelectric dams were proposed that would flood the Grand Canyon, the Club decided to go to the barricades. If that meant risking its tax status, well, this was the Grand Canyon. Could there be a more worthwhile cause?

On June 9, 1966, the Sierra Club ran a full-page advertisement in the *New York Times*. It was headlined: "Now only you can save the Grand Canyon from being flooded . . . For profit." The following day the IRS notified Sierra that this was proof of significant lobbying and that, "pending further review, donors to the club could no longer deduct their contributions."

The uproar was as magnificent as it was unexpected. Editorials in newspapers across the nation chided the tax collectors. Political cartoonists depicted the Sierra Club as a noble David, battling the IRS Goliath. Our membership ranks increased exponentially. Best of all, Americans who had previously paid no attention now began to oppose the dams.

There was no turning back. When dam proponents argued that flooding would improve the ability of tourists in power boats to view the canyon walls, the Club ran a second ad. This one asked: "Should we also flood the Sistine Chapel so tourists can get nearer the ceiling?" The dams were dropped, and Congressman Morris Udall, D-AZ, summed up the impact: "The conservationists' victory in stopping the Grand Canyon dams marked a turning point in history. . . ."

It was also a turning point in Sierra Club funding mechanisms. The Sierra Club Foundation, which had been established in 1960, began to serve as our banker in all things scientific, legal, and educational. It is now the repository for our "soft" money and pays for clearly tax-exempt activities. A separate fund of "hard" money is kept as the Club's treasury and may be used for our more outspoken efforts to effect legislation and promote membership growth. In 1960, the foundation began with $3,797. In 1987, it managed almost $9 million in assets, including trusts. We treat our foundation cousins much as you would treat very rich relatives.

The setting for the Long Island meeting was certainly appropriate. We stayed at a motel, but the meeting the next day was held at an old estate that was straight out of *The Great Gatsby*. In the 1930s, I was told, when the big old houses that once dominated this section of the island became too costly to maintain, many of their owners donated them to the municipalities or to land trusts. They are great white elephants, but they are also magnificent ghosts whose very existence is evocative of an era that may never be repeated.

When we had hammered out the details of the foundation's role in the Centennial Celebration, local activists took us on a hike in the Muttontown Preserve, a string of once-upon-a-time estates that Mother Nature is aggressively reclaiming. In this climate, even these remarkable residences will soon be gone, gobbled up by a combination of humidity, vegetation, and frost.

I was near the head of the group when we came out of the woods into a clearing. A sprawling stone mansion had once stood there, I was told. The evidence could be seen in two curved stairways that seemed to soar out of the weeds and underbrush, then rise with fantastic grace to meet . . . nothing! It was a metaphor for the beauty mankind is capable of creating, and for the evanescent character of our work. Without unceasing diligence, our efforts are temporal; they will be consumed by a more natural world. Briefly angry, I forgot that I was on nature's side. Then I reminded myself that this place was abandoned by human choice. There was no conflict here, just peaceful reclamation. I was on a short trip, and I was not far from home, but that moment in the woods ranked with the best of all the other pinch-me experiences in my year as President.

Going back to East Haddam required retracing a two-and-a-half hour drive the length of Long Island, reboarding the ferry, disembarking in New London, and then driving half-way across Connecticut. I started out at dusk, feeling intrepid. I reached home in time for a late pizza and talk with my family, but I was exhausted, crabby, and seriously wondering how I was going to keep up this level of activity.

The Sierra Club budget is decided at its September Board meeting, so I had plenty to do — via e-mail and telephone — for the next few days. One piece of e-mail received my special attention. There was a big meeting of multilateral development banks (MDBs) coming up in New York at the end of the month and the Sierra Club had been asked to write an essay for a newsletter that would be published during that meeting. Since the essay would appear over my signature, I wanted to be certain that we made easily understood points that would hit home to the development types in the audience. At the same time, I wanted to be certain they could not color themselves green just by publishing our words.

Only months before, a formal environmental assessment of a loan's potential impact had become a required World Bank procedure. I was skeptical. It sounded good on paper, but it would only work if the bankers understood why it was important. In the article, I pointed out that nine-tenths of all tropical forests would disappear within the next fifty years if current rates of deforestation were allowed to continue, and I recited the damage that the resulting global climate change would do to the world as we know it.

"Structural adjustment loans, comprising 25 percent of bank lending in 1989, and sectoral adjustment loans are currently excluded from mandatory World Bank Environmental Assessment requirements," I pointed out, and then I hit hard on the need to assess cost for environmental damage. "MDBs," I said, "must... incorporate environmental protection and the conservation of natural resources into all development decisions. These would include national accounting systems that treat irreversible or costly resource degradation as a loss, not a gain, against estimates of gross national product." I also called for policies that would reduce or eliminate pesticide subsidies, that would reform energy pricing, and that would eliminate subsidies for timber extraction as standard operating procedure.

What seems so clear to me — that environmental degradation is a threat, not only to environmental and social well-being, but to economic growth and development too — is apparently a very difficult concept if the purpose of your life is to make sums of money multiply by lending them to developers. I know that many bankers, especially the younger ones, are beginning to recognize the impact their actions have and I hoped others would consider our viewpoint if it appeared in their press.

This was also a period of considerable anxiety for the Merrow family. Annie had done well in the East Haddam school system. As a matter of fact, she had done so well that her father and I decided she needed more of a challenge. There is an excellent private preparatory school, Loomis Chaffee, north of Hartford, where we took Annie for an interview. She decided to apply for a highly competitive place in the freshman class — and she was accepted! Now we had to face three problems. First, the tuition was expensive, and I was not working in the traditional sense. Second, the commute was fifteen to twenty minutes beyond her dad's plant. She would have to be in a car for two hours a day; she was too young to drive; and I was often away. Third, she would be leaving old friends and familiar activities — not a teenager's favorite situation.

It was not Annie, however, who seemed troubled that week. She went off to a freshman field day in high spirits. When she came home, she talked enthusiastically about the team-building exercises (they scaled walls, swung on vines, and in what they called a "trust fall," jumped into one another's arms). Meanwhile, Arthur and I redid the budget for the hundredth time, and reassured one another that our elderly cars would thrive on the added mileage. We also searched our consciences about abandoning our hometown school system. We are both staunch believers in public education and we both have a record of activism on its behalf. In the end, the decision to let Annie pursue this educational challenge (which *she* had earned) was based on what seemed best for her, not what made us feel best about our philosophies. Loomis was going to be a challenge, not only for Annie, but for the entire Merrow family. I suppose that was another thing in its favor.

On Tuesday, September 11, Annie officially began high school. I dropped her off and then drove back to Hartford for a visit with state Senator John Larson, the man who had appointed me to the Fees Task Force. Like most lawmakers, he sets great store by the concept of a central pot of money that can be allocated by elected officials as the overall needs of the electorate change. Separate funding for separate departments was, generally speaking, not his cup of tea. However, he recognized the need for assured environmental funding. I promised him I would watch for problems and keep him informed if I found any.

On Wednesday I had reservations to fly back to San Francisco. Arthur took Annie to school, but the airport is near her school and I decided to stop by for a final hug. It was a mistake. First of all, I was driving what we refer to as "the car that wouldn't die." This terrible clunker gets me around and is "environmentally correct." However, at Loomis one is more likely to encounter BMWs and shiny four-wheel drive vehicles. I knew that Annie would be out in the playing fields at this hour, so I drove up one side and down the other, looking for her. Annie, on her second day, still trying to establish an identity for herself, was mortified.

Even worse, the setting seemed to make this particular good-bye especially difficult. I was so proud of her in her new school, so confident that she would meet the challenges here and succeed magnificently. And I hated not being there day in and day out to see it happen. I started to hug her, but she turned away, her eyes brimming with tears. I saw her swallow hard, and take a deep breath. She didn't cry, but I felt her anguish. It was a time in her life when she needed both parents and plenty of support.

What did she get? A scary new school, a mother who never stayed home, lost friends. I was on the verge of saying "I won't go" when another girl called out and Annie turned to her, ready to get on with her new life.

"I will go," I said aloud, but more to myself than to her. She had her life. It was necessary for me to make sure I had my own. But I had to blink away the tears as I drove out the gate.

The annual budget of the Sierra Club for FY 91 was based on expected revenues of $52,017,212 and was passed at a meeting in San Francisco held September 14-15, 1990. That is a simple declarative sentence — but what a world of twisting and turning, dodging and feinting it took to make it possible! There were vastly differing ideas on how to spend those dollars.

The Board met for two days in the library of our San Francisco headquarters. This is a lovely room, full of sunshine and old oak bookcases. One wall is covered with original Ansel Adams photographs that would inspire even the most prosaic bean counter. A good thing, too, for we were doing some close calculating that weekend. We chewed our way through a long agenda, listening to pleas from every segment of the Club and, I'm afraid, not being very responsive in many cases.

Michael and I had spent my first day in San Francisco choreographing the meeting. We thought we had planned a smooth show, but all hell broke loose when it came time to discuss the expense of the Centennial Campaign. The people who believe that the Club *must* be run by volunteers if it is to maintain its strength were adamant that staff must keep hands off. Volunteers are the driving force in the Sierra Club, not only according to the by-laws, but as standard operating procedure. But we were amateurs at this kind of big-time fund raising. We had never had a large donor program, and we were discovering that it was about as manageable as a balloon on guy wires.

To convince very wealthy people to give money, you must first tell them precisely what you are about. We soon found that there were as many different versions of the Sierra Club vision as there were Sierra Club members. There were also more practical problems. It costs money to raise money. We believed that celebrating the Club's one hundredth anniversary by blowing our own horn would yield a big payback in the future. But who would pay now, and if they did, what would they be owed when the money started rolling in? Exact reimbursement? A percentage? All the returns? It was like being in the fourth dimension. I tried to be serene and even-handed. If we were to come out of this united, then it was up to me to lead the way — but oh, how I loathe battles over money. It makes me glad I've always been relatively poor.

On Monday, my head still swimming with numbers, I flew home. At least there I had some miles between me and all the turmoil. Unfortunately, those miles can be easily wiped out these days by electronic gadgets.

The Club was, for instance, in the middle of a hassle about the conflict of interest of an Atlantic Chapter member. It had already generated a two-inch stack of legal hard copy. In very brief terms, Jim Carr, a former Chair of the chapter, had become Director of Planning for the Love Canal Area Revitalization Agency. He made no secret of it, absented himself from chapter meetings where Love Canal was discussed, and abstained from all votes on the subject.

Nevertheless, the Atlantic Chapter has a policy opposing the resettlement of Love Canal, and Jim's new job made some members extremely uncomfortable. They succeeded in passing a vote for a recall election and advertised it in the chapter newsletter, which goes to nearly 42,000 members. They also issued a press release, on Atlantic Chapter letterhead, and made a series of statements to the media describing the chapter's "conflict of interest problem."

In the meantime, an ad hoc committee established by the national Sierra Club reported: "Ordinary difference of opinion ...is... being confused with unethical behavior...." Concerning the press release, the committee added, "Some of the release might be interpreted as libeling, slandering, or defaming the character of Jim Carr.... We are still researching the potential exposures...." In other words, there was the real possibility of an expensive and embarrassing lawsuit here.

The Board of Directors, and certainly the President, has a duty to protect the Club from exposure to liability. On September 21, via e-mail, I approved a letter to the Atlantic Chapter advising them that Jim Carr was not guilty of any legal conflict of interest and reminding them that "Sierra Club specifically encourages expression of differences of opinion." I suggested that they reconsider the special election and warned them, if they per-

sisted, that the national organization would scrutinize any charges
and statements made, as well as the backgrounds of the election
committee. I also forbade further public statements, press releases, or electioneering.

At the same time, the debate about low-level radioactive
waste was also bubbling along. The Board of Directors' Executive Committee had voted to have the North Carolina Chapter
withdraw its petition to the Nuclear Regulatory Commission,
but I knew that I would be dealing with hurt feelings for months
to come.

Fortunately for groups like the Sierra Club, we can al' ways
count on some villain to come along and unite us. In other words,
thank God for George Bush and his environmental policies! On
September 21, we put out a press release charging that the
findings of an administration task force on the spotted owl
problem was "playing fast and loose with our environmental
laws to suit its own political agenda."

Months earlier, President Bush had created a Task Force
headed by Department of Agriculture Secretary Clayton Yeutter
and charged with developing alternatives, "not constrained by
existing law," to implement the Interagency Scientific Committee recommendations for protecting the northern spotted owl. In
contrast to the Interagency Scientific Committee, which was
composed of scientific experts, the Yeutter Task Force was composed of Bush administration political appointees.

As environmentalists expected, the Yeutter Task Force had
come up with recommendations that set timber cutting levels in
violation of the National Forest Management Act and insulated
them from the National Environmental Policy Act. Not only the
forests, but the protective laws we had worked so hard to enact
were in danger. "Circumventing the law and destroying our
ancient forest ecosystem — critical habitat for the threatened
spotted owl — is a short-sighted approach that will not serve the
timber workers or the environment well in the long run. Rewriting environmental law is not an acceptable solution," we said.

We were especially aroused about this one because two
members of Congress had released a Department of the Interior
study — the administration's own study — which had been
suppressed. It suggested several proposals to mitigate job impacts in local communities and to reduce projected timber job

losses while sparing the ancient forests from decimation, all of which the Sierra Club supported. Evidently the administration preferred to ignore potential worker protection in its single-minded determination to cut those big old trees!

The Task Force recommendations were also received unfavorably by many members of Congress. Senator George Mitchell said, "The administration has spent three critical months trying to chart a political course around the Endangered Species Act and other federal environmental laws. . . . The administration says that the plan they have developed strikes a balance between conservation and economic concerns. . . . But what kind of balance is there in a plan that seeks to void every major environmental law governing management of federal forest lands?"

Sometimes being the President of the Sierra Club was an experience in extremes. The same week that I was nearly talking to myself in my frustration with Secretary Yuetter and his crew, I was booked into the University of New Haven, with a variation of my Japan speech on global warming. I got lost on the way and arrived late, but it didn't seem to make much difference. About sixty young men and women in the student union half-listened to me while eating brown bag lunches. They didn't seem very worried about global warming. I tried, but I couldn't reach them. Oh well, at least the Club made some money on the honorarium I had received.

From New Haven, I drove into rural eastern New Jersey to a meeting of the Club's Northeast Regional Conservation Committee, where I gave a workshop on lobbying skills. It was a pretty camp setting, complete with sleeping bags and gorp. Maybe I'm getting a little old for bunk beds, though. I've done fifteen years of meetings at church camps and scout camps, and sometimes I get wistful about industry representatives in their cushy motel rooms. On the other hand, the people at these meetings are so real, so welcoming, that you mostly forget about the lack of creature comforts and privacy. This was no exception. I felt instantly at home — but I drove five hours back on Sunday, thinking happily of my own bed.

The next morning, September 25, I enjoyed the special privilege conferred on all Sierrans by the Internal Revenue Service and federal election laws. Since our tax status has been taken away and since we have created a legal entity called "The

Sierra Club Political Committee"—a political action committee (PAC)— we are free to campaign (within complicated rules) for candidates with good environmental records.

Although our national political action committee endorses specific congressional candidates, normally the choice of who to support is made at the local level. In New Haven, a very special woman was running for Congress on whom we all agreed. Rosa DeLauro is the product of a family that has, for many years, been deeply enmeshed in politics. She served as the good woman behind, first, a New Haven Mayor, and later, Senator Chris Dodd. Yet nothing about her suggests "politics as usual." At 9:45 a.m. I reported to her headquarters. Before 11:00 a.m., at the Connecticut Marine Studies Center on New Haven harbor, I proudly gave my endorsement of Rosa to the media.

The next day, my former boss, Betty Gallo, was staging her annual lobbying conference. I gave a workshop entitled, "Getting Legislators to Say 'Yes.'" Betty's conferences do not attract the lobbyists for big business. They don't need to know about her kind of persuasion; they have plenty of money to spend. The attendees are mostly lobbyists or volunteers from the so-called "do-gooder" ranks. I have been watching these people grow in professionalism for more than fifteen years. They care about their causes; they are eager to go that extra mile; and, over the years, they have become extremely adept at the art of persuasion. The wonder is not that we win so many rounds, but that the big-money boys never understand why.

At home, via computer, I was deep into preparations for a very exciting event. Sierra's Native American Sites Committee and its James Bay Task Force had organized a weekend in Great Whale (far, far northern Canada), which would be attended by several Kaiapo Indians from Brazil, a Gwich'in tribesman from Alaska, a half-dozen other activists, a sprinkling of media folks, Freeman Allen, and me. We were to meet with the Cree and Inuit people to discuss the issues of indigenous people and the James Bay hydro project. To keep the Kaiapo from freezing in the harsh climate, we had arranged for the Patagonia Company to outfit them in arcticwear over their feathers and loin cloths. I pointed out that Sierra Club representatives get cold too, but the Patagonia people paid no attention.

Also via e-mail, I was in touch with Mike Traynor at the Sierra Club Legal Defense Fund. Our side had presented the document they asked for, outlining how we could continue to work together. He called it "very disappointing" and even went so far as to question its ethics. He accused us of "wimping out" by compromising on an old-growth forest issue. I had the feeling that we were communicating from different planets. All in all, a very disheartening prologue to negotiations scheduled for the end of the month.

I flew back to San Francisco on September 28 with a heavy heart.

October 1990

— ✑ —

"The James Bay project is the dream — some say obsession — of Quebec's Premier, Robert Bourassa," Time magazine reported in a special feature on the world's most extensive hydropower project. "Is it really needed?" the magazine's headline asked.

By the autumn of 1990, more than 1,000 Cree Indians from the Canadian island of Fort George had been relocated and thus deprived of their traditional way of life. Their ancestral hunting grounds were flooded over, and the local fish soon became inedible because of mercury contamination stemming from the creation of a reservoir upstream. Thirty percent of the Indians tested had high levels of mercury in their bodies. Rates of alcoholism, suicide, vandalism, and family violence were soaring.

Despite ten years of protest and court suits, however, there was more to come. HydroQuebec, a government-owned utility, was planning to build another $31 billion worth of dams for electric power, much of it to be sold to the northeastern United States. If they did, according to Ian Goodman, a Boston-based environmental consultant, massive disturbance of ecosystems would result in an area as big as New England, New York, and Pennsylvania combined. He likened it to a giant science experiment.

On October 5, the Montreal Gazette reported that two native chiefs from the Brazilian rainforest, leaders in the fight to stop a huge hydroelectric project on that continent, had arrived to confer with the Cree. Matthew Coon-Come, grand chief of the Quebec Cree, said the two regions had much in common. "We are both losing, by the actions of others, our resources and, consequently, our way of life," Coon-Come said.

The Cree and the Inuit (the other inhabitants of the region) bitterly resented the loss of their lands to supply power, not just for Quebec, but so that people in New England and New York "can keep running their air conditioners and hair dryers."

By mid-October, the New York Times *reported, environmentalists in the United States were trying to derail the sale of power from HydroQuebec to U.S. utilities. Indians, Eskimos, and Canadian and U.S. environmentalists charged that HydroQuebec had given short shrift to energy conservation, the environment, and the rights of indigenous peoples, according to the* Times.

In Washington, D.C., untroubled by energy problems in subarctic regions, the U.S. Congress continued to hammer out a new Clean Air Act. On October 27, by a vote of 89 to 16, the U.S. Senate granted final Congressional approval. The 700-page bill (the original, back in 1971, had been 41 pages long) was sent on to the White House, where President Bush was expected to sign it. The New York Times *described the new law as a "measure that transforms the twenty-year old original law from a path-breaking but narrow statute into an ambitious plan to cut contamination from every sizable source of air pollution in the nation."*

It was a big day for the environment in the U.S. Congress. On the same day, Congressional negotiators agreed to keep vast tracts of coastal waters off limits for oil and gas drilling. Interior Secretary Manuel Lujan talked of a Presidential veto but was unable to sway federal lawmakers. Indeed, the October 27 decision, which affected 135 million acres of the Continental Shelf, significantly expanded areas the Bush administration had earlier set aside in hopes that restrictions on other areas would be dropped.

"The lawmakers' decision," the Times *noted, "was the first clear sign that oil disruptions caused by the Iraqi invasion of Kuwait had not reversed the decade-long aversion to offshore drilling in Congress."*

As the month ended, at the United Nations Church Center in Manhattan, two powerful movements joined briefly when fifty feminist leaders met to demand a bigger role for women in decision making on the environment and development. Women from Latin America, Africa, Asia, Europe, and North America adopted a six-point action plan: full participation by women in environment policy at all levels; freedom of choice in family planning; redefinition of development on the principle that investment must not destroy the environment; increased education

*and information on the environment and development; protection of
natural systems; and development of a code of Earth ethics.*

_____

ฉะ

If I flew to San Francisco with a heavy heart over our dispute
with the Sierra Club Legal Defense Fund, that feeling only
heightened as I worked with the Planning Committee the last few
days in September trying to set up a strategic plan for the Club.

Planning presents some challenging hurdles to organizations like the Sierra Club. First, because we place such a high
value on volunteer management and because we are so diverse,
good policy (or, at least, policy that will be accepted) has to have
as many people's fingerprints on it as possible. It can be a
damnably tedious job to touch all those bases. Sometimes I felt
as if each of our 620,000 members had to be individually informed on everything.

However, the most frustrating thing about "planning" for
Sierra is that we cannot know exactly what we are planning for.
We are, I sometimes think, not unlike the Atlanta Center for
Disease Control. We have no way of guessing what epidemic
will sweep America, or when, but plan we must. You never know
when an outbreak of a new disease like AIDS will occur — who
could have predicted global warming? — so you have to be ready
for all eventualities.

On October 1, things got even more disheartening. Five
Sierra Club leaders sat down with six Sierra Club Legal Defense
Fund attorneys, to discuss our mutual grievances.

The problems between the Sierra Club and the Sierra Club
Legal Defense Fund had been bubbling along under the surface,
for some time. Unfortunately, they came to a boil while I was
President.

Environmentalists work to protect the world's natural resources in many different ways. We lobby for new laws, we
publish educational materials, we vote for leaders who have
demonstrated concern, we testify at public hearings, we boycott
products, we stage demonstrations, and—very often— we take
to the courts. Because typically such lawsuits are brought by

ordinary citizens with little money, public interest law firms working on environmental cases—particularly the Environmental Defense Fund and the Natural Resources Defense Council—have played a critical role in shaping the environmental movement.

The Sierra Club Legal Defense Fund (SCLDF) is also a public service law firm. A spin-off from the Sierra Club, it has no direct, legal tie with us, but we are its biggest client. We provide SCLDF with approximately a half million dollars in income each year and they continue to use our name (which, we are convinced, draws many dollars more to their own funding efforts).

Being a legal defense fund, they tend to seek solutions in court. Sometimes the Sierra Club finds that approach alone inadequate. In the case of the ancient forests in the American northwest, for example, we believe that the solution has to be political. Even if the law is with us, there must be a base of support broad enough to keep the lawmakers on our side—or they will change the law.

A great deal of money is involved in the sale of timber from those forests. Jobs, international relations, and the rights of indigenous people also must be taken into consideration. The people involved are passionate for lots of different reasons (even if the media does tend to report the whole matter in terms of one species of owl), so when we realized that SCLDF was making public statements in direct contradiction to our policies, we began to worry more than ever about whether it was a good idea for them to do so using our name.

At the early October meeting, the lawyers started out by insisting that we use their agenda, not ours. Then they announced that they would not even discuss the licensing agreement we had prepared, and that our proposed restrictions on their activities were "not negotiable." They also informed us that their claim to the Sierra name was "relatively unassailable," and called our promise to pay them $500,000 a year for legal services "a step backward." We finally agreed to negotiate the license, the question of their lobbying, and their ability to make statements using our name, each separately in smaller groups.

Actually, had we but known, the entire session was summed up as it opened. SCLDF's Don Harris walked into the conference room and laid a long, narrow case in the middle of the table. He said it was a shotgun. We took it to be a quasihumorous comment on our "family quarrel." When we were leaving, one of us asked what really was in the case. Don opened it up; it was, indeed, a shotgun.

I kept telling myself he meant it as a joke. Was I losing my sense of humor?

My big trip to Great Whale was coming up in a few days. I flew back to Connecticut and woke up the morning of October 3 completely disoriented. This was happening more and more. When I first woke up, all the traveling would be blended together and I would not be able to remember whether I was in San Antonio or Tokyo, Lake Tahoe or Washington.

I had learned to stay calm. "You'll remember where you are in a minute," I would tell myself, "no need to panic." This time it took longer than usual, but I finally recognized the room. It was my own home.

There wasn't much to pack; Great Whale is not a fashion center. I caught up on the housework, attended a Fees Task Force session at the Capitol, ate lunch with an old friend — and on October 5 flew to Montreal to meet with the Cree, the Inuit, the Kayapo, the Gwich'in, and the Canadian press corps.

It was pouring rain as I came off the plane. Even the lights of the city and the glare of the airport failed to dispel the feeling that I had entered some sort of 1950s *film noir*. A man in a raincoat met me, welcomed me in a mixture of French and English, and led me to a room where Cree and Kayapo Indians were just starting a press conference. I had not expected this, but I managed to smile at the cameras and say that the Sierra Club would be fighting on both sides of the border for energy conservation and the rights of indigenous people.

We had been told that in Quebec, if you had no claim to being French, you were nothing. As a result, we were depending heavily on the guidance of a man named Jean-François Turmel. Although we had never met, I had heard an array of adjectives about him: spartan, dedicated, fanatic, brilliant, and austere, to name a few.

Arrangements had been made for me to stay at Turmel's house. As we drove slowly through the sopping streets, I squinted between swipes of the windshield wiper, trying to see where we were headed. It was too dark and too wet to make anything out. Eventually we pulled up at a very small house on a tree-lined urban street. It looked to me like the setting for a John LeCarré rendezvous.

Inside, the rooms were sparsely furnished — but the hospitality was unstinting. M. Turmel, who always put his cause ahead of creature comfort (and assumed that everyone else did too), had invited ten of us to sleep in his two-bedroom house. Another woman and I made for the smallest bedroom where we separated the twin mattress from its box spring. As I settled down on the mattress, I heard her remark, "Well, at least we're out of the rain."

The band of people who gathered at the Montreal airport the next morning included environmentalists, reporters from the *New York Times, Audubon* magazine and other publications, and our host, Grand Chief Matthew Coon-Come, leader of the Grand Council of Crees in Quebec, but, sadly, it did not contain our friends the Kayapo. They had received word late the night before of more violence in their region and had been obliged to hasten home. Should we go on without them? The consensus was that since we had come this far, it would be irresponsible to leave the Cree and Inuit with no sounding board at this late date.

I eyed with dismay the little twin-propeller plane that would take us hundreds of miles north, but it was the only way. There are no roads to Great Whale yet — which has, of course, been a plus for ensuring the cultural survival of the native people. From the other side, I have heard it argued that HydroQuebec will "rescue" these primitives from their backward ways.

Another traveler, Rich Fedele, the Chairman of our Atlantic Chapter, was frowning at the plane. I knew immediately that he was a fellow sufferer of air sickness. When I asked, he not only freely admitted that he was, he offered me half of his last Dramamine. Sierra brotherhood!

We flew north over lush farmland and forests. The further north we flew, the more wild and uninhabited the land beneath us. After two hours in the air, we were above the LeGrande project — the giant dam, spillway, and enormous reservoir that were built during the first phase of the project. Our pilot dipped and circled so that we could see the grave of a drowned river and comprehend the implications for the native people and for wildlife such as caribou, whose migration patterns have been disrupted.

I was feeling quite smug, since my half a Dramamine seemed to be working, even as the people all around me were starting to look green. As we flew on toward Great Whale, however, I felt the familiar queasiness, the hot flashes that precede a full-blown case of air sickness. I caught Matthew Coon-Come's eye. He was a solicitous host — but beneath that he had exactly the same air as my Japanese hosts watching me and my family cope with the crab dinner. I gritted my teeth and did not relax until we began to circle for a landing.

We call it Great Whale. On the map of Canada it is Grande Baleine, but to the people who live there — and have done so since long before the white man's language — it is really two closely nestled villages, the Cree village of Whapmagoostui and the Inuit village of Kuujjuarapik. They share a sandy spit of land where the Great Whale River empties into Hudson Bay.

The Great Whale runway was gravel and very bumpy, but it felt wonderful to be on solid ground. Our gear was tossed into pickup trucks and we were driven the mile or so to the "town hall" of Whapmagoostui, where I was surprised to see that civilization — in the form of computers, fax machines, and copiers — had arrived ahead of us.

Matthew Moukash, representing the local government, welcomed us and assigned us in groups of two to Cree homes where we would sleep. A Canadian woman and I were driven to a small, prefab ranch house. No one was there, but the door was open, so we left our gear and walked back to the village center. All of Great Whale is built on sand. There is no grass in the village — and no trees. We trudged on through the sand, passing more homes, modern, but very small and very close together. There is no paving and no landscaping. We saw snowmobiles in the front yards and teepees in the back. These people, we learned, lead double lives. In their town homes, they have TVs, VCRs, all the amenities. But they spend six months or so each year in the bush, hunting and trapping.

I saw evidence of my host's hunting prowess the next morning, when I got up before anyone else in the house. In the dish drainer were two handsome, freshly killed ducks, waiting to be plucked and cooked for the community feast that night. Those two magnificent birds really got to me. They said: this is how these people live. They do not order their meat from the supermarket. They have learned how to extract a living from the wilderness, but without destroying it.

A few of us took a walk down to the banks of the mighty Great Whale River that first afternoon. The day was grey and sleety — hat and mittens weather. Standing on the shore, the river looked to be about a quarter mile across at its mouth. It is the lifeblood of the village, providing both transportation and fishing. If HydroQuebec had its way, it would be reduced to a trickle. The arrogance! The James Bay Power Project was not just tinkering with nature. This was a major rewriting of Mother Earth's script. An area the size of France would be flooded, twenty rivers flowing though 350,000 square kilometers of northwestern Quebec funneled into vast reservoirs. Some of the rivers would be reduced, others simply submerged.

The Great Whale portion of this grand scheme included three power stations with a total capacity of 2,890 megawatts, and the diversion of two other rivers as well. In many cases increased flow would cause erosion, with silt deposited wherever the rivers slow. Vegetation along the shore and under the new reservoirs would be destroyed, causing the release of mercury and algae blooms that will eat up oxygen in the water and kill off the fish. In most cases, shoreline vegetation and habitat would be impossible to restore, because the water levels would change periodically, based on demand for power. As the magazine *Canadian Geographic* reported in March 1990, "Scientists do not have enough information to predict the consequences. But in such a complex and fragile environment to which plants and wildlife have   adapted successfully but precariously over the millennia, the impact could be catastrophic."

That evening we attended a traditional feast arranged in our honor. A two-room teepee (two tents, side by side, with a bridging room between them) had been set up near the village school. We lifted the flap and walked into another world.

The floor was covered with fragrant spruce boughs, gathered, I am sure, at great effort from the small, scrubby evergreen trees just outside the village. There was a cooking fire at each end. Ducks and geese turned on spits hung from wood pole frames over the fire. There were sticks wrapped with "snakes" of bread dough slanted toward the fire, baking. There were pots of who knew what cooking, tended by older women wearing traditional sealskin parkas. One of them caught my eye and nodded gravely as I came in. It was a very special moment — to be so far from home and all that was familiar, and still to be welcomed into the culture and families of the native people.

As we broke bread together, we acknowledged an important bond: our respect for the land and our desire to find a way to save it from the greedy and their thoughtless followers. There were speeches in Cree and Inuit, and ancient blessings. We ate wild goose, ptarmigan, caribou spare ribs, bannock (fried bread), herb teas, and mashed potatoes. (I don't know where potatoes fit into the native diet, but they surely tasted good — hot and familiar!)

After dinner, we went back to the town hall for more strategy talks. The Cree had challenged the first phase of James Bay (the LeGrande project) in the mid-70s and had won in the lower court. HydroQuebec appealed and the Cree victory appeared to be going down the tubes. Seeing the handwriting on the wall, the Cree settled for money damages but made no promise that they would not fight the next phase.

Their settlement money explained the modern machines in the town hall. What elegant irony. They were using their "blood money" to let the outside world know they had already been wounded and expected worse to come. The electricity would be sold in the northeastern United States and the Cree had decided to reach out to people across the border, appealing to them not to accept this dirty power heedlessly.

We were grateful for sleep that night. My roommate and I were displacing the two teenage daughters of the family from their bedroom. The walls were covered with posters of the New Kids on the Block and Johnny Depp. There were also photographs from school, much like those in Annie's room back home. Except for superficial differences of skin and hair color, these people are much like us. I think it is significant that, with feet in both worlds, they chose to make their stand to protect their ancient ways. They have been offered massive amounts of money to shut up and go away.

The next morning we were out early, exploring the village. I'm embarrassed to say that most of us behaved just like tourists, searching for some souvenir to take home. We found the local Hudson Bay Company Store but I held out. I wanted to buy native crafts, preferably from the people who had made them. To me, a souvenir ought to distill what you have experienced in a place.

I did eventually buy a small, carved soapstone walrus from the co-op shop maintained by the community. I gave it to Annie, but sometimes I like to touch it and remember that faraway place. It is wonderfully smooth to hold. It has the carver's name scratched in the bottom in symbols I don't recognize. I hope he knows how much pleasure his work has brought to us.

We were scheduled to go in boats, the next day, to see a waterfall on the Great Whale River that would be dried up by the proposed dam. The wind was too strong, however, and so instead we took a hike across the tundra. This is not hospitable country, but its very bleakness has its own beauty. I was reminded of the rocky coast of Maine, except that the trees were miniatures of those in Maine. There were blueberry bushes and an abundance of crunchy gray reindeer moss. Our hosts were eager to show us the land they loved and depended on for sustenance.

The community center is a modern, bright, cheerful building with a kitchen and a meeting hall. You might find its duplicate in any Connecticut village. After strategizing there most of the day, we returned in the evening to a potluck supper. As the guests, we were invited to help ourselves first from the heavily laden tables. There were game meats and all sorts of intriguing casseroles. Near the head of the table was a large bowl of something grayish, of pudding consistency, with dark spots all through it. I passed it by, but not without being ashamed that I wasn't more adventuresome. Later I learned that it was a mixture of pemmican, bear grease, and blueberries. Harvard Ayers, the head of Sierra's Native American Sites Committee, loved it, but he was the only one who did. The rest of the food was wonderful, and very welcome after a day in that cold climate. We finished up with a giant sheet cake, decorated with flowers and welcoming words in English and in Cree.

Speeches followed. The Cree language is lyrical, and pleasant to the ear. They start each speech with a word that sounds like "ouwatchiwa" with the accent on the "watch," spoken with a downward movement of the head. It's a greeting, much like aloha or shalom, I suppose.

I had arranged for two sets of children's books (one for the Cree school and one for the Inuit) to be shipped ahead of me. Now it was time for me to make a presentation. I compared the native peoples to the canaries miners use to test the air deep underground, and said they were pawns in a giant attempt to see how far mankind could push back environmental limits. I assured them that we care about the environment, but also that we care about people. We knew that if they could not survive in their native land, being sustained by the earth, then we—all of us— were living beyond our means.

Traveling with us was Louie John, a Gwich'in Indian from Arctic Village, Alaska, adjacent to the Arctic National Wildlife Refuge. His way of life, entirely dependent on caribou (*gwich'in* means caribou people), is threatened by drilling for oil to serve the hunger of Americans for cheap oil. There was an instant bonding between the men of these two distant but similar cultures, each threatened by a civilization in another land. We watched videos about both countries and talked and talked and talked. We straggled out of the community center at midnight, into the ever-present wind and needles of driving sleet.

At seven the next morning, we reversed our arrival ritual. Back I went on the same little two-propeller plane — this time with no Dramamine. The flight was smooth, with only one stop to let off Matthew Coon-Come at another Cree community. I spent the last night in Montreal in a hotel room by myself. Lord, how I love hotel rooms! I feel so wicked, so hedonistic, so . . . waited upon.

We do not have a TV at home, which makes watching television in a hotel a sort of stolen pleasure. On this particular night it was especially heady. As I tuned into the news, my bête noir from Houston, Brit Hume from ABC, was announcing a film clip of someone, I forget who. Instead the station aired the wrong clip and then switched immediately back to Hume. The usually suave newscaster was caught in a moment of fury, throwing his pencil on the desk.

"He's lost it!" I laughed, slapping the bed in glee. "Way to go, Brit! You show 'em the old poise!" By the time I realized how much noise I was making, the station was airing the right clip. I continued to beam throughout ten minutes of gloomy news, and on into the night.

No question about it, the trip to Great Whale was one of the pinch-me experiences of the year. It was shadowed, however, by the fact that Annie's school, Loomis Chaffee, was observing Parents Weekend at the same time. At odd moments I would imagine my daughter trying to tell her friends and their families where her mother was.

"My mom had to go to Great Whale," she would say, "because some Indians from Brazil are visiting the Cree who were flooded out by HydroQuebec." At this point, I knew, their eyes would roll and they would remark on the weather. They were thinking, I was sure, that Annie's mind had come unhinged as a result of some stress, and probably suspected her parents were divorcing.

When I told her I would not be there for Parents Weekend, Annie said that a major souvenir would be required to make up for a loss of this magnitude. I didn't mind. The child would have to be a dolt not to try to extract something for herself out of all this — and Annie is no dolt. I brought her the carved walrus, created out of native stone, by an Inuit artist, a true piece of Great Whale.

In Connecticut, U.S. Congressman John Rowland was running for Governor on the Republican ticket. The Sierra Club endorsed his Democratic opponent, Bruce Morrison, a Congressman with an outstanding environmental record. I felt that the Connecticut chapter acted too soon. Morrison was clearly the shining environmental star, but part of the fun of political strategizing is figuring out when to get into the race. It's an art, not a science, however. We had a third-party candidate, former Senator Lowell Weicker, also in the race. The longer we withheld our endorsement, I theorized, the more pledges all three would make for environmental protection. Although I thought we moved precipitously, it was clear that I would never have advocated endorsing Rowland, a me-too environmentalist with no real understanding of the issues.

I had, therefore, been surprised when a Rowland aide called to say that the Congressman wanted to nominate me for one of the second annual Theodore Roosevelt Conservation Awards. It would be presented at the White House, I was told, by President Bush.

Vanity flapped her wings like a great white turkey vulture and settled on my shoulder. "The White House!" I said. "A national environmental award!" I said. "Yes!" I said. "Oh certainly, yes!"

A little later, common sense set in. I believe in America; I believe that right will triumph; I believe that the Sierra Club (and its President) deserve recognition. However I am not so naive as to think that national awards are passed out at the White House, on the say-so of non-endorsed gubernatorial candidates, by Presidents who have been embarrassed at economic summits.

On inquiry, I learned that all members of the U. S. Congress were asked to make nominations, but that I was the only one nominated from Connecticut — and that all nominees automatically receive an award. Eventually, I was sent a notice that the ceremony would take place on October 22nd.

I queried a few friends in the Sierra network. Most of them were enthusiastic. A wonderful honor. . . we need more bipartisanship. . .you'll meet influential public policy makers, they argued. Others were more cynical. You'll pose for pictures with Rowland, they warned, and end up in his campaign literature, looking like an endorsement.

I doubted that, but I thought perhaps I should bring all this out in the open. I called the Rowland headquarters and talked to the man who had originally contacted me. We examined all the fine points, and agreed that I would accept the award only if it would not be used for campaign purposes. In return I promised never to mention the award in connection with the Sierra endorsement of Bruce Morrison. The talk was amicable and I hung up feeling, for the first time in weeks, comfortable, even excited, about the honor I was about to receive.

Ten minutes later the telephone rang. It was Congressman Rowland in person. "Listen, Sue," he said, "I think we ought to forget this whole Roosevelt Award business. Frankly, the White House never liked the idea from the beginning." Somewhere, someday, archivists (perhaps putting the White House attic in order) will find a plaque or a scroll with my name on it. "Who in the world was Sue Merrow?" they'll wonder.

The good people at Common Cause were still giving me a salary (I had taken a leave from my other part-time job as a lobbyist) and had been very patient about the mere fragments of time I was giving them in return. But now their twentieth anniversary was coming up. For the next few days, I threw myself into preparations for its celebration.

I confirmed the hall and hired the caterer and checked out the speaker and made calls to see who was coming to the Common Cause party. On October 13 there were torrential rains, but Arthur and Annie and I dutifully drove into Hartford.

This was a half-day reception for 60 people. It had a total budget of $400. Sitting at home on my desk were the details of a five-day Sierra Club meeting in November that would involve 200 people and cost upwards of $20,000. I also wanted that to be perfect. Yet my anxiety about this big Sierra meeting was no greater than my anxiety about the Common Cause party. I don't know whether it's me or if this happens to everyone, but the zeal to perform well does not seem to be related, in my psyche anyway, to the scope or magnitude of the job.

The political season was in high gear by now. I spent the next few days at fundraisers and press hits for various statehouse candidates. The afternoon of October 15 found me on the shores of Long Island Sound with Bruce Morrison, the Democrat who wanted to be Governor. He had chosen to make an environmental pitch in Stratford, with the Great Salt Marsh in the background.

I was really excited about this one. Connecticut's tidal wetlands, and this one in particular, have been the site of a twenty-year battle between developers and conservationists. I am always happy to help educate people about the reasons that a salt marsh, in its primal state, is so valuable.

Developers, of course, recognize the human desire to renew ourselves by the sea. They understand that what John Muir felt in the wilderness, many of us also experience at the shore. They figure that people will appreciate being supplied with a water view, and so — there being a nice profit involved — they build along the shore, and when the solid beach is used up, fill in marshes so they can build some more.

In the sixties and seventies, marine scientists sounded an alarm. Half of Connecticut's coastal marshes had already been lost, 25 percent more were somewhat damaged (including the Great Salt Marsh itself), and they feared we would damage Long Island Sound irreversibly if the filling wasn't halted.

Marshes, to the casual observer, are a beautiful but useless no-man's land. You can't swim or hike there. You can't sail a boat. If you don't want the salt hay, or a place to dump old tires, they seem a great waste of valuable space. Wrong. Those marshes are teeming with life. It is there that newly hatched fish take their first meals of phytoplankton. The food chain that ends when a beaming waiter places a succulent lobster before you probably began amid the shallow, sun-warmed, nutrient-rich waters of a coastal marsh.

The Connecticut General Assembly recognized the value of these marshes early on. After a decade of persuasion from environmentalists all over the state, it passed a Coastal Area Management Act meant to preserve such areas from harm. Since the law went into effect, very few acres have been lost — but the constant pressure from developers continues. Facing the TV cameras, Bruce Morrison swept his arm out to encompass the marsh and called it "the cradle of life," while I beamed in the background. (I just wished the people of HydroQuebec could be as enlightened. Those twenty rivers also cradle life!)

On the 16th I made a quick trip to San Francisco. By then we were deep into planning for our big November Board meeting, fondly dubbed "the circus" because there is always action in at least three rings. Agendas and arrangements had been flying back and forth via e-mail, but we had hit the limits of electronic communication. Sometimes the ringmaster just has to look the lion tamer in the eye in order to assess the dangers afoot.

Many of the upcoming events would be fun. On Friday night, for instance, the annual Sierra Follies was scheduled. This year we were doing "The Sound of Musings" with tunes stolen straight out of the mouths of the Trapp Family Singers. Everyone was having a ball with parodies. "Climb every mountain" was now "Save every mountain." "My favorite things" had turned recyclable, as in "bundles of newspaper, tied up with strings." A puppet number was being put together to the tune of "Lonely Goatherd." It dealt with support for state chapters and began, "Out in the states was a lonely state chair, Lady-with-a-lobby-with-too-much-to-do." My favorite, however, took off on "How do you solve a problem like Maria?" Our version went, "How do you solve a problem like Sununu?"

Also on the plus side, we had a top expert on data-based demographics to make the keynote speech at the Annual Meeting on Saturday. The world is changing; Sierrans need to know the trends. Another plus: progress had been made on the aid to states I advocated in May. We were about to hire a program director and would announce that forty-five grant requests had been approved at the annual meeting.

Some other things, however, were not going to be so pleasant. The Atlantic Chapter problem, for instance, had disintegrated into chaos. Early in October I sent out a letter asking that they not have a recall election and — if they insisted on going ahead — outlining the rules for such an event.

My letter was not too well received. The Atlantic Chapter is our second oldest and third largest regional group. Feelings were high; recriminations were the order of the day. The chapter leaders were refusing to cooperate and some well-motivated activists were resigning in disgust. I knew it would be cause for concern at the annual meeting.

Most thorny of all was the problem the Club as a whole was having trouble adjusting to the idea of mounting a Centennial Campaign. A promotion of this magnitude is not the usual Sierra Club enterprise — but, hey, we are one of the oldest environmental organizations in existence. Our hundredth birthday ought to be a big deal.

Unfortunately some of the people we hired had not worked out. There were strong objections from a few members about the way the money was budgeted. The idea of having commercial sponsors for big events stuck in some craws (even though the companies would be thoroughly reviewed for environmental purity). I didn't expect "the circus" to find a solution, but I knew there would be plenty of debate.

I caught the redeye for home on Friday, October 19. Just the day before, Doug Scott had announced his resignation — after seventeen years with Sierra — as our Associate Executive Director for Conservation and Communications. Doug had started out as a Sierra Club volunteer at the University of Michigan right after the first Earth Day. He was sometimes prickly (when we deserved it); he was generally solid in a crisis; and he was always a dynamo. It was hard for me to think of the Sierra Club and Doug Scott as separate entities. There was no quarrel. Doug simply wanted to spend more time with his family than his Sierra duties allowed (Doug traveled as much, if not more, than I did). He had taken a job in Washington state as Executive Director of a community theatre and art center.

A community job sounded just right for Doug. I remembered how much a part of his community he had been when the
Merrows stayed with him over the Fourth of July, and how much
fun his wife and daughters were. It must have been very tough
on him all these years, being away from them so much. But that
didn't make losing him any easier for the Sierra Club. I knew that,
just as we all remember where we were when we heard about the
Kennedy assassination, Sierra Club members would always
recall the circumstances under which they heard that we were
losing Doug Scott.

The reason for the redeye flight was a bat mitzvah for the
daughter of my friend and fellow lobbyist, Judy Blei. I got
through that with pleasure and even managed, the next day, to
fill in for Senator Chris Dodd, who was unable to make it as the
guest speaker for the Housatonic Valley Association's Annual
Meeting. On the 22nd, however, jet lag got me. Aside from one
political fund raiser and one conference call regarding the Centennial Campaign, I sat quietly at home and thought about all the
other environmentalists who were receiving Teddy Roosevelt
Awards from George Bush that day. Lucky for John Rowland,
our paths didn't cross that day!

The plight of indigenous people had been one cause among
many before I went to Great Whale. Indeed, I could become just
as passionate about an endangered bird or rodent as I could
about a human tribe. After all, humans are supposed to have the
brains to adapt to new circumstances, while lesser species simply
give up the ghost.

The loss of all races was the ultimate environmental catastrophe, and it was more likely to come from destroying a critical
ecosystem than from flooding out some Indians, from overuse of
petroleum fuels than from relocating a handful of small villages.
Or so I argued before my trip to Great Whale. Meeting those
native people, seeing their plight, hearing their leaders describe
how families had been disrupted and deeply-held values scoffed
at, ignited a fuse of anger deep within me.

If you have a shred of human decency, you care if a race is
being wiped out. You want every variety of person to have a
place in the Museum of the Human Race. The groups that we call
"primitive" have usually figured out how to sustain themselves
while staying in harmony with nature. When we lose them, we

are one giant step further along the road to ultimate ecosystem collapse.

We mock religious missionaries for trying to impose their beliefs on primitive peoples. We are embarrassed by the violence with which the West was won. "Ugly American" and "carpetbagger" are terms of opprobrium, both of which describe people who think they know better than the local inhabitants of a place. What, then, makes it all right for us to move entire tribes of indigenous people for the sake of so spurious a value as "progress?"

Hence I was delighted when the Sierra Club decided to give its second annual Chico Mendes Award to the Penan Indians of Sarawak, Malaysia. The award commemorates the Brazilian rubber tapper who was martyred in the struggle to defend the Amazon rainforest and the livelihood of the people who live in and depend upon it. Last year we gave it to the Kayapo Indians who were also protesting Amazon rainforest decimation (and who later joined me in Canada to protest the HydroQuebec project).

The deforestation rate in Malaysia is believed to be the most rapid in the world — as much as two million acres per year. Timber companies, having found a rich market in modern Japan, have been working so fast that they have logged in heavy rains, and in some cases even used floodlights so they could work twenty-four hours a day.

In Sarawak, some half-million people depend on the nondestructive use of forest resources for a large part of their livelihood. As hunter-gatherers, the Penan are the most severely affected. They rely solely on the forest for everything they need to survive — food, water, medicines, home building materials, hunting implements, and crafts.

The widespread logging has resulted in severe erosion of their forest homelands, as well as contamination of rivers and destruction of plants, animals and ancestral grave sites. Dietary deficiencies and health problems are growing more and more common.

The government, of course, claims that the forests belong to the state. "But," say the Penans and other tribes, "we were here before there was a state!" Their other pleas — "You have the world; leave us the forest. . . . If logging happens on our land, it is the end of our community. . . . When our lands are taken, it is the same as killing us....We have no choice but to defend ourselves from extinction"— also fell on deaf ears.

As a result, in September 1987, they began peaceful blockades of the logging roads leading into their traditional territory. Over two hundred Penan and scores of other natives were arrested during numerous blockades in the past three years. The harsh treatment the prisoners received — and the fact that they would risk prison to save their homelands — brought the plight of Sarawak's rainforests to world attention.

One result was the current tour of one Kelabit and two Penan tribesmen, the first Sarawak natives ever to travel outside Malaysia. The tour, called "Voices for the Borneo Rainforest," was organized by Japanese and Canadian environmental and human rights organizations. Over a two-month period, the tribal delegation was scheduled to travel to Australia, Canada, the United States, Europe, and Japan.

In Washington, the Congressional Human Rights Caucus and Foundation were working with Sierra Club to present Sierra's Chico Mendes Award "for extraordinary courage and leadership, at the grassroots level, in the universal struggle to protect the environment."

On October 24 — after a speech to student activists at the University of Connecticut campus in Hartford, a few hours' work for Common Cause, and a visit to a United Auto Workers "event" for former Congressman Toby Moffett, who aspired to be a Congressman once more — I boarded the 4:27 train to Washington.

A peaceful night at the Bellevue, a morning at the D.C. office, and off I went to Room 2168 of the Rayburn House Office Building. It is one thing to make friends with Brazilian natives dressed in Patagonian skiwear. It is quite another to meet tribesmen from Borneo in scarlet loincloths and feathers. They were handsome men, tanned and muscular, with shoulder-length black hair and flashing brown eyes. They wore carved wooden bracelets call "jongs" (two of which they presented to me later). One of them was carrying a blow gun.

Although they looked perfectly composed, I knew from my own travel experiences that they were under a great deal of stress. One of the people making their travel arrangements told me that, though they were booked into comfortable hotels, they slept on the floor. After being on show all day, I guess it was asking too much to expect them to experiment with new concepts like "bed" when they needed a good night's sleep.

I had been given a script. *"Djian awe,"* I said (welcome), *"Amee nekedeng ngan ka-ah lem tusah iteu* (we stand beside you in your struggle)." They seemed to find me vastly amusing. Their wide grins lit up the room. I smiled back and launched into my speech. *"Hadja iteu ngan kellunan eh djelleng ga-ga...."* We were all having a fine time but I could see goose bumps on their shoulders. They are used to tropic climes. I knew they must be freezing.

These are a peaceful people. Their blowguns, for instance, are never used against another human being. Yet now they are like fish in a puddle that is drying up. Only their government can help them, and it shows no inclination to do so. I felt enormous frustration. What can Americans do to help?

The ceremony rolled on. Several Senators endorsed the award. Human rights activists sang the praises of the tribesmen. When it was finished, however, they faced their biggest test. Ben & Jerry, a gourmet ice cream company that often donates to environmental causes, sent in several gallons of Rainforest Crunch ice cream, a flavor created to help market tropical products without destroying the forest. Dressed in practically nothing, seated on cold leather and wood chairs, shivering in 65 degree heat, these men who had spent their lives in the tropics spooned down their ice cream and, shivering, grinned some more. Anything for the cause!

I had to hurry back home to Connecticut, however, to clean the house. Arthur's parents were coming from Buffalo for a long weekend. Let me tell you about my mother-in-law. She is a dear lady and very savvy. We share many values and interests, but on the subject of housework we come from different planets. Her favorite sound is the clatter of grit being sucked up a vacuum hose. When she visits me, she cleans. As a bride, I found this embarrassing. Eventually I came to see it as a blessing. She is a "neat freak"; I am known politely as a "casual housekeeper." People like me need people like her. After twenty years, we had come to an accommodation. I promised not to tell anyone that she cleaned on vacations. She promised not to tell anyone why!

All through the month, by letter, telephone, and e-mail, I had been receiving reports on the progress of the Clean Air Act Amendments of 1990. As I left Washington, I was told that the bill could come up in the House at any moment, in the Senate by evening.

By the time I woke the next morning, our victory press release was written. We lauded Congress for at last making possible reductions in smog, acid rain, emissions from coal burning power plants, and cancer-causing industrial pollutants. We praised them for mandating cleaner gasoline and phasing out chemicals that deplete the ozone layer. Then we went all out in urging President Bush to sign the act at once. "The American people can breathe a sigh of relief now that Congress has passed the historic Clean Air Act of 1990," I was quoted as saying. "This redletter day was a decade in the making."

It was indeed. I went out to my back yard and stood staring at the pasture, remembering the ten years of toil that had gone into this day. Then I did just what I had advised the American people to do. I drew in a lungful of Connecticut air, knowing it would now get better, and breathed a sigh of relief.

November 1990

As October's brilliant colors faded along the Potomac's shores and a bleaker November landscape took shape, environmental activists in the national capital were locked in a bitter struggle with two U.S. Senators who were seeking to amend the Interior Appropriations Bill.

Frank Murkowski (R-AK) had been trying since the invasion of Kuwait to open the Arctic National Wildlife Refuge in Alaska for oil and gas leasing. When he announced his intention to use the appropriations bill as his vehicle, a storm of environmental protest arose. In the end, despite a good deal of saber rattling, he decided not to offer his proposal.

Senator Bob Packwood (R-OR) was also defeated in his attempt to undermine the Endangered Species Act through an amendment to the appropriations bill. Packwood proposed to ask the Endangered Species Committee to address the question of the spotted owl vs. logging. Since this committee is comprised mostly of pro-timber administration officials (it is nicknamed the God Committee for its power to decide, literally, whether a species lives or dies), the amendment could have allowed continued logging in the ancient forests for as long as ten years.

A number of Senators argued vehemently against circumventing the process outlined in the Endangered Species Act. At the conclusion of debate, the Senate handed environmentalists a big victory by voting against the Packwood amendment, 62-34.

On November 4, 1990, the New York Times Magazine published an article by environmental writer Trip Gabriel on the Earth First! phenomenon in the northwestern United States. The five-page article described the organization's impassioned and sometimes illegal efforts to prevent logging of old-growth forests.

Gabriel estimated that some 3,000 citizens had participated in the Earth First! Redwood Summer endeavor and that their focus on the issue caused other, more law-abiding environmental groups to pursue court action. As a result, the author said, "Pacific Lumber and state officials announced a temporary moratorium . . . on harvesting the world's largest unprotected virgin redwood grove, a 3,000-acre tract, known as Headwaters Forest."

The Times article went on to describe a system of beliefs dubbed "Deep Ecology," which holds that human beings are not meant to exert dominion over the earth, that all species have equal title to the earth's bounty. Many Earth Firsters, Gabriel said, pass over issues like clean air, clean water, and the greenhouse effect because "for Deep Ecologists, the real hot-button issues are overconsumption and overpopulation."

The article quotes one Earth First! leader as declaring that people are going to die "because they've overshot the carrying capacity of the planet" and concludes that "environmentalists of all stripes share the anxiety that the life-support system of the planet is perilously out of balance, that we are running out of natural resources while we choke on toxins and subvert our own climate."

On November 6, in voting booths across the country, Americans seemed to agree, but cautiously. In the first major election since Earth Day Twenty, candidates for Governor and Congress who had campaigned on "green platforms" were swept into office. Stunning victories and major upsets from Maryland to Texas to Oregon and a dozen states in between prompted election watchers to declare that the Decade of the Environment had begun.

However, specific programs designed to improve natural resource protection and calling for either life style changes or more taxes were generally defeated. The comprehensive "Big Green" initiative in California not only lost, but dragged gubernatorial hopeful Dianne Feinstein down with it. New Yorkers rejected an environmental bond issue for an important landfill/recycling program and narrowly defeated another $2 billion bond proposal for land acquisition. In Oregon, where current bottle-return bills originated, a bill that would have required more recycled and recyclable materials in packaging was defeated.These defeats seemed to indicate that the national mood, influenced by uncertainty in the Persian Gulf and growing state and federal deficits, had taken a turn for the conservative.

A widespread acceptance of the preservation ethic was demonstrated on November 8, however, when Attorneys-General from ten *states banded together to propose guidelines for the claims manufacturers make for products advertised as degradable, compostable, or recyclable. The states' lawyers also said that broad declarations such as "environmentally friendly" and "safe for the environment" ought to be based on scientific evidence. In response, companies like Dow Chemical and Procter & Gamble vehemently proclaimed their innocence.*

An even sharper cry of pain came from the International Monetary Fund, which had been termed "one of the world's leading architects of environmental destruction" in a New York Times *advertisement run by the Rainforest Action Network. "The fight against poverty," responded IMF's director of external relations Asisali F. Mohammed, "is the only way to avoid a situation where people are driven to destroy irreplaceable environmental assets, such as rainforests." Mohammed invoked the Persian Gulf crisis as a reason for keeping IMF's capital base strong and concluded, "The best prospect for preserving the environment worldwide is to be found in encouraging and assisting countries to develop their economic potential . . . . "*

More positive signs of industry's willingness to consider environmental protection as part of the cost of doing business had come earlier in the month, when the McDonald's Corporation agreed to eliminate its plastic foam hamburger box following a joint study with the Environmental Defense Fund. Then, on November 25, one of the environmental movement's traditional enemies, the mining industry, announced the conclusion of negotiations that proved that even they could accommodate to new trends.

"We would rather see the money go into environmental enhancement than the pockets of lawyers," said the Senior Vice-President of Viceroy Resource Corporation, as he announced that his company would be mining gold near the California-Nevada border on public land with the blessing, or at least the acquiescence, of environmental watchdogs. A coalition of six environmental groups, represented by the Sierra Club Legal Defense Fund, had spent two years resolving issues of cyanide poisoning, aquifer protection, waste disposal, and reclamation presented by the proposed mine. The final agreement allowed the company to extract an estimated $290 million in gold in return for implementing costly new environmental concessions.

At a packed White House ceremony on November 15, amid massive media coverage, President Bush signed the Clean Air Act of 1990 into law. The long-awaited signing ceremony was attended by Vice-President Dan Quayle, First Lady Barbara Bush, congressional leaders, industry leaders, and representatives of environmental groups, all of whom cheered the President's declaration that "every American expects and deserves to breathe clean air."

"Clean, hot air!" some environmentalists complained as the United States effectively blocked an international accord for reducing greenhouse gas emissions at the Second World Climate Conference in Geneva. More than 700 scientists, representing 135 countries, called on the nations of the world to take immediate action against global warming. Of the industrialized nations, only the U.S., the world's biggest producer of greenhouse gases, refused to make a commitment.

"This is definitely a setback," said Alden Meyer of the Union of Concerned Scientists. "It's clear that the Bush administration has no intention of budging on this." Mostafa K. Tolba, head of the United Nations Environment Program, warned that the threat of global warming is "potentially more catastrophic than any other threat in human history."

Legislators from the United States, Europe, and Japan seemed to concur when, on November 17, they announced plans to introduce parallel legislation in their own countries to deal with climate change, deforestation, and other threats to the environment. These legislators, all members of Global Legislators Organization for a Balanced Environment (GLOBE), told reporters that their initiatives would put pressure on national governments to act more decisively on threats to global ecological systems. GLOBE listed reduced energy consumption worldwide, international timber agreements (particularly in the Malaysian state of Sarawak, which they described as approaching "ecological suicide"), a treaty protecting the ecology of the North Pacific Rim, and "burgeoning human population growth in the developing world" as priority concerns.

ɘ

There is nothing more restorative than autumn in New England. I am exhilarated by the colors and the crisp air, cheered by the pumpkins and corn and gourds that signify another bountiful harvest. Most of all, I love the tasks of preparing for winter. Snow shovel, firewood, storm windows, weather stripping: each check on the list increases my feeling of security. My horizons close in and small creature comforts — a seat by the wood stove, a hot bath, flannel sheets — fill me with content.

Why, then, was I flying to Florida (to Orlando, to be specific) on Friday, November 2, 1990? Why was I trading my cozy farmhouse again for an impersonal motel room?

FinCom called! The Sierra Club's Finance Committee was meeting in advance of our circus meeting, to make sure that all accounts were balanced and answers readied for every conceivable question.

It was the usual routine: arrive Friday night, socialize a bit, begin meeting Saturday morning, and finish meeting Sunday in time to fly home. We were in Orlando at a fine Sheraton Hotel, but, believe me, this was no trip to DisneyWorld. We sat in a meeting room all day Saturday, hunched over balance sheets. I felt like a character out of Dickens.

Unfortunately, I had to play Scrooge, not Bob Crachit. The numbers were bad. Our new-member growth rate had slowed. The income we counted on to back planned expenditures was not being generated at what we considered "reasonable expectations." We had invested $250,000 in direct mail and would not see a return for some time to come. We had been trying to control spending, but clearly we needed to try harder.

At the end of the day, the meeting planners announced a surprise treat. "Sue," they said, "you've come so far and worked so hard, you deserve a reward. We've made reservations for all of us for dinner at a unique restaurant here. They specialize in oysters, and they serve them every way anyone could possibly think up."

Shades of the Hokkaido crabfest. I hate oysters!

Good sport that I am, I trooped along, smiling. The restaurant had an interesting ambiance — sawdust on the floor, oilcloth on the tables, and Elvis Presley, I think, issuing from a distant jukebox.

"Well, madam President," Michael Fischer beamed, "how do you like them? Baked in butter? Fried? Raw on the halfshell? Or maybe you'd like to try the oyster stew?" This was not Hokkaido. Diplomacy was not involved. I knew my friends truly wanted me to enjoy myself. "I'll have the swordfish," I said. "Well done."

After a pleasant two days at home, I flew on Wednesday to San Francisco. The circus was about to begin.

In actuality, the annual meeting of the Sierra Club and the November meeting of the Board of Directors would not occur until that weekend. For three days beforehand, we prepared.

All the Sierra permutations were involved: the Foundation Board of Trustees, the Council, the Board of Directors, the Regional Vice-Presidents, and, of special import this year, the Centennial Campaign Planning Committee. The action took place in five locations — the Cathedral Hill Hotel, the Lombard Hotel, the Sierra Club Foundation on Sansome Street, the Sierra Club headquarters (where my office was), and a nearby Unitarian church.

We began at 7:00 p.m. on Wednesday night with a meeting of the Council's Executive Committee and, simultaneously, a New Delegate Orientation Session. An array of committees engaged in a frenzy of meetings all day Thursday and Friday, culminating at 7:30 Friday night with the annual Follies.

In our own version of "The Sound of Music," I played the grandmother. I was in the kitchen rehearsing (this is not a very polished production; we don't get together until the day of the show) and missed the opening act, some very cool vocalizing by the Regional Vice-Presidents. I proudly claim credit for starting the Sierra Club Follies several years ago. It was an idea I borrowed from Byron Kennard, a Washington, D.C. activist whose works in the environmental movement are legend. The important thing, to me, is that we are making fun of ourselves. This is a way, if we have lost it, of restoring our perspective on reality.

It also allows for the venting of a good deal of internal frustration. When our lead singer, to the tune of "Edelweiss," crooned, "Hey, Dan Weiss, hey, Dan Weiss, Henry Waxman will greet you. Through the night, you will fight. Dingell will not defeat you," it was a clever way to recognize one of our hardest-working staff people — but it was also a gentle way to satirize the Weiss feisty character.

The stirring "Climb every mountain" was even more stirring when it became "Save every mountain, clean every stream; cancel every highway, then we'll build a dream." No fiery speech could have done more to excite our loyalty to the Club. I know I had a large lump in my throat and tears in my eyes, when the curtain came down.

Saturday began at 7:45 a.m. with a Council business meeting and ended at 7:30 p.m. with a reception hosted by the Great Lakes Bi-National Committee (the Great Lakes ecosystem is shared by the United States and Canada)—their way of lobbying for a greater share of our interest in their issues. Saturday also included a two-hour annual meeting, a five-hour centennial meeting, and a three-and-one-half hour meeting of the Board of Directors. At the very center of the annual meeting agenda was the presentation of a telescope to Doug Scott. We knew it would fit nicely in his new home in the San Juan Islands of Washington state. More than that, we wanted something that would symbolize the vision and far-sightedness he had, for so many years, brought to the Sierra Club. I made the presentation. I told them all that I had been privileged, as Sierra Club President, to spend a year flying with the eagles — and that Doug Scott had been one of those eagles.

Sunday we were at it again by 7:30 a.m. (breakfast for the Council Executive Committee), spending three more hours on a meeting of the full Board of Directors and another two of its Executive Committee.

It takes great skill to carry off such an event. The Club spends a lot of money training its volunteers to run meetings efficiently and to participate in them effectively. Our payback comes at the circus in November as consensus is achieved on dozens of knotty issues.

By the time we were finished that weekend, the Sierra Club had adopted its Conservation Priorities for 1991-92. At the state level, we would focus on preservation of biological diversity, implementation of the Clean Air Act, and municipal solid waste. At the federal level, ancient-forest protection, preservation of the Arctic National Wildlife Refuge Wilderness, global warming (which included auto fuel efficiency), and national parks were listed. We also decided to launch smaller campaigns on international development lending (*re* tropical forests), on overpopulation, and on reauthorization of the federal Resource Conservation and Recovery Act (RCRA). Under a final heading, "Other Campaigns," we listed defense and energy facilities cleanup, Great Lakes water quality, James Bay, reform of the 1872 mining law, transportation and the highway trust fund and wetlands protection.

It appeared to me that we had completed a mammoth meeting, only to find we had created a mountain of work for the future. But there was real progress on several issues. I took personal delight in announcing that we had hired a veteran Sacramento lobbyist, Paula Carrell, to serve as our new state issues coordinator.

Our main speaker, Peter Francese, galvanized the membership on an issue with which the Board was already familiar — changing American demographics. The charges of elitism, so often hurled against the environmental movement, find a readymade stereotype in the Sierra Club. It is true that the Club has been dominated by white males—but, they happen to be the ones who began the fight to save our natural resources! As a woman, I certainly can't claim these white males are antifeminist; they elected me to their highest office. And, as a long-time environmental activist, I know first hand how difficult it has been to get inner-city minorities, blacks or Hispanics, to be concerned with conservation issues. I have been told by more than one minority leader, "My people need decent homes and jobs. We are not ready to fight for the rivers and the woods." Yet that too is changing. Urban leaders have begun to understand that their environment is most often ill-used because they have been focused on other issues. In our turn, we recognize that the fights still ahead of us *must* involve a diverse population if they are to be won. Environmentalists are starting to think about the role we might play in broader issues of social justice.

In addition to Peter Francese's warnings, a report from our own Education Committee stressed the skyrocketing figures of Hispanic and Asian populations in American cities. This, I believe, is where the action is going to be in the next decade. If the Sierra Club has not found a way to communicate with these groups, and to work with them, then we are simply not going to be part of the new policies and solutions that will evolve. I think that would be very sad, for we have a great deal to offer. Let me give one example. The most poverty-stricken areas around the Great Lakes are reporting serious toxic pollution problems. The local black community councils cannot ignore this — but neither are they likely to find an easy solution. Sierra's expertise could make a difference, but only if we are sensitive to their agenda and the need to forge a real collaborative working partnership.

The Sierra Club needs to pull into its ranks all the urban people whose neighborhoods have been split by a smog-causing highway, all the families who live near old factories with yards full of buried hazardous waste, all the men and women who have eked out their food supplies by fishing in a polluted river. We need blacks and Cambodians and Cubans and Arabs and Chinese in leadership positions—and we need to be welcome in their boardrooms, too. And don't talk to me about "tokenism." When someone can tell me a better way, I'll be happy to listen. Evidently our membership agrees. One result of the circus was a new policy goal: at a minimum, the same proportion of minorities in our membership that is found in the general population.

Tuesday, November 13, was one of the darker days in my career as Sierra Club President. I had driven to Palo Alto the night before and checked in at a conference center, where the environmental engineers of Hewlett Packard, nationwide, had assembled. That morning I rose, donned my credibility suit, and went in search of the muffins and coffee that are a feature of every such convention. Sure enough, I found breakfast and a friendly welcome in a sun-drenched foyer just outside the meeting room.

I was in the heart of Silicon Valley, where the computer industry has a history of toxic water pollution. I had not written my own speech, but I knew what was in it: a challenge to those despoilers of the green earth to change their practices and join us in saving the globe. When the meeting began, I was led into a windowless chamber, full of engineers. I half-listened to the opening speakers, then stood up to scold them all.

Well, as it turns out, *these* were the good guys—the ones who had taken it upon themselves to try to influence company policies to be more environmentally benign. I had committed a cardinal sin in speech making: not knowing enough about my audience. Instead of being confrontational, I should have been conspiratorial. They didn't much like what I said — and I, exhausted by the circus, confused by their response, drove back to San Francisco feeling I had let everyone down. I guess they agreed. I never did get a thank-you note.

On Wednesday I flew to Billings, Montana. No mistake this time—I was on my way into the belly of the beast. The Wyoming Heritage Society was holding its annual public forum on Friday. The topic was "Marketing and the Environment," and I strongly suspected I was lunch. "Heritage Society" may sound like an innocent name, but its letterhead includes a tag line: "Wyoming's Advocate for Business and Jobs." These were the big boys, I had been told, when it came to cows, mining, gas, and oil — all the villains we greenies love to hate, in one well-heeled package.

The stopover in Billings was to aid the Montana Chapter in its rejuvenation of their Billings Group. I spent the entire day doing media interviews and tried to be inspirational that night at an organizational meeting with local activists.

These United States are vast and varied. Persuading citizens in Montana to worry about natural resources is far more difficult than persuading citizens in Connecticut. In my home state, we are so densely populated that we can easily see the harm we are doing to ourselves. In Montana, under those big skies and with those wide-open prairies, the concept of finite resources seems much less critical. Because of this, and because so many local incomes depend on using natural resources, it takes a bit of courage to be an environmentalist. You can get your tires slashed if your bumper sticker says the wrong thing.

After the Billings meeting, our field representative, Larry Melhaff, drove me to his home in Sheridan, Wyoming. I slept there but was ready at 6:30 a.m. for his assistant to drive me to Casper in his little pickup truck. By now I owned two credibility suits. I was wearing the second one, with my best gold earrings. I suspected that the Heritage Society's expectations of me included a wardrobe of T-shirts, Birkenstocks, and a peace symbol necklace. If this was a set-up, I counted on those earrings to make them relent.

I arrived too late to hear the first speaker, an anti-environment columnist from the *Detroit Free Press*, named Warren Brookes. Instead, the moment I arrived, they whisked me and Brookes off to a local TV station where I found myself answering questions about the environment and the economy. I tried to make it hard for Brookes to hate me by being sweet and friendly without ceding him any points. Later, when I learned he had spent the morning ridiculing environmentalists and trying to debunk global warming, I regretted my good nature.

We made it back to the forum in time to hear a luncheon speech, "Can We Drill in the Arctic?" The speaker, Robert O. Anderson, is president and CEO of Hondo Oil and Gas, and former CEO of Atlantic Richfield. He thought we could — and

To Sue —
Thanks for
your support
Bruce

Thirteen years of lobbying led to the passage of the Clean Air Act of 1990. Congressman Bruce Morrison, here with me in 1988, went on to run for Governor of Connecticut in 1990.

The love of wilderness runs deep in all environmental activists. In 1987 the Merrow family visited Yosemite, so important in the history of the Sierra Club. That's Half Dome in the background, Annie and Arthur with me in the foreground.

The Merrow home in East Haddam, Connecticut. The house was built in about 1813.

The dining room of the Merrow home. The table has been the site of many envelope-stuffing parties.

Photo by Bruce Cook

The headquarters of the
Sierra Club at 730 Polk
Street, San Francisco,
California.

SIERRA CLUB

SIERRA CLUB

Sierra Club Presidents find themselves rubbing shoulders with a lot of interesting people. Some of the most fascinating for me were the Penan tribesmen (above), and television journalist Charles Kuralt (below).

The "ecotour" group that went to Costa Rica in February 1991. I am fifth
from the left, top row; our guide, Jorge Morra Escalante, is third from left,
bottom row.

Photo by Elizabeth Feryl

Sierra Club meets Rainbow Coalition: Jesse Jackson and I posing in an ancient
forest during his tour of the Pacific Northwest. The men to Jackson's left are Bill
Arthur, Sierra Club Northwest Field Representative, and Andy Kerr, of the Oregon
Natural Resources Council.

The ultimate "pinch-me" experience was our trip to Japan. The Merrows were invited to tour the Young Corporation, headquartered in this Golden Pyramid structure.

Photo by Windell M. Smith

In May 1991 I presented Dr. Wangari Maathai with Sierra Club's Earth Care Award.

The invitation to the reception in my honor that Senator Chris Dodd threw at the Capitol in June 1990; my press pass from the Economic Summit in Houston in July; the soapstone walrus that I bought for Annie in Great Whale, Canada, in October.

More souvenirs from my year as President—bracelets made by Penan tribesmen (jongs); crafts from Costa Rica; and a bottle of elixir from the Young Corporation in Japan.

Arthur and Annie joined me at the podium during the Annual Dinner Awards Ceremony in May 1991, as my year of presidency came to a close.

The next stage of my life: a campaign photograph of me, as I ran for First Selectman (i.e., Mayor) of East Haddam. With me is Roger Gandolf, who ran for Second Selectman.

should. For the Sierra Club, this is heresy. The coastal plain of the Arctic National Wildlife Refuge is the last such pristine ecosystem in the world. There is nothing else quite like it, anywhere. The oil companies admit there is only a one-in-five chance that they will find oil there, but if they do, it will be cheap oil that can be fed into the Alaska pipeline and quickly distributed. (When I say "cheap oil," understand that I am talking about the company's developments costs; the price you pay at retail will not, I can assure you, be cheap.)

The worst part is that *we don't need it*. Or we wouldn't, if we really tried conservation. I listened to Mr. Anderson's remarks with a sinking heart. If we couldn't agree on this, we were not likely to find many other points of common ground.

Chatting with the other folks at the table, I began to understand the mentality of a hostage. We all want approval from the people around us, even when we are surrounded by villains. And these people were not villains; they simply have not come as far down the environmental path as I have. They all claimed to love the environment. They valued their state's vast open spaces and enjoyed what they called "the great out-of-doors." Unfortunately they also depended for their livelihoods primarily on exploitation of the land and its natural resources. At one point, the Heritage Society's President summed it all up. "We must develop and utilize our natural resources and our people," he said.

The concept that resources are finite, that there are limits to the amount of pollution air and water can take and still bounce back, that all species interact in a web of life so complex that — to guarantee human survival — all must be maintained: I heard little indication that any of these ideas had crossed the minds of the people present. Maybe that was because we environmentalists have not communicated clearly enough; or maybe it was because they are smart enough to see which side of the bread is buttered. Either way, they were not bad people — just slow to evolve. They have so *much* in the way of natural resources; the problem has yet to come clear to them.

At 3:00 p.m., according to the program, Susan Merrow of the Sierra Club would share the spotlight with Alexander Trowbridge, past President of the National Association of Manufacturers. Now there's a combination!

Sandy (as I came to call him before we were done) talked about garbage. Now Wyoming's population is such that while it has a normal complement of two U.S. Senators, it merits only one Congressman. Coming from Connecticut, where we have slightly more people than acres, I just could not get excited about Wyoming's waste disposal problems, and I suspected that the audience couldn't either. It was a safe subject for him.

When my turn came, I tried to persuade them that they could lead comfort-filled lives while respecting nature's limits. I presented statistics proving that environmental protection can add to the gross national product. I talked about new growth industries in pollution control devices and ecotourism. I assured them that the Sierra Club fully understands that you can't have a healthy environment in a devastated economy, and called on them all to become activists in preventing global warming and in energy conservation. I hope they heard me.

After the meeting, several people came up to say hello and assure me they agreed with me. The room was mostly full of men, and they were almost entirely dressed the same: cowboy boots, ornate belt buckles, and sports jackets. The hat-check room was awash in wide-brimmed Stetsons. My gold earrings buoyed me in this sea of bolo ties and made it possible to maintain my composure. Until, that is, a more hostile gentleman confronted me. "The trouble with you environmentalists is that you never will admit it when you've made a mistake."

"Of course we will! That's silly," I rejoined.

"OK. Tell me one mistake you've made."

My brain was spinning. For the life of me, I couldn't think of an example for him. Yet I had to say something. I remembered a remark David Brower once made. "We should never have let them build the Glen Canyon Dam!" I blurted out.

"Ha!" the man shouted, raising both hands. Before I could recoup, he had turned away.

I was standing alone, still trying to think of a mistake we had made, when one of my hosts approached with a slender, bespectacled, bald man wearing an eerie, beatific smile. "Ms. Merrow," my host said, "I'd like to introduce you to former Secretary of the Interior James Watt." The Sierra Club once collected 1.3 million signatures on a petition to get rid of James Watt — but he was polite. He offered his hand and I took it.

In my head was a vision of one of my favorite cartoons. Two bears are talking. One, toothpick in his mouth, is saying, "So I sez to him, 'You're not THE James Watt, decimator of wilderness, scourge of the plains?' And he says to me, 'Yes I am' — so I ate him." We shook hands and I kept on moving. After all, the two of us did not have much small talk to make to each other.

The Heritage Society took about twenty of us out to dinner that night at a private cattlemen's club. It was very elegant— nouveau Victorian decor, great rounds of beef, and chafing dishes full of delectable edibles, which we ate in a greenhouse sort of room, full of exotic plants.

As an extra benefit for its forum speakers, the Society had promised a side trip to Cody, Wyoming, and the museum there on the following day. Sounded good to me; I assumed the entire dinner party would be together again. To my surprise, only Sandy Trowbridge and I had accepted the invitation. He and I and the society's President, Jim Nielson, were joined by executive director Bill Schilling and his family. A private plane was waiting for us at the tiny Casper airport.

The trip took a bit more than an hour and was a welcome adventure. The Wyoming topography below us was brown and treeless, almost lunar. I regarded this whole outing as a perk. I had no speech to make, no press dates to keep. I could relax. . . that is, until I saw the mesa up ahead and realized that was where we were going to land.

My knuckles went white gripping the arm rests, my stomach started to churn. It is one thing to throw up in the impersonal surroundings of a transcontinental jet — and quite another when you are sitting next to the former head of the National Association of Manufacturers. I bit my lip and stayed very quiet until we were down.

Cody is Jim Nielson's home town and he is on the board of directors of the William Cody Museum there. We checked in at a motel and then were driven to the museum. It has a large display of interesting Cody memorabilia and a wing devoted to Western art, with a fine collection of Frederick Remington's work, some impressive paintings by N. C. Wyeth, and the works of several more modern painters. A third wing is devoted to the Plains Indians, including a depiction of the massacre at Wounded Knee. All in all, it was like opening a window for me into a world about which I knew very little. The people around me began to make more sense viewed from that perspective. I was very glad I had the opportunity to see the museum. I wish everybody from the East Coast could.

Sandy had stayed at a dude ranch in the area many years before and wanted to see it again. Jim Nielson obliged by driving us to Sunlight Canyon, a spectacular place where the desolation of the November landscape gave way to a panorama of mountain peaks, framed by tall evergreens. We had dinner that night in a hunting lodge, Absaroka by name, where local people had been invited to meet the traveling dignitaries. A dinner of game hen and slabs of cherry pie was served beneath the glassy-eyed gaze of bear and elk heads, mounted and hanging on the wall. Everything in the place reflected the words of the old song: This land was made for you and me.

I am an old hand at sleeping in forest outposts. Bunks and sleeping bags and mattresses of pine boughs I take in stride. Nevertheless, I was pleased to be delivered back to my comfortable motel bedroom. When I tried to settle down for the night, though, the peculiar Absaroka mood held fast. I felt as if I were inside a Jack London short story. The stars, as I walked outside just before bed, lacked the blurry overlay of smog I have come to expect. They seemed to blaze. And the silhouette of the horizon, blocky in shape, faintly opalescent, was so unlike the horizon in Connecticut that I might as well have been on the moon. It was beautiful and I was being treated like a head of state. Yet I felt guilty. So far on this trip, I had engaged in no serious arguments, laid no heavy blame. Should I have hurled invectives instead of trying to build bridges? Maybe my detractors had been right when they said I was too nice to be President of the Sierra Club.

The preservation of the Yellowstone ecosystem is not guaranteed because two major parts of it have been set aside as national parks. The private land I had been seeing for the past two days is also a living, breathing part of that system. The life within the park cannot be separated from the life outside of it simply by drawing a line on a map. They depend on each other — and I had not heard anything since leaving Billings to indicate that the people here understood this important fact.

Men like my hosts have jeopardized so much of their children's heritage — and yet they took for themselves the name

"Heritage Society." It seemed to me that fact alone demonstrated their innocence. I wanted to absolve them of every crime save naivete . . . and knew that it was more likely I was the one being naive.

I stood under the stars and listened to the wind scratching at something in the distance. I remembered Jim Nielson's pride in the Cody Museum. I remembered standing side by side with Sandy Trowbridge studying an Indian sculpture. It seemed to me wonderful that leaders of the Sierra Club and the National Association of Manufacturers had found even that much common ground. The warmth of their proffered friendship made me hope that our time together would lead to a continuing dialogue. I knew that I had done some growing that day. I hoped the others had too.

Five days later I sat in my father's dining room in Maine and dished up our Thanksgiving dinner. My husband, my daughter, my father, and my brother and his family were my entire universe for those few days. There was a heaviness in the cold air, a promise of snow. The wind came in off Penobscot Bay full of ice crystals. Midmorning, my father turned up the oil fire in the old cast iron stove and passed around hot chocolate while the turkey browned in the oven.

I babble without letup about my travels to Arthur and Annie. I am, however, curiously reticent when I am with my brother and father. I suppose I am afraid that they — like the men in Wyoming — might find me hard to comprehend. That is something I would not want to know. It didn't matter, though, on that Thanksgiving day. All I wanted was to hear the local gossip, and to brag about Annie's English compositions, and to reassure myself that my father was content in his life.

The smell of the sea, the sound of wind in the tall pines, and the sight of acres of pastures on the drive to town, each outlined by neat stone walls, seemed to me ample reason for giving thanks. Before we ate, I read a prayer from a dog-eared scrap of paper that had been folded up in my appointment book, waiting for just such a time. I think I had copied it from a poster long ago.

"Thank you, Lord," it said, "for each new day you give to me, for earth and sky and shining sea, for rainbows after springtime showers, autumn leaves and summer flowers.

"For winter snowscapes so serene, harvest fields of gold and green, beauty shining all around, lilac scent and robin sound, stars that twinkle high above, and all the people that I love. Amen."

I felt a moment of soaring content — but almost as soon as we began to eat, part of me was planning next Saturday's trip to San Francisco.

December 1990

If a community destroys so much of its usable water that it has to build an expensive water treatment plant, should the value of that plant be included in the country's gross national product? Traditionally it would be, but in December, when the Dutch government put the question to Rofie Huetig at the Netherlands Central Bureau of Statistics, he said, "No!"

Huetig's negative response was portentous because his government had asked him to devise a system of national accounting to reflect the damage done to the air, water, soil, and animal and plant life, and to account for the cost of maintaining or restoring them. The Netherlands is believed to be the first country in the world officially to study so-called "green accounting."

"You can only count the treatment plant as value added if you have first entered the ruined drinking water as a loss," Huetig said. He added that the same rule should apply to systems that clean up smog or restore any natural resources lost to development.

"Ecological economists," according to the New York Times, *"hope that a new framework for national accounts will lead to a fundamental change of national goals and even a redefinition of progress."*

In a related study, done for the U.S. Congress and made public later the same month, the U.S. Environmental Protection Agency estimated that 2 percent of the country's gross national product tally came from goods and services to control pollution and to clean up the environment. According to the EPA, that is about half of what the nation spends on clothes and a third of its military allocation.

EPA went on to predict that the figure would rise to 2.8 percent by the year 2000 and, as a result, make it very difficult for some municipalities to afford pollution control facilities. Cleanup of waste, particularly hazardous materials, was singled out as the fastest-growing and easily most expensive environmental initiative. Total 1990 costs were placed at $100 billion. By the year 2000, the analysis said, that figure could rise to between $148 and $160 billion.

The demand for environmental accountability when large facilities are built was recognized in Hawaii, where a federal judge ruled that the development of a 500-megawatt geothermal power plant in the Wao Kele O Puna rainforest required a federal environmental impact statement. The judge pointed to the $49.7 million in federal funds involved when ruling that the plant was not, as justice department attorneys had argued, merely a private and state project.

In Washington, D.C., the National Conference of State Legislatures (NCSL) was targeted for heavy lobbying by both environmentalists and oil interests when it met for its annual State-Federal Assembly in mid-month. Against a background of increasing global anxiety about oil supplies in Kuwait, the NCSL was debating a resolution that urged opening Alaska's Arctic National Wildlife Refuge to oil and gas development. Following days of tension and some harsh charges from both sides, the NCSL Environment Committee defeated the resolution 11-9.

On the same day, meeting in Paris, the Council of Ministers of the European Economic Community agreed to study a plan that would give an official "green label" to products that were created with concern for the environment. One proponent, Carlo Ripa di Meana, the European Commissioner for the Environment, said the plan was designed to speed environmental action through competition instead of by law.

As economists, attorneys, state legislators, and consumer advocates debated an array of "macro" topics, scientists from New Mexico zeroed in on a "micro" topic: the kangaroo rat and his role in the web of life. Reported in the journal Science, *a fifteen-year study conducted by biologists at the University of New Mexico found that the kangaroo rat species, collectively called a guild, controlled the nature of its habitat. Removing the guild (while leaving other rodents) changed a desert plain into an arid grassland area in only a decade, the researchers said, and illustrated the inordinate influence seemingly innocuous animals can have on the environment.*

The concept of keystone species, animals and plants that exhibit an effect on the habitat exceeding their size or number, was first recognized twenty-five years ago. In this new study, the kangaroo rat appeared to influence, indirectly, the rate of snow melt, the number of birds, and the kinds of vegetation. All of this eventually turned the land into a completely different habitat.

❧

The blues hit me in San Francisco, at the end of a meeting of the Centennial Campaign Planning Committee. I could be glib and call it "panic about the meaning of life," and in a way it was. However, more likely it was anniversary depression. The next day, December 1, 1990, I would commence my eighth month in the Sierra presidency. My year was more than half over — and what had I accomplished?

Certainly I had seen the country, and had a great time for myself. I'd made a few points in Japan. I'd "told it like it is" to the press, especially at G-7. But I had also ridiculed George Bush for his apparent lack of strategy, his dearth of milestones. I wandered out of the meeting room, frowning, back to my own office and closed the door. I too held the title President. If I were to be measured as stringently as the Sierra Club measured George Bush, how would I hold up?

My self-doubt lasted through the plane ride, next day, to Eugene, where I was to be a speaker at the Oregon Chapter's annual banquet. It began to fade once I reached the home of Sandy and Bert Tepfer, my Oregon home away from home. These staunch activists make no room for doubt; they know what they are about.

The banquet was held at a downtown hotel. Unfortunately the management placed us in between a noisy auction and a noisy prom—so I had some excuse if I didn't strike fire in the heart of every member of the audience.

I remember two things happily from that night. The first was the salmon. They take it for granted in Oregon, but this New Englander smacked her lips. The second was a handmade basket I bought for Annie. I remember thinking that I would fill it for Christmas with soaps and other sweet-smelling things. Even when she was 3,000 miles away, thinking about Annie cheered me up.

The entire next day was devoted to airplanes. East Haddam, Connecticut, is a *long* way from Eugene, Oregon. The day after was devoted to resting up at home. On December 4, I got back into harness. A posh photo gallery in Manhattan was featuring the original prints from two elegant picture books Sierra had published. The Centennial Committee was using the opening of the exhibit as an opportunity to entertain potential donors, the kind with very deep pockets.

What a complex organization we are. People think the Sierra Club is all hikes in the wilderness, but here we were, munching hors d'ouevres as casually as if they were trail mix, adapting almost as well to the canyons of Manhattan as we do to the arroyos of Arizona.

The photographs were of the Alaskan wilderness, very beautiful. I was proud to be a part of the whole event. I did not stay over in Manhattan, however. I took the last train back to New Haven and then drove an hour to East Haddam. I got in shortly before 2:00 a.m., and slept four hours. Then it was time for chores.

Throughout the year, I tried to be at home in the morning if it was humanly possible, so that I could take care of the animals. Arthur and Annie have to leave our house by 6:30 a.m. if he is to drop her off at school. During basketball season (her favorite sport), many times they don't get home again until 7:30 at night. Since he takes on so much of the burden of her transportation, it seems only fair for me to make an effort to ease his mornings by tending the livestock.

In Hartford they were still wrangling about how to pay for the Department of Environmental Protection — fees or General Fund. I spent the next day putting in my two cents and the next few days tending to other local matters.

On Sunday, December 9, I drove to the Stamford, Connecticut, Presbyterian Church to give a talk on recycling. They were such good people, and I was so reasonable. I brought my own little portable display of garbage—actually examples of ill-designed over-packaging— and spouted scary figures about landfills and dioxin, but my heart wasn't in it for two reasons.

First, it always makes me feel uneasy to endorse saving the world without leaving the kitchen. Many people get so excited about reusing raw materials that, I fear, they have no energy left for the big jobs — like finding out how a Senator is going to vote and telling him why he shouldn't, or raising money to hire professionals to make a film that will have an impact on everyone who sees it, or taking time to understand the relative risks for waste disposal options currently available. I don't mean to sound impatient. Recycling is right! Do it! But don't think that saving newspapers, or starting a compost heap, is all there is.

In all matters environmental, we must know the dangers, understand the solutions, and influence public policy through lobbying and education. That's why the Sierra Club has been so successful. Demanding that lawmakers establish recycling as government policy is the real job. Without that, washing out our tin cans will never be enough.

Second, some shadow of my earlier dissatisfaction still haunted me. I felt as if I should be doing more — and then I felt guilty because these really were wonderful, concerned people, reaching out to ask how they could help save the planet. And I was being a self-centered grinch.

A thousand points of light. That is how George Bush, campaigning for President, described Americans who volunteer to help others. It was an image with almost universal appeal — each of us picturing ourselves as a star, or maybe just a candle, against the engulfing darkness. Sierra Club members were intrigued. More than one of them wondered aloud: "Could he mean environmentalists too?"

Well, sure enough, he did! On December 13th, something called the Points of Light Foundation was having a meeting in Washington. President Bush would address representatives from major volunteer organizations — and the Sierra Club was invited. Now remember that I had already been dis-invited to the White House. I was relieved to note that this meeting was being held in the Old Executive Office Building. Maybe this time I wouldn't be scratched.

I'm joking. The truth is, I would not have gone to such a meeting ordinarily. (Not that Sierra would ignore an invitation from the President, even one as obviously self-serving as this, we would have sent a staffer.) However, a more meaningful invitation had also arrived for the same day. A group of environmentalists were being given time to talk to Secretary of State James A.

Baker about global warming and other worldwide environmental health problems. I had been planning to fly to San Francisco on the 13th, but the chance to talk to Baker was pure gold. I told our Washington office that I would attend both meetings.

Now arose the airlines problem. My seat to California was booked and paid for. It would be a sinful waste not to have someone use it. At the last minute I sent our good friend, Bob Howard, to fetch Annie from school and put her on the plane in my stead. I arranged for Annie to be met in San Francisco, but I forgot to call the dean of girls at Loomis. Believe me, I heard about it later. Sending a strange man to pick up your daughter at a private high school is frowned upon, to put it mildly.

The TPOL Foundation meeting was interesting because the George Bush in front of us seemed in no way related to the angry individual I had last seen in Houston. The President was urbane, relaxed, and witty as he talked to us about the delights of being a volunteer. He was even charming when a man in the audience had the temerity to point out that our attendance here in no way endorsed budget cutting for programs that should be supported by tax dollars, not charity.

There must have been two hundred of us there—Camp Fire leaders, candy stripers, scout masters, United Way fund raisers, people working against AIDS, for abused women, with drug addicts, on all sorts of humane missions. I'm sure it did them all good to see the others, and to bask in the approbation of the nation's chief executive. I was happy for them, but I couldn't escape the feeling that I was there by mistake. And, anyway, I was a lot more excited about my 2:00 p.m. meeting with Secretary Baker.

I rushed back to the office so that I could be thoroughly briefed by Dan Becker, Melanie Griffin, and other staffers on the latest world events. It was nearly noon — we were deep into rainforest politics — when a call came from Baker's staff. They were sorry Mrs. Merrow had not made the meeting. Should she be included on the follow-up mailing list?

Not made the meeting? It was still two hours away!

"Oh, didn't you get the message? It was pushed up to ten a.m. It's already over."

I was beyond tears. I had postponed being in San Francisco. My innocent daughter had flown cross-country all by herself. I had spent time and too much of Sierra's money on a useless trip to Washington. I had missed the opportunity to persuade a key member of the Bush administration about the critical need for environmental protection. I was even beyond swearing. I went back to the Bellevue, turned on the television set, and watched game shows without comprehending what was on the screen.

Annie had arrived safely in San Francisco, been greeted by friends out there, and was waiting for me when I arrived at the Richelieu late that day. Waiting for me at the office was a tall stack of paperwork. Perhaps the most interesting item was a brief but thoughtful document from one of our policy gurus, Gene Coan. Gene raised a lot of questions about the siting of waste disposal facilities. Mostly they dealt with what I sometimes call the Eternal Conundrum: if a thing is in any way environmentally malignant, should it absolutely be opposed; or is it better to face the inevitable and work to make it as benign as possible?

Crack the shell of that question and you will find inside another series of questions: Our relationship with NIMBYs. Whether we should oppose hazardous and nuclear waste facilities more resolutely than municipal refuse structures. The morality of demanding local disposal as an incentive for quantity waste reduction.

Gene was starting at the beginning, as a good philosopher should. He wanted to know with whom and when and where to hold the debate and was suggesting that our Conservation Coordinating Committee begin "an electronic dialogue" on the subject. This seemed a sensible way to get a handle on the low-level radioactive waste problem, which was still bubbling along and would certainly get hot again, probably at the January meeting.

As it happened, the ConsCoordCom had met just a week before and debated a good many related items. I felt confident that Gene's queries were in good hands. Paula Carrell, our new state/provincial director, attended. The Club had already spent $202,800 in grants to various states. We were helping to hire lobbyists, print materials and buy computer equipment in eleven states and two Canadian provinces. Forestry in Minnesota, clean air in Texas, toxics in Arizona, and James Bay in Quebec would all benefit.

Additionally, Gene Coan had contacted all concerned about three issues of special interest at the state level: Clean Air Act implementation, solid waste, and biodiversity. Paula, in her turn, had written to every local chapter, enclosing a questionnaire that sought information on their issues, priorities, and coordination methods. With staff like that, who needs a President?

Interesting question!

Lawyers, for one. Our Ohio Chapter was all set to intervene in proceedings before the Ohio Public Utilities Commission and, because of short deadlines, needed emergency approval. They wanted to present evidence that increasing energy efficiency is a cost-effective means of reducing the pollutants that result in acid rain. I concurred.

Our Lone Star Chapter was also seeking quick approval of a legal intervention concerning ranching on Matagordo Island; and the Santa Fe Group of the Rio Grande Chapter wanted to take on the State of New Mexico and the Los Alamos National Laboratories regarding air pollution from municipal waste incinerators. I approved both.

The Canadians, for another. We were about to begin negotiations with the Sierra Club of Canada — which has a conglomeration of subsidiaries — and there were dozens of pesky questions concerning, for example, parity with U.S. chapters, outings coordination, and cost of membership services, all needing careful consideration. I put that one aside for homework.

And, third, the Atlantic Chapter, already in trouble with the national Board of Directors, had, on the one hand, asked us to postpone placing them under suspension and, on the other, come out publicly in support of a grandiose wilderness proposal being made by the Alliance for the Wild Rockies. Not only did we disapprove the scheme, the letter could jeopardize sensitive relationships with hitherto friendly congressmen. Unfortunately singer Carole King, no lover of the Sierra Club, had a copy of the letter and was expected to make it public on national television. There were a half dozen memos about this on my desk. One, headed "Brace yourselves," asked, "How can we extricate ourselves gracefully from this tar pit?" My favorite concluded, "Flies bite elephants all the time, but elephants survive essentially unharmed. So will we."

Although I was diligent in addressing my in-box, most of my time on that trip was taken up with a meeting of our Planning Committee. Among a host of other items, we did in-depth interviews with three consultants on strategic planning.

I don't suppose there is an MBA program in the country that could teach me what I was learning in my current position. I flew home on December 18th dreaming about becoming a corporate executive — in a good "green" company, of course — and at last bringing home some real money.

My holiday rum balls are famed in three states. It was time to forget about global warming and concentrate on creating some Christmas warmth at my own hearth. Aside from a Fees Task Force meeting in Hartford, I attended no more meetings in 1990.

We were embroiled in a couple of other interesting issues, however. Our Alaska Chapter, for instance, had set up, and was already widely advertising, a trip to Lake Baikal in Irkutsk, Russia. That's a no-no! My computer clattered with wrath as it transmitted objections from Peter Bengtson, the Chairman of our National Outings Committee. The Outings Committee has been running trips for close to ninety years. We had 320 planned in 1991, using about 650 volunteer leaders and staff. Four of these were to Russia (they would gross an estimated $33,225) and a fifth had been cancelled on the theory that the market was currently too thin to support another trip. The proposed Alaska Chapter trip was viewed as being direct competition.

Now, all outings to foreign countries require advance approval from the Sierra Board of Directors if they are to be advertised as Sierra trips. The liability we take on is considerable and prudence is warranted. Many of our Outings Committee members were initiated in the tradition by their parents. All of them go through a careful training period and hands-on screening before they are allowed to take leadership responsibility. The folks in the Alaska Chapter know all this. I guess they just got carried away.

It's no fun, especially at Christmas time, to tell someone who is all excited about a trip, that he can't go — but sometimes life just isn't fun. Within days we established two committees, one on outing standards and another to deal with "trips longer than ten days, international trips, and trips into neighboring chapters." Before the month was over, the Board's Executive Committee issued an official statement saying we would approve no more chapter-organized outings to foreign countries until we could complete a "major review of chapter outings policy."

Christmas, in 1990, was dimmed for all Americans by the imminent threat of war in the Persian Gulf. Upwards of 400,000 young men and women had been mobilized. It seemed that we all knew some family, somewhere, in danger of being snared by Saddam Hussein's oil-slick tentacles.

Immediately after the invasion of Kuwait, I had been hopeful that Hussein's actions would force a more rational energy policy in the United States. With our access to Mideast oil threatened, surely, I reasoned, we will begin to take energy conservation seriously. By mid-December, my naivete was clear. Energy Secretary James Watkins had evidently made a sincere effort to draw up a reasonable national energy strategy, but everything leaked from the White House indicated that the Bush administration was not buying it.

We all knew the White House was lobbying its own Department of Energy to drop proposals for tightening auto fuel efficiency standards and most other conservation measures. Budget Director Richard Darman was quoted as calling the strategy "antimarket" and thus "antithetical" to the administration's economic principles. Efforts to increase the use of non-gasoline fuels were criticized as a federal subsidy for the alternative-fuels industry. Yet they were apparently willing to subsidize the oil industry with a Gulf war! It made me shudder.

I reacted in two ways. I turned inward, and concentrated on building a gingerbread house with Annie. I turned outward and spent long hours sending and receiving e-mail messages about how the Sierra Club should respond to this national madness.

In the week before Christmas, I:

* Finished my shopping. I had been trying to buy Arthur both an anvil and a butterfly net (he's a very interesting man), but anvils are hard to find. I settled for the net.

* Encouraged my colleagues to plan a Mass Mobilization that would tie the grassroots efforts now focused on auto fuel efficiency, protection of the Arctic Wilderness, global warming, James Bay, keeping oil rigs off our coasts, and other energy conservation issues into a single, gigantic assault on anything less than a conservation-based national energy strategy.

* Expanded our usual stereotypical gingerbread house into a model of our farmhouse, complete with el and center chimney.

* Agreed to help with a nationwide Citizen's Safe Energy Policy Petition. The petitions, besides being circulated at every public meeting we could get to, would be published in *Sierra* magazine, hundreds of environmental newsletters, and paid ads in small daily papers. The message: Stop being held hostage by big oil companies! Prevent future Mideast crises! Save our fragile environment! Stop oil spills! Curb global warming! Plus space for special local concerns. We set no goal for the number of signatures, but we knew we were talking in the millions.

* Moved in — when Arthur burned the home-grown raspberry jelly he was making for Christmas gifts — and filled the empty jelly jars with my own homemade chocolate sauce.

* Kept close tabs on a joint Sierra Club-Senator Timothy Wirth press conference in Washington. Our chairman, Mike McCloskey, called the national energy strategy being announced that day "a lump of coal in the stockings of all those who care about the health of the planet we are leaving to our children."

* Helped Arthur find a suitable evergreen tree in our woods and then helped Annie trim it with tiny white lights and our collection of handmade ornaments.

* Approved a January timetable for the Mass Mobilization campaign that would integrate the many Sierra Club structures into a cohesive effort, so that we could go public with the campaign by February 15.

* Shored up the roof of the gingerbread house when it collapsed.

*   Began serious brainstorming about public events — at gas stations, beaches, state capitols, public utility offices — that would garner media coverage of our Mass Mobilization.

*   Turned out seven dozen holiday rum balls, four pounds of chocolate peanut butter fudge, and assorted other candies.

*   Worked out the agenda for the January meeting of the Board of Directors.

We spent Christmas Eve, as is our custom, with valued friends, David and Annie Bingham in the neighboring town of Salem.

Annie always makes breakfast on Christmas morning — after she feeds the livestock — and it is an important meal, usually bacon and eggs and coffee cake and sparkling cider. We don't open the presents until we have eaten and then we open them slowly, savoring each one before we go on to the next. This year we hurried it up a bit, however, because we were driving to Vermont to have Christmas dinner with Arthur's brother and his family, as well as the senior Merrows.

We slept in Vermont and the next day drove down to Beverly, Massachusetts, for our annual visit with Arthur's elderly aunt and uncle. They have no children and always make a great fuss over us. We stayed with them that night, and the next day travelled to Boston to visit the Museum of Science there. I include all these details because they lead up to the moment — inside the museum — when my life changed.

Of course we all change, all the time. We grow wiser, or more experienced. Our values develop in different ways, depending on what happens to us. Mostly, however, we are unaware of the change. This was different—like a squiggle in my psyche, like some disjointed part of me falling into place. I watched a movie at the Museum of Science called "The Blue Planet." And as I watched, the anxiety I had carried with me all month, the self-doubt, the ennui, melted away. It was a moment of epiphany for me and two weeks later, at the January Board meeting, I found the words to share the experience. This is what I told them.

"During the holidays, I found myself at the Museum of Science in Boston in their Omni Theatre. The screen surrounds the audience overhead and on all sides, and the movies are so realistic that the management gives instructions on how to deal with motion sickness. The movie, "The Blue Planet," featured those pictures of the Earth from outer space that we've all become familiar with, only this time interspersed with close-up shots of environmental degradation.

"We saw pictures from outer space of rainforests on fire, then — up close — pictures of the Mississippi delta with its plume of eroded sediment, interspersed with pictures of agriculture and the chemical industries that contribute to its problems.

"Most movingly, it showed the silhouette of the Earth against the backdrop of the rest of the universe. It was easy to pick out the fragile, pale blue shell of our atmosphere. It's only four or five miles thick — the distance from my house to our local post office. And within it, and depending upon it, is all life — everything we love and hold dear.

"The message was clear. The pictures, words, and music conspired to be a deeply stirring call to act, to make a start, to put things right with this blue planet before it is too late.

"As the lights came up and the two or three hundred other people in the room began to file out, I wanted to say, "Go out and do something. Get mad. Get involved. Get up on your hind legs." As they filed by they seemed unmoved by my silent exhortation, and I realized that the chances were very good that no one in that room had been given the gifts and the resources that I had at my command to do something, to get mad, to get involved, and to make a difference.

"I thought about the resources that I have as the Sierra Club President: this microphone and a whole room full of the smartest, most committed people I know listening to me; the bully pulpit; ninety-nine years of credibility; even some discretionary money; and people return my calls.

"I thought about what I need do to get ready to be worthy of this title, and to lead like a person with a mission. I've begun to start each day — and I commend this to you — by saying into the mirror, 'The Sierra Club is a means, not an end.'

"Now, I love the Sierra Club a lot. It's my work, my family. It's Annie's sibling. But it's a means, not an end, and I want to start behaving as if I believe that, and more like someone on a mission. Someday, when my grandchildren ask, "What did you do in the moral equivalent of war, Grandma?," I don't want to say that I wanted to help but I was too busy working on the budget or worrying about office efficiency.

"If we believe that the Club is a means, then we must believe that, not only can we save this planet, but that there is no more important thing we need to do everyday. It's so easy to become like Edward Abbey's 'Men with their hearts in a safe deposit box and their eyes hypnotized by desk calculators.'

"I believe that when we are people on a mission, a lot of other things fall into place. I keep coming up with an image of people furiously filling sandbags and building a dike to protect a place they love. They have a singleness of purpose. They know what they need to do, and their conviction draws people and resources to help. They take chances. They're bold. There's no time for bickering. Their case statement and needs lists practically write themselves. I'd like for us to behave more like those people, more like we have just as urgent a mission, and it lies outside the Sierra Club.

"I believe that our mission has to be to save the planet from the intertwined issues of global climate change and the horrendous lack of leadership from Washington on a rational energy policy. And these are all tied up with the Arctic National Wildlife Refuge, automobile fuel efficiency, rainforests, and population. We can make a difference, because we have to. And as your leader, I'm going to act like I believe that. That doesn't mean that I'll work any less hard on the Centennial or on the Board's agenda. I just mean to put them in a different perspective. I believe that if I do, the perpetuation of the Sierra Club will begin to take care of itself.

"We have daunting goals, but we know how goals work. You break them down into pieces, into something you can get a grip on, something quantifiable. Then you think about them, and work toward them, every day.

"I recently heard a review on the radio of a just-published autobiography. I don't remember whose life it was, but the reviewer remarked that the writer had had the arrogance to write, 'If only I had been a better writer, I could have stopped World War II.' Now I didn't think it was arrogant, because I had actually had a similar thought. If only I were a better speaker or more of a poet, I could slow down global warming. I could stir people like you to act. Well, I'll soon hit the road to try my hand, and I appreciate the chance to practice my speaking skills on you. The poetry will take a little longer, though. It will be a long time before I don't have to borrow the words of others. I'd like to leave you with the words of a poet, Lawrence Collins:

'The planet you're standing on
looking out at the stars
is the Earth,
the third planet from the sun,
and the mildest
and softest
of the nine.

If you can stop, and let yourself look,
let your eyes do
what they do best.
Stop
and let yourself see and see
that everything is doing things
to you
as you do things to everything.

Then you know
that although it is only a little planet,
it is hugely beautiful
and surely the finest place in the world
to be.

So watch it, look at it,
See what it's like
to walk around on it.

It's small but it's beautiful.
It's small but it's fine,
like a rainbow,

like a bubble.'"

January 1991

On the night of January 16, at 7:00 p.m., U.S. President George Bush began a military campaign to evict Iraq from Kuwait. Waves of bombs and cruise missiles launched from naval vessels fell on Baghdad and other targets in Iraq and Kuwait, touching off a brief and victorious war — but one that carried a price tag in terms of environmental disasters greater than any before in modern history.

Before the war was finished, three gigantic oil spills, 300 oil wells burning out of control, and a two-month bombardment of fragile desert and coastal ecosystems disrupted harvests, filled the air with hundreds of thousands of tons of soot, caused greasy black rain to fall in Iran, destroyed commercial fishery stocks including shrimp, and killed birds and aquatic life (cormorants, sea turtles, sea cows, and dolphins especially) in great numbers.

Scientists generally agreed that, even without the climatic cooling being predicted by Cornell University's Carl Sagan and others, the effects of the war on the area's ecology — in terms of disruption of food chains, destruction of critical habitat, and decimation of species — would be felt for decades to come.

Although, by the time it ended, America was a nation at war, January 1991 began in relative calm.

Supercomputers, capable of performing billions of mathematical operations in a second, were being touted as an exciting new environmental tool early in the new year. U.S. military forces had used them to simulate the potential damage to the environment if Kuwaiti oilfields were set on fire. Cray supercomputers at a California research company, able to store and retrieve the large amounts of data needed to understand complex chemical interactions in the atmosphere, found that little of the smoke generated by such fires would reach the upper atmosphere.

This was disputed not only by Sagan but by University of California scientists who have used supercomputers to predict climatological effects of a nuclear war and who believe that oilfield fires could block out sunlight and cause regional cooling.

Supercomputers were also being used to determine the lifespan of smog and to set up hypothetical simulations in which alternative anti-pollution options could be tested.

"Because the use of supercomputers leads to cost-effective regula-tion," an EPA official said, "there is going to be money to buy these tools." Smog researcher Gregory J. McRae, at Carnegie-Mellon Uni-versity, agreed. "The cost of the supercomputer is peanuts compared to what you can save," he said. Thousands of times more powerful than a desktop computer, supercomputers cost between $3 million and $30 million each.

A scientific assessment of national environmental priorities was also being pushed by EPA Administrator William K. Reilly as the new year began. Concerned that Americans sometimes misplace their envi-ronmental anxieties, Reilly told U.S. Congressmen that "a study by a board of scientists who advise the EPA has determined that global warming is among the highest environmental risks, while hazardous waste is among the lowest.... People rated them the other way around in public opinion surveys," according to the New York Times.

The EPA's Science Advisory Board study also listed habitat destruction, depletion of the ozone layer, and loss of biological diversity as high-risk ecological threats. Oil spills, the escape of radioactive materials, and leaking underground storage tanks were designated as relatively low-risk problems.

Few, if any, Americans got that message, judging by the nation's reaction on January 25 when word of a major oil spill in the Persian Gulf reached the airwaves. Described as being ten miles long and 35 miles wide, the slick was originally believed to contain the equivalent of 11 million barrels of oil and to be 50 times the size of the 1989 Exxon Valdez spill off the Alaskan coast.

Environmentalists had described themselves as sick at heart because their country had gone to war over oil, but had been hesitant to protest the air strikes ordered by President Bush, mostly because of the wave of patriotic fervor sweeping the country. However, the gigantic oil spill, plus news that the White House had waived the legal require-ment for environmental assessments of Pentagon projects, had a gal-

vanic effect. Small groups began to gather in opposition to the war, and many of them were environmentalists. Two giant movements, one for peace, one for a healthy globe, had at last found common ground.

ða

Sleet, snow, slush, and columns of mercury that couldn't make it above the zero mark took over Connecticut as 1991 arrived. The weather was like a great, wet sheepdog, emerging from an icy pond and shaking cold droplets in unwelcome directions. It was nice to know that my calendar contained two trips to California and one to New Orleans during January.

Faith Middleton, Connecticut's public radio maven, invited me to appear live on her "Open Air New England" call-in show the second day of the month, to describe my perspective on the most serious environmental issues. I listed our energy policy and all its concomitant concerns, and added that the biggest problem was retrograde leadership by the federal government.

I expected angry phone calls, but apparently none of our listeners disagreed. The calls I did get were thoughtful and intelligent. People picked up on the Arctic National Wildlife Refuge question. They also were worried about low-level radioactive waste. I thought I recognized a couple of the voices — friends pitching me soft balls. The whole experience was more fun than I expected, although it is a bit weird to have a conversation with another person while you're both wearing huge headphones.

For the next two days I played wife, mother, and Common Cause coordinator as best I could. A conference call about the Centennial Campaign kept me from one of Annie's basketball games. I hated that.

On January 5, I was scheduled to attend a retreat for the ELECT Board of Directors in Wallingford, Connecticut. When it ended earlier than I expected, I decided to make up for yesterday's absence to Annie. She had a game that afternoon at Kent School, which is as far west as you can go in Connecticut. I was already halfway there, so I called Arthur and made arrangements to meet him in Waterbury. It was a crazy thing to do — especially since there was a sleetstorm going on — but I thought Annie would be pleased to see both her folks in the stands.

When we got there, well into the third quarter, Loomis was behind and Annie — who is not the strongest player on the JV team — hadn't played yet. I ached for her to have a chance to play, but dreaded it at the same time. In the fourth quarter, the coach put her in. Although she didn't make a basket, she did (according to Arthur) do just the right thing several times. Loomis achieved a one-point victory and we all rode home happily together. We stopped at a sandwich shop for an all-too-infrequent family outing.

·The next day I journeyed northward for a quick visit with my father. I hadn't seen him since Thanksgiving. I returned the same day because I wanted to help with the chores at home and also because the next morning I was being interviewed by a reporter from a local monthly magazine called *Hartford*. As I chatted with the reporter the next morning, she let it drop that I would be part of a section entitled "Intriguing People." Intriguing? Me? I am more apt to think of myself as an old gray draft horse. Oh boy, if my friends could see me now!

By noon I was in Hartford eating lunch with an old buddy, former state legislator and energy expert Joel Gordes. I was picking his brains about the electricity-buying habits of Northeast Utilities — hoping to discourage them from purchasing "dirty" HydroQuebec/James Bay electricity. I felt another pang of guilt that I wouldn't be able to do much myself since my time was so finely divided. I would have to hope that I could plant a few seeds and that others would take up the cause.

I spent the next day in Hartford as well, visiting my former employers, the Clean Water Coalition, among others. The new legislative session was about to open, always an exciting time, and I wanted to cheer them on. I enjoyed it so much that I made time to drop by the Capitol the day after that and listen to the Governor's opening speech, before heading to the airport and the plane to San Francisco. Hartford's streets were a slushy mess. California may have smog, but it doesn't make your feet wet.

In California, personnel problems with one of the staff people in our main office prompted us to call in an industrial psychologist. (I hadn't even known there was such a profession.) We didn't solve the problem — eventually the employee and the

Sierra Club parted company — but it was an instructive session. Most of that four-day trip, however, was devoted to a Board of Directors working session on the Centennial Campaign and the January Board meeting itself.

This particular meeting is usually small and therefore held in the library of our Polk Street headquarters. Our agenda was bursting at the seams; it was good to tackle it in the gentle dignity of that room, under the lofty grandeur of the Ansel Adams photographs.

Michael Fischer gave us an update on our budget picture. It had not improved since the Florida meeting. Indeed, for two straight months revenue had fallen behind our projections. If things continued at this rate, Michael told us, we could be facing a half million dollar shortfall by the end of the year.

We maintain a so-called "prudent reserve" of nearly that amount. Nevertheless, it was time to start cutting. Michael outlined a program in which all vacant positions would be left vacant, travel would be sharply reduced (no small sacrifice for peripatetic Sierrans), and direct mail membership fluctuations would be reevaluated.

There was some good news: a $12,500 foundation grant for James Bay was one item, a near-final draft of the Mass Mobilization Petition — with language that read like poetry — was another. Nevertheless, the unhappy fiscal situation made us all cranky and uncertain as we tried to sort out the lines of authority, communication, and accountability within the Centennial Campaign.

But the campaign plans were so big, and so unlike our usual activities, and so expensive! Was it right to take such a gamble during the current economic downturn? The two hours allotted for the working session proved to be woefully inadequate. Much had to be left for a more formal meeting scheduled later in the month.

We knew from colleagues across the country that all the other environmental groups were also seeing reduced income flow. We were not doing anything wrong. . . just sharing a general spate of bad times. Still, I wished we could postpone being one hundred years old for a year or two.

I flew back to Connecticut on the 14th — the weather had dried up a bit, thank heavens — and stayed there for four days.

During that time, Michael Fischer and I made a painful decision. To this day I don't know whether we were right or wrong. We decided that if war came — and everything pointed to that — it would be wrong for the Sierra Club to oppose it while our soldiers were risking their lives.

Accordingly, on January 16, only hours before the bombardment actually started, we e-mailed a statement to all Club leaders and staff. It said, in part, "Should a peaceful resolution not be achieved and war break out, human lives will be lost. There will be widespread media coverage of these losses and of the soldiers' friends and families here at home. Now is a time for all of us to be especially sensitive to the suffering of these losses. Should this occur, we will know what caused it. But our saying so will not bring these lives back or decrease the suffering . . ." Not all our members agreed. Certainly many other environmental groups only turned up the volume of their outcries against an oil-based war. We had placed ourselves in a precarious position. While freely condemning the administration's policies, we wanted to refrain from criticizing the war they caused.

Although I was unsure of myself on this major issue, my judgment had recently been validated on another important concern. The federal government (after a good deal of prodding from many environmental groups) decided to require formal environmental assessments of the social and environmental impacts of loans proposed by the World Bank.

For the Sierra Club, this was something to crow about. We sent out an op ed article over my name calling for "speedy delivery" from multilateral development banks "of social and environmental goods in their programs." I talked about deforestation and its link to global warming which, I said, "could mean the end of living and the beginning of survival." I closed by telling the world, "There is mounting evidence that environmental degradation is a threat, not only to environmental and social well-being, but to economic growth and development as well."

It was a good, solid article. I didn't write every word, but I believed them all. It ran in many daily papers and I was proud that it had my by-line.

On the 17th, *Hartford* magazine sent a photographer to take a picture of me for its "Intriguing People" section. I wanted to look the part, so I suggested that I wear a business suit but pose out in the pasture.   I sat on the edge of the watering tub there, with a scoop of grain, while horses and sheep gathered and slobbered over me. Now I know why we don't feed animals while wearing good suits.

When the photographer had all he wanted of that pose, we moved down the pasture and I stood next to various rocks and trees. It was bitter cold. By the time he was satisfied, my hands and feet were blue. After he left, I thawed out in the bathtub. Annie was worried. She had never seen blue toes before. At least Annie thought I was intriguing.

Since we do not have television, I was not, like millions of others around the globe, glued to CNN almost from the minute the U.S. began bombing Iraq. I have to admit, though, that whenever I was near a set, I joined in. Those incredible early photographs — Larry Register fumbling with his gas mask, the bombs falling outside the windows in Baghdad — horrified me every bit as much as any battlefield atrocity I saw photographed in Vietnam, perhaps more.

Those first few days were for me, and I suppose for most of my countrymen, powerfully emotional. I had to work hard to keep one part of me — the woman whose country had gone to war — under control so that another part — the Sierra Club President — could calmly exercise whatever wisdom she had in choosing strategies for the group.

In Washington, the U.S. Congress went back into session mid-month. Our Capitol lobbyists reported that action was slow, and attributed the general apathy to the war.

Rep. James Jontz, (D-IN) , assured us that he would again offer his ancient forest legislation (ultimately determining how many acres could be cut), but he balked at making it more stringent as some of our members were urging. Our lobbyists agreed that the job this year was to line up more supporters so that the bill would pass. Making it tighter at this time would only discourage those already supporting it.

Reading their reports, I felt a real rush of satisfaction. For so many years the industrialists and cattle barons and mining companies and timber moguls simply out-waited the waves of reformers. The Sierra Club was going to be one hundred years old next year. We had proved we could out-wait them.

We had lost the ancient forests bill last year. We would try harder this year. If we lost again — well, we'd still be here the year after, and for all the years it takes to get these unique habitats protected. Unfortunately, in this case, we were racing against time. The trees were going fast.

The Sierra Club's Delta Chapter (Louisiana) was holding a weekend-long annual meeting and had asked me to be their after-dinner speaker. Ted Buckner, a local activist, met me at the New Orleans airport and introduced me to his city through a well-planned auto tour. We stopped for coffee and pastry in a little coffee shop in the French Quarter.

I had grown more blasé with each new Sierra Club trip and had not bothered to pinch myself for quite some time. As I sat sipping that bitter, aromatic brew, however, I realized another pinch-me experience was in the making. That evening we went, with some fellow Sierrans, to a little café where they served all the dishes I had always heard of. Jambalaya, crawfish pie, filé gumbo, blackened catfish, shrimp étouffé, sweet potato pie: I managed at least a taste of every one.

My host's apartment was delightful — half of an Old New Orleans house, with high ceilings and marble fireplaces. I was enchanted with the city's architecture and ambiance. Whimsical, yet beautiful houses were painted in pastel shades and ornately decorated with wrought iron. The streetscapes, too, were beautiful. An old trolley car system travels down the "neutral zone" (median strip to the rest of us), providing eye appeal as well as public transit.

The city was already deep into Mardi Gras preparations. It seemed to me a lovely way to live — to be able, as soon as Christmas was over, to start looking forward to a week of revelry, parades, and parties. I decided these people were definitely more laid back than their northeastern cousins.

Charmed as I was, I had a hard time remembering that this beautiful city sits in one of the most heavily polluted states in the nation. Twenty percent of the hazardous waste from the whole country is disposed of in Louisiana. There is a huge petrochemical industry, accompanied by all the problems of offshore oil drilling. Elected officials have been beset by a series of scandals. The Sierrans here are a beleaguered lot. They face odds that we Northeasterners can't even imagine.

One ray of light on the Louisiana environmental scene is a new method of taxation that would tie a company's pollution record to the amount of taxes it pays on business property.

Highly innovative, the new regulations were not yet fully approved but were already causing quite a stir. No other state has tried anything like it.

It works this way. Normally the state tries to encourage business expansion by granting property tax exemptions. Between 1980 and 1989, for instance, corporations spent $25.8 billion on capital projects in Louisiana and were exempted from $2.6 billion in taxes. Simultaneously the state's cancer rate began to threaten the national record, local schools were woefully underfunded, and millions of tons of toxic chemical wastes poured into the air and water, creating miles of irreparably polluted rivers and marshes.

An organization that was not primarily concerned with the environment, the Coalition for Tax Justice, pointed out that the exempted projects produced millions of tons of toxic waste, and that companies receiving the tax breaks were routinely violating Louisiana's environmental laws.

Under the new system, each company applying for an exemption would have to be scored first on its environmental violations, the amount of chemicals it releases, and other factors. The score helps determine the size of the exemption.

I heard the idea praised and I also heard it criticized — both for not doing enough and for doing too much. Whatever the outcome, it is a sign that a state with a dismal environmental record is trying to do something about it.

One of the saddest examples of Louisiana's endangered natural resources are her marshes and bayous. The local group took me on a tour of the Jean Lafitte National Park. We walked about a mile on boardwalk built over the wetlands. It was just what you would dream of: hanging Spanish moss, large wading birds, slow-moving water. I could all but see a pirogue sliding over the water, poled by a tall, lean man with a black mustache.

The Cajuns lived off these bayous for a century and a half. They found ways to stay at the top of the food chain, but also to maintain it. It took the rest of us far less time to foul the ecosystem and begin to destroy it, not just for the fish and birds and mammals, but for the Cajun population — and for all our children.

The Delta Chapter was holding a meeting in the afternoon. I arrived in time for a lunch of black beans and rice. The main celebration was held that night in a remodeled warehouse, now a restaurant famed for its Cajun dancing. We had the back room to ourselves for a buffet of — you guessed it — jambalaya, crawfish pie, and filé gumbo.

When I spoke, I tried to relate my feelings about the Blue Planet to the particular ways in which it was threatened in Louisiana. I'm not sure the timing was all that good, however. The dim lighting on stage, the buzz of the busy restaurant outside, and the sounds of a band tuning up for dancing were distracting. I knew perfectly well that people were there for fun, not exhortation. I wound up as fast as I could — and we all danced into the wee hours.

As my plane lifted off from New Orleans the next day, I did pinch myself—and vowed to bring Arthur and Annie back to see this magical town some day.

I was traveling from Louisiana to Connecticut, two very different places from the point of view of culture, lifestyle, and climate. Yet they—and a good many other states—have one problem in common: water quality.

While many western states have to worry about having enough water, that is not a big problem in either Louisiana or Connecticut. Having enough clean, usable water is, however, another story.

Americans get their water from a variety of sources. Urban residents usually depend on a public or private municipal water system. Out in the country, artesian wells are the most common source of drinking water, but shallow "dug" wells and springs also add to the overall supply.

Water, like air, exists on this planet in a reasonably stable amount. It evaporates from the earth's surface, is held in the sky in the form of water vapor and comes back to us as rain. Some of the rain water washes over the earth and finds its way into recognized water courses: brooks, streams, rivers, marshes, bogs, ponds, lakes, the ocean. The remainder seeps into the earth itself and is stored in below-ground aquifers. The important thing to remember is that as water gets dirty, clean water does not automatically take its place. There is only so much water, and dirty water has to be purified before it can again be used.

Polluted water is cleansed through a complicated biochemical process, which is carried out in surface waters such as streams, swamps, and marshes, or as the water seeps through the ground.

Unfortunately, as population density increases, the burden on natural purifying mechanisms increases and may cause them to break down. More septic waste, for instance, is the direct result of more human users. More industrial waste, more erosion, more siltation come with growth and development.

Governments have tried in many different ways to tackle the problem of maintaining enough clean water for the needs of growing populations. The Federal Water Pollution Control Act (copied in many ways, I am proud to say, from earlier Connecticut law) has resulted in the establishment of a massive bureaucracy designed to give permits for water degradation, and then to monitor and enforce water protection statutes.

Industries, municipalities, and many other entities are now almost universally forbidden to discharge wastewater into public waterways without a permit. Efforts to cleanse wastewater, using the "best available technology," before it is released are required. Municipalities once were encouraged to build sophisticated sewage treatment plants via the "carrot" of government funding. Since that has now greatly diminished, we depend on the "stick" of penalties such as fines for manufacturers and towns that continue to pollute.

Of course, not all municipalities have sewers. Many families depend on private septic systems to handle household wastes. Toilets flush and washing machines empty into a large concrete tank, below ground, which overflows into a series of drainage fields. This is fine if the soil is sandy and not too compact. However, where the land is wet or where clay abounds, ordinary septic systems often don't work.

The rapid housing growth in the first half of this century just about used up the land suitable for septic systems in many states. Officials now are under heavy pressure to allow development in more questionable areas. In some cases, where they have succumbed to that pressure, the results have been disastrous and local governments have had to resort to expensive municipal sewage systems to correct them.

But sewage systems are no panacea. Once they are installed, the pressures for growth redouble. Acreage that was totally (and obviously) unsuitable for building before the sewer pipe was installed along the edge of the road now becomes a temptation. If a town desires industrial and commercial growth, sewers can be a big first step. On the other hand, if a semi-rural atmosphere is the goal, or if for other reasons (to hold down school taxes, encourage farming, etc.) the town desires to stay as it is, sewers can be extremely disruptive.

Even with the most expensive tertiary treatment sewage plants, however, there comes a time, in the face of too-heavy population growth, when natural systems simply can no longer manage to keep the water supply pure. Communities that refuse to recognize the limits nature imposes—communities that refuse to live within their means as defined by their natural resources—eventually pay a heavy price.

Exacerbating the problem is our sad human history of undervaluing and filling in swamps, marshes, and bogs. These wetlands are the simplest, cheapest, most effective way we know to cleanse large volumes of water. Nature set up a complex mechanical and chemical process for us—a system far beyond anything our own technology can duplicate—and, too often, we seem hellbent on destroying it. That is why environmentalists so closely watch the Bush administration's fealty to the President's campaign pledge of no net wetlands loss.

Water quality concerns do not stand alone, of course. How much waste we have, how we dispose of it, and what chemicals it contains all influence the leachate that leaks out of landfills and into aquifers. The gases emitted from power plants and industries turn our rain water into a dilute acid—which in turn affects the vegetation nourished by the rain, the buildings and monuments it washes over, and the quality of the water we drink.

Finally, as we in Connecticut well know, and as the people of Louisiana are learning, the toxic waste buried today will endure to sabotage land values decades hence—and not only land values, for water is a natural resource on which, quite literally, our lives depend.

Three days at home, mostly working for Common Cause, and then — back to San Francisco. Before leaving, on the 22nd, I e-mailed my fellow directors some good news about the budget. Our membership numbers had picked up and the deficit was not as bad as had been expected — only about $300,000, although that was nothing to rejoice about, certainly.

There was good news from other directions about that time too.

- A "risk evaluation" of the Alaska chapter's proposed trip to Russia had shown serious insurance problems, but not so serious that we couldn't approve it. We let them use the Sierra name—this time.
- The Atlantic Chapter was moving along with its reorganization. The threat of suspension had been postponed, and they had passed a motion rescinding their earlier resolution on the Wild Rockies. Another rift healed.
- A flurry of concern about the levels of pollution in the southeastern United States gave promise of increased environmental activism throughout that region. The area is sometimes described as a "sacrifice zone" because of environmental and human health neglect by the state governments. It was high time its people demanded action. I was especially pleased because the protestors came from all races and walks of life. Perhaps this would help us increase the number of minorities working on environmental problems.

My initial emotions about the war, all mixed up with national pride, excitement about fighting for the oppressed, and a lust to win, came abruptly into focus in San Francisco on January 25. I was spending a day and a half with the Centennial Campaign Planning Committee. There were perhaps ten of us seated around a table, deep in discussion, when one of Michael Fischer's aides came in and whispered in his ear. Michael left the room and returned a few minutes later, a little pale. With trembling voice, he told us that the Earth's largest oil spill had just happened in the Persian Gulf.

The members of the Centennial Campaign Planning Committee, chosen for their affluence and sophistication, are probably the most conservative on the Sierra membership roster. It didn't matter where you perched on the political curve that day, however. There was universal shock.

For the sake of the national TV cameras in Michael's office later that afternoon, we managed to recover our composure and our rhetoric, at least concerning the folly of America's oil addiction and the immorality of ecoterrorism. Silence on our part was no longer a viable option.

I managed to put the war out of my mind for a Finance Committee meeting on the 26th and 27th. There wouldn't be a Sierra Club to take a position if we didn't solve our fiscal woes. I flew home on Sunday, arriving around midnight, but still managed to be up by 6:00 a.m. so that I could see Annie's face before she went to school.

That afternoon I was a guest of the Trillium Garden Club at a church hall in Groton, Connecticut. After the tea sandwiches and punch, about thirty ladies listened to me talk about garbage and global warming. It was a far cry from sitting in San Francisco drafting statements for the national press. On the other hand, these women write their elected officials faithfully. They are the grassroots we boast about as the heart and soul of the movement.

President Bush was going to talk about energy strategy in his State of the Union message the coming week. On January 28, we put out (from San Francisco) a national press statement challenging the President to base his strategy on efficiency and renewable energy resources.

"It is inconceivable that, at the same time lives are being lost in the Middle East, the administration maintains the energy policies of the past and offers no vision for removing oil-dependency as a factor in future conflicts," I was quoted as saying.

Our language was cautious. For instance: "'We believe that this nation's overdependence on oil helped to create the conditions that drove the world to war,' said Merrow." The *Hartford Courant*, our country's oldest existing newspaper, came closer to expressing my true feelings four days earlier when it accused the President of not being "entirely on the level" about the relationship between the war and our oil dependency when talking to the American people.

The month ended cheerfully. Our public affairs people had arranged a one-day media tour for me in Manhattan on the 30th. I dug out the gold earrings and caught the 7:15 train from Saybrook to New York.

Two public affairs staffers and I rendezvoused at the offices of *Good Housekeeping*. Our goal was simply to get on its editor's Rolodex, to be called on when they needed a spokesman for environmental issues. We were pleasantly surprised when she did more than just take our cards. She rolled out the red carpet for us, then called in her boss, John Mack Carter, so that we could all be photographed together.

Who would think that *Sports Illustrated* would be an outlet for Sierra Club views? The editors there treated us like celebrities. They have done some excellent reporting on the Arctic, so I was pleased to make the connection.

Seventeen magazine, which was just starting a regular column on the environment, was next. This is a powerful venue for reaching teenagers, and we have a serious story to tell people of that age. The meeting went extremely well.

Three very different magazines, reaching three very different audiences—but every one of them eager to hear what we had to say. As I relaxed on the train that night, I decided that we must be doing something right after all.

Had I kept the promise I made to myself in Boston a month before? I believed I had. I had behaved like a woman with a mission in points as far removed from one another as a church hall in Groton, a bayou boardwalk in Louisiana, a boardroom in San Francisco, and the editorial offices of *Sports Illustrated*. No one person can save our Blue Planet, and the war had made the job a good deal more difficult — but the word was spreading.

February 1991

＊

Through the first three and a half weeks of February 1991, America and her allies kept up a massive air war against Iraq. Environmental news took second place to military reports, but environmental concern did not lag.

On February 7, Senate Majority Leader George Mitchell and forty other Senators introduced a global warming resolution. It stated that it was the sense of the Senate that the United States should adopt specific greenhouse gas reductions by a certain date and that industrialized nations should reduce their CO_2 emissions.

At about the same time, delegates from 130 countries assembled in Chantilly, Virginia, for a United Nations-sponsored ten-day conference on global warming. This was to be the first in a series of five such meetings, to culminate in June 1992 in Rio de Janeiro with the signing of a treaty to take new economic, environmental, and scientific steps to curb the warming.

Although the meeting was opened by Michael Deland—head of the U.S. Council on Environmental Quality—brandishing a twenty-two-page "action agenda," the United States made no promise to reduce production of carbon dioxide. Indeed, his plan allowed a 15 percent increase in CO_2, supposedly balanced by reductions in CFCs and other greenhouse gases.

Environmentalists pointed out jubilantly that this was the first public admission by the Bush administration that global warming was a significant problem. They were not, however, impressed by the "action agenda," noting that the President had already guaranteed such reductions to lessen depletion of the ozone layer. "He's selling us the same horse twice," they said.

No one can say for sure which parts of the world will benefit and which be harmed by global warming, but some things are clear. Smaller coastal nations and island kingdoms will be especially hard hit by flooding because their people will have no place to go. Some predict millions of environmental refugees will pour into areas such as northern Europe and central North America, which are expected to become more temperate, while the world's richest food production areas will suffer drought and drastically reduced harvests.

"In general," according to a UN study, "populations most vulnerable to global warming are in developing countries, in the lower-income groups, residents of coastal lowlands and islands, populations in squatter settlements, slums, and shantytowns, especially in megacities." In short, populations that do the least to cause global warming and are least able to help themselves will probably bear the brunt of it.

While the Chantilly conference was going on, the U.S. Congressional Office of Technology Assessment released a new study saying that the United States has the necessary technology to reduce carbon dioxide emissions by 35 percent by the year 2015, but that it could cost the American economy as much as $150 billion a year. The report said that such reductions would require dramatic changes in how Americans use energy.

The Chantilly conference closed with little more than an agreement to meet in June in Kenya. Observers attributed this to the continuing opposition of Bush's Chief of Staff John H. Sununu, who is said to fear that reducing the use of oil and other fossil fuels could lead to economic stagnation.

From another viewpoint, a group of Environmental Defense Fund and Cornell University scientists warned that, once started, warming trends could accelerate on their own, even if CO_2 and CFCs are reduced. A study (termed "provocative" by the New York Times), published in the British journal Nature, showed that, over many different time scales, the amount of carbon dioxide in the air increased following a warm period. The authors speculated that warm weather might cause release of CO_2 from such natural holding areas as forests and wetlands.

In Brooklyn, early in the month, the only guilty verdict to result from the 1988 "Syringe Summer" was handed down against Geronimo Villegas, the Vice-President of a defunct medical laboratory. Villegas was charged with dumping vials of blood, some contaminated with hepatitis B virus, in waters off Staten Island and New Jersey. The summer of 1988 was noted for the medical waste that washed ashore on metropolitan beaches, outraging the public and ruining business for many seaside ventures.

Although Villegas faced a million-dollar fine and thirty-six months in jail, he was written off as a mere "midnight dumper" by law enforcement officials, who are using criminal statutes more and more to prosecute polluters.

Under criminal law, instead of civil fines for the company, top officials can personally pay fines and go to jail. Environmental attorneys explained the new trend as a way to get the attention of those corporation heads who decide a company's environmental policies. The deterrent effect, they said, is vastly increased when personal freedom is at stake.

Industry spokesmen, however, decried the resorting to criminal penalties. They said that often the people at the top are unable to keep track of actions by underlings, and that people make mistakes for which prison is an inappropriate punishment.

On Friday, February 8, the Bush administration's long-awaited National Energy Strategy was leaked to the press. While doing everything possible to encourage the search for domestic oil and the construction of nuclear power plants, it called for only token efforts at energy efficiency.

Faced with a major war in the oil-rich Persian Gulf, the President had chosen to make the nation less dependent on foreign oil through deregulation, tax breaks, and new areas of oil exploration, but no less dependent on oil in general.

"None of the proposals would encourage motorists to reduce their use of gasoline, the largest single use for oil in the United States," wrote Keith Schneider in the New York Times. Indeed, one section of the Bush strategy proposed weakening an existing regulation that requires automobiles to become more fuel efficient.

Times business writer Matthew L. Wald concluded, "The problem with a nation whose oil production satisfies barely half its oil appetite is not its appetite, the Bush administration has apparently concluded, but its production."

David S. Broder, a syndicated Washington columnist, listed the flawed National Energy Strategy as yet another proof that the President's heart and mind were not into domestic policy. Broder said the strategy was the "product of a serious intellectual and political effort sustained over eighteen months" by its principal author, Secretary of Energy James D. Watkins, and declared that it "deserved better" than the petty bickering and leaks by administration leaders that preceded official release of the policy document. "Bush allowed his aides to trivialize the Watkins effort by last-minute nitpicking," Broder charged.

In various public statements the following week, Bush said the nation must avoid "unwise and extreme methods" such as "excessive" mileage standards, and declared himself committed to "the power of the marketplace."

When the plan was finally officially unveiled on February 20, it was praised as a "good start in a reasonable direction" by the President of the American Petroleum Institute, even though some aspects of it did not live up to industry hopes.

In Congress, Senator Albert Gore (D-TN) called the proposal "breathtakingly dumb" and predicted "a battle royal." Senator John Glenn (D-OH) regretted an energy policy that relies on "fragile coalitions and the prosecution of a war."

The opening up of the Arctic National Wildlife Refuge to oil exploration was especially controversial. "The White House staff equates energy efficiency with sacrifice, and apparently doesn't mind sacrificing the Arctic National Wildlife Refuge," a senior scientist at the National Resources Defense Council said.

Encouraged by the Bush policy, Senator Frank Murkowski (R-AK) reintroduced his long-touted legislation to authorize drilling in the Arctic. Also reintroduced was a bill drafted by Senator Richard H. Bryan (D-NE) to increase automobile fuel mileage standards.

Representative Phillip R. Sharp (D-IN), Chair of the House Energy and Power Committee, proposed a requirement for states to promote energy savings, and for enhanced conservation via mortgage requirements from federal lending agencies and conservation planning from the customers of federal power agencies.

In light of the new National Energy Strategy, the lawmakers to watch, however, became Bennett Johnston (D-LA), Chair of the Senate Committee on Energy and Natural Resources, and Malcolm Wallop (R-WY), ranking minority member of the House Energy and Natural Resources Committee. Their joint bill, which eventually embodied many of the President's proposals, also called for token encouragement of alternative fuels and conservation projects.

A strong supporter of more oil and gas drilling, even in environmentally fragile areas, Johnston seemed a likely partner for Wallop, who had declared that America's energy policy could be summed up in one word — "import" — and that it should be changed to three words — "made in America."

While high-level energy policy debates captured most of the media's attention, the disastrous results of oil drilling run amok continued to deface the Persian Gulf.

"The Gulf is out. Bye-bye, Gulf," the manager of the Saudi Fisheries Company declared in describing the state of the once-flourishing shrimping fleet there. He said the industry was unlikely to recover for a decade. Shrimp spawning areas had been choked with a layer of oil more than a foot thick.

Other sources reported that thousands of oil-coated cormorants, grebes, and other shore birds were washing up on Saudi beaches, and that the nesting grounds for rare sea turtles had been destroyed. David Olsen, an American working with the Saudi government, summed it up: "It's a graveyard out there."

At the end of the month, New York Times columnist Tom Wicker declared the 1980s "a foolish decade." His reasons: earlier American support of Saddam Hussein coupled with the dismantling of energy conservation programs instituted by Presidents Nixon and Carter. Wicker recalled that Carter had termed energy independence "the moral equivalent to war."

"President Bush's continuing energy myopia," Wicker wrote, "raises the hard question whether the sacrifices and bloodshed of Desert Storm may have to be undertaken anew, when some future oil crisis finds the U.S. still dependent on hostile potentates, far-off sheikdoms, and its own gas-guzzling addiction." The New York Times also worried about the President's vision when it editorialized, "The energy policy now taking shape within the Bush administration is distressingly blind to the oil addiction that underlies the dispatch of 500,000 American troops to the Persian Gulf."

On February 24, after Saddam Hussein ignored a deadline set by the United States, allied forces stormed into Iraq and Kuwait, turning what had been an air war into a desert death struggle. Vitaly N. Ignatenko, a Soviet Union spokesman commenting on Moscow's failed effort at mediation, remarked, "We see, from high above burning oil facilities, the continued destruction of the ecosystem. We still hope that common sense will prevail."

ào

When we had time to get our wits together, we remembered that the Sierra Club did indeed have a policy about war. Paraphrased, it says simply, "Peace is better for the environment than war." It was time to say so loudly and clearly. On February 1, I wrote to my fellow directors, so advising them. Later, in an article in *Sierra* magazine, Carl Pope would remark that when the war began, "The environmental trumpet, if sounded at all, quavered and faltered." We were now free to blow our horns.

I spent the first day of February in the Common Cause office in Hartford, catching up. One of ex-Congressman Toby Moffett's former public relations people dropped by, looking for leads to a job. A great many young men and women call on me asking for help. They want to earn money while pursuing their consciences, but I'm not usually able to be of much assistance. Enviro jobs are very few and poorly paid, especially when you are just starting out. I knew that I would soon be out networking, hat in hand, just like him.

The next day my good friend Molly McKay and I, along with our two daughters, set out on an adventure. We were going to Washington to "Celebrate Wild Alaska." This was a huge four-day gathering, planned for over a year, to commemorate the tenth anniversary of the passage of the Alaska Lands Bill. It started out as a grand reunion, but its timing was such that it became an incredibly angry and moving rededication to keeping alive what had been accomplished and to keep from losing ground. The energy storm clouds looming everywhere seemed to threaten Alaska's wild land especially.

The literature for Celebrate Wild Alaska was almost embarrassing. Dripping with "big names" from Jack Lemmon to Teddy Roosevelt IV, the sponsorship list included major foundations and more Senators and Congressmen than you could count. If there was an environmental organization not listed, well, I have never heard of it.

Annie is totally enamored of Union Station, the lavishly restored terminus of our train trip. When we arrived, she and Marnie McKay (one year younger) pleaded to be allowed to stay and explore its shops. They said they would come to the hotel by taxi when they had had enough. Washington is one of the most dangerous cities in the world; they were only twelve and thirteen; but when Molly said OK, I swallowed hard and went along with it. I guess I am an overprotective mother. They arrived just fine a couple of hours later.

The celebration was fabulous. Five hundred people, most of whom had never seen Alaska and never would, came together because the Alaskan wilderness was, for them, an important symbol—not merely the only place of its kind in the world, but a place exactly as God created it, pristine, original, undefiled.

Many of us were old warhorses, activists who had cut our teeth in the 1970s on the Alaska Lands Bill and others like it. We talked openly of our shame that we had, during the wasted '80s, allowed energy policy to slide right off the environmental agenda. Now, ten years later, thanks to the National Energy Strategy about to be announced, we had a real live enemy again, and a mission — to save the Arctic National Wildlife Refuge. There were also, I'm pleased to say, plenty of younger people, galvanized by Earth Day and by the renewed threats to fragile ecosystems inherent in the Gulf war.

For two days we listened to speeches and attended workshops dealing with Alaska's history, natural resources, archaeology, wildlife, and cultural lifeways. We heard from people like Alaskan Senator Frank Murkowski and Secretary of the Interior Manuel Lujan, but their words did little to quell the growing resentment towards the current administration's energy policy.

Under the Alaska Lands Bill, Section 1002, some 1.5 million acres along the coastal plain of the Arctic National Wildlife Refuge were placed in a special-study status and were therefore not entirely secure from oil development. This area is the biological heart of the ecosystem. It is the largest onshore denning area for polar bears and the calving grounds of the porcupine caribou. The only untouched Arctic ecosystem left on this planet, it is home to musk oxen, Arctic fox, and a host of rare plant and animal species. And it is the object of intense greed on the part of oil companies who want to drain off whatever oil is there and pump it via the Alaskan pipeline down to Valdez and Prince William Sound.

Even the Department of the Interior admits that there is only one chance in five of finding oil in the 1002 area. If they do find a supply, however, it will be finite. In the end the oil will be used up, the wilderness will be violated, and we will still have the same energy problems.

Most frustrating of all is that, damn it, *we don't need it!* We import 1.7 million barrels of oil from the Persian Gulf area each day. Section 1002, at best, would yield .29 million barrels of oil per day, and there is only a 20 percent chance that it would yield any at all. The Bryan Bill, if enacted, would reduce oil consumption by 2.5 million barrels of oil per day — more than the total oil we can get from the Persian Gulf and Section 1002 combined.

After two days of revving each other up, we broke up into pairs to do some targeted lobbying on Capitol Hill. This kind of "lobby week" — sending throngs of people, briefed and well organized, to buttonhole lawmakers — is a specialty of the Sierra Club. I always enjoy it.

My partner this time was Marylin Blackburn, a young Black woman who had won the Miss Alaska title several years ago. Marylin lives in Atlanta now, but her willingness to come out and witness for the resources of her home state was much appreciated. We were assigned to selected swing voters in the Black Caucus. The Black Caucus is traditionally open to environmental lobbying, but it was nice to come with a Black environmentalist at my side for once.

On Monday, Molly and I put our daughters on the train back home. Their fathers would take over when they got there and send them off to school the next day. We did sneak away one night while they were still in Washington to see Mel Gibson's movie version of *Hamlet* in one of Union Station's ten theaters. Annie counted this as a double blessing — another look at Union Station *and* Mel Gibson, all in one night. Slyly, I thought of it as exposing her to Shakespeare.

The finale of the celebration was a banquet at the Washington Press Club. The event was dedicated to Morris Udall, a great hero of the Lands Bill, who could not be there because he was hospitalized with Parkinson's disease. A tribute to him by John Seiberling, the other famous veteran of the Lands Bill, left me and many others wiping away our tears.

On February 7, Molly and I took an early train back to Connecticut. The train splits in New Haven, some of it going along the shore route to New London and Boston, some of it going north to Hartford. I said goodbye to Molly there and headed for Hartford and a meeting of the Fees Task Force at the state capitol. I hiked from the train station to the Legislative Office Building, across the park in a sleety rain, my suitcase and briefcase banging against me with every step. I wasn't sorry, though. The enviros and Mike Meotti, one of our favorite state

Senators, were split about the idea of appointing a business ombudsman within the Department of Environmental Protection, and I wanted to see how it played out. Arthur picked me up there later, on his way to get Annie at school.

I heard about the leaked version of the National Energy Strategy as I was returning to the Common Cause office on February 8. I had just had a tetanus shot (getting ready for a trip to Costa Rica next week) and was not feeling too happy. This news, though it was fully expected, sent my spirits plummeting. As Melanie Griffin, from our D.C. office, said to me via e-mail the next day, "It's hard to believe that the administration picked all the worst options and none of the good."

In our speeches, Sierra Club officers had been saying that a good energy policy must pass two litmus tests: respect for the Arctic wilderness and diminished fuel use in automobiles. "The President's proposal doesn't even pass the laugh test," Melanie complained, but none of us smiled.

The official Sierra statement went out over Michael Fischer's name. He accused President Bush of mounting "an all-out assault on the environment," and of continuing "this nation's march down the wrong path. . . ." The National Energy Strategy was termed "nothing more than an answer to the prayers of the oil, nuclear, and auto industries."

The fat was in the fire now. Our Mass Mobilization plans had been honed over the last couple of weeks into a national "Kick the oil habit" campaign. We knew that the official and final version of the National Energy Strategy would come out around February 19. We set February 20 as a target date for commencing that campaign and taking on a new legislative initiative, the Johnston-Wallop Bill, about which we were hearing some alarming things.

While all this was going on, we had Dan Becker down in Chantilly, Virginia, monitoring an international meeting on global warming. When it was over, Dan complained that all they had done was "argue about the shape of the table." Generally federal officials ignore us, but this time the chief negotiator for the Department of State told reporters, "The shape of the table can sometimes be very important." We were deeply flattered.

Thank God for the talented and hard-working Sierra Club staffs in Washington and San Francisco, and for my volunteer colleagues across the country. I was able to take February 9 off and watch Annie play basketball against Deerfield Academy. Loomis lost, but it was still fun.

On the way home, Arthur dropped me off at the Hartford Sheraton, for my 6:30 a.m. flight the next day to Costa Rica. I settled in at the hotel and returned phone calls, a never-ending pursuit.

As President of the Sierra Club, I am automatically a member of the Sierra Foundation Board of Trustees. Generally speaking, Trustees are people of means. It is their tradition to meet in an exciting place, to spend considerable time at it, and to pay their own way. I was not paying my own way (the Club was) and so, that night at the hotel, I had some qualms. I assured myself—and it was true — that it was imperative to maintain good relations with the Trustees, especially with the Centennial coming up. I felt uncomfortable about being away from home and work so long, but I told myself I deserved a vacation. I began to feel a little better.

I got to the airport bright and early, but not quite early enough. The increased security because of the war had brought chaos to the Bradley terminal. I stood in an endless line, fully expecting to miss my flight. My panic grew as the minutes crawled by and no progress was made. Finally I squeaked through and was on my way to Boston, where I had to change planes for Miami.

In Miami I joined up with some Sierra friends. We had a smooth flight down to San José, Costa Rica, where I spent the next week, feasting my eyes on exotic sights, learning new things, sampling strange foods, and forging new friendships, insulated from the world outside.

Costa Rica has no army. It spends its money on education and has a literacy rate higher than the United States. It is a clean, stable country, and has therefore enjoyed a good deal of ecotourism lately. People come to it because it *is* clean, stable— and beautiful to look at.

We stayed the first two nights at a posh new hotel, where I was sorry to see that the jelly came in little plastic containers and the water glasses were covered in Saran wrap. They probably throw all that unnecessary plastic into a landfill, which will grow until, eventually, it spoils the very ambiance that brings the ecotourists here in the first place. The road to hell is paved with good intentions.

Having arrived all befuddled from celebrating Alaska and dealing with energy policy, I lacked such necessities as sunscreen and bug spray. Borrowing proved to be a good way to make friends with the others in our group.

When we had finished the business portion of the trip, we traveled by bus to see the Poaz volcano. We had a dedicated and highly organized guide with us for the trip, Jorge Mora Escalante. We were only an hour or so outside San José when he directed the bus to a little roadside stand for a rest stop. There he introduced me to the cashew plant. I had never seen the cashew fruit or thought much about where the nut comes from. It is orange-red and shaped like a Delicious apple, but with a nut shell attached to the top. It was only the first of the plant and animal species I was to meet for the first time in the next day or so.

Poaz, an active volcano, was shrouded in fog. We couldn't see down into the crater. As a consolation prize, we hiked up to look into the old crater. Just as we got to the top, the clouds broke and we had a view of a great, placid bowl of azure water. There were birds everywhere. I'm not a birder, but even I was enchanted by the tiny hummingbirds, darting about.

Back at the parking lot, Jorge produced a gigantic picnic lunch: cold chicken, pasta salad, brownies, the works. I sat at a picnic table in the sun, chatting and munching. The sun didn't feel that hot, just nicely warm, but it is strong. Even in my borrowed sunscreen, by the time we reached Monteverde my face was scarlet.

Monteverde was settled by some farsighted Quakers. They knew enough to protect the country's water supply by setting aside a vast forest preserve that you reached by way of a 25-mile, uphill, winding dirt road. The dust found its way into every crevice of my body! The hillsides were barren, denuded by deforestation. But the higher you went, the better you could see the cloud forest in the distance, verdant, misty, infinitely mysterious.

The forest preserve is famous for its bird populations, especially for the resplendent quetzales, said to be the most beautiful bird in the New World. Very large, it has a scarlet breast, iridescent green wings, and long tail feathers, green with blue highlights. You have to search for the quetzales in the tree canopy above your head — and when you find one, it is a memorable occasion. We also saw the nests of the ora pendulas, a big brown bird with a bright yellow tail that hangs huge nest bags from the palm trees.

We saw toucans as well, and toucanettes, and morpho butterflies, and strangler figs (hollow in the middle because they have killed the host plant). But we did not see the famous golden toads, which supposedly exist nowhere else in the world.

These toads, I was told, are evidently part of an amphibian crisis being experienced worldwide. The golden toads come out to breed once a year, and in 1987 there were thousands of them. In 1988 only three were reported. In 1989, with the whole country watching for them, only one appeared. In 1990 there were none— they had vanished. No one knows why the planet is losing so many amphibian species. They are known to be susceptible to heavy metal pollution, but that does not seem a broad enough explanation.

In Monteverde we visited a women's collective, called the CASEM, where the local women marketed crafts. There is a strong environmental link here. Women who can earn money on their own are more likely to use birth control, which leads to a lower birth rate—and many believe that population growth is at the heart of all environmental problems. I was pleased to support these women by buying handmade craft items to take home.

On Friday, in the dry forest of Lomas Barbudal, we saw a wonderful family of monkeys watching us from the canopy. Later, at a watermelon break (our guide always seemed to have cold melon at the right moment), Jorge showed his skill at spotting these howler monkeys in the tree tops as they sat checking us out.

We stayed that night in a resort hotel near Putarenas. I wondered what the native people thought about us, arriving in our air-conditioned buses to swim in private pools and hide from the sun under thatched cabanas. The arrogance (I blushed) of touristas in general, but of my group in particular, to come here and tell them not to exploit their environment!

The next day we toured a national park, Carara, where we saw alligators from a distance and a scarlet macaw close up. The macaw stuck her head out of a hole in a tree very near to where we were standing. Then she flew off, revealing her splendid plumage. Macaws are high on the list of birds that get smuggled into the United States. I am told that they bring enough dollars from exotic bird fanciers to feed a Costa Rican family for a year.

That night, back in San José, we had dinner with the Minister of National Parks, Mario Boza, and a woman who has worked hard to educate people to live gently on the land, Lirio Marquez. Boza is a dark, handsome man in his forties who speaks excellent English. His aggressive land acquisition program has helped Costa Rica become such a tourist attraction.

It is curious that Costa Rica, with one of the highest rates of deforestation in the world, also has one of the best park systems and the most progressive park management. I suppose the two balance one another to some degree. There are other contrasts here, especially between the rich and the poor. As in the United States, it is the poor who put up with most of the pollution. I can't help but think that something has to give, in both countries.

On the flight home the next morning I had time to do some serious thinking. I had just spent a week as that creature about whom I have such mixed emotions: the ecotourist.

On the one hand, it seemed to me I had been good for Costa Rica. I had only looked, taken nothing away except a bag full of craft items (which was good for the economy). The money I paid out to hotel keepers and restaurateurs stayed in local hands. If they had not had that money coming in, who knows what they might have done — mined, manufactured, or in some way exploited nature. Isn't it better to earn a living by showing off your natural resources, rather than digging them up?

The problem is that, once started, it can get out of hand. Recently, for instance, I saw a full-color, sixteen-page brochure (glossy paper, not recycled) touting New Zealand as the environmental destination of the 1990s. The inside front cover informed me that because "ecotourism" is "quintessential New Zealand," it "can offer you vacations of rare quality." So far, so good. I was truly impressed, until I got to the part where we would "soar (with the aid of a bungee strap) like a butterfly from a bridge over a river chasm." I just flat out do not believe that such activities can be carried out while maintaining ecopurity. Where bungee jumping can penetrate, new hotels can spring up in places they were never meant to be, and roads can be carved into mountain ridges simply because gringos love the view.

The Sierra Club has been a major sponsor of "outings" almost since we began. We have two firm rules: take nothing but pictures; leave nothing but footprints. That works well in American wilderness areas, but where an indigenous culture is involved, photography can be cause for resentment, and local entrepreneurs are hoping you'll leave dollars as well as footprints. Ecotourism and outings seem to be more like distant cousins than brothers.

Concern about these matters prompted a conference in Miami last November, attended by more than 400 people. The success of that conference, in turn, prompted an invitation from the chief environmental officer of Belize, the capital of British Honduras in Central America. He urged the Club to sponsor a similar conference in his city in December 1991. Should we involve ourselves? It seemed to me, coming home from Costa Rica, that the travel industry probably could use a watchdog like us. We had helped the world to preserve its natural wonders. Now we had a moral obligation to save those wonders from people who came, albeit in good faith, to admire them.

I spent February 18 at home in East Haddam, but the energy situation was too hot (if that is a pun, forgive me) to allow time off, and on the 19th I took the train to Washington for our energy press conference there. The strategy had been carefully mapped out in my absence. We had linked the Johnston-Wallop bill (now called the Energy Security Act of 1991) and the Bush National Energy Strategy together. Although Johnston-Wallop offered some conservation strategies, they were too few, and it called for oil exploration in the Arctic National Wildlife Refuge. We decided to fight for our viewpoint against both of these proposals.

Fifteen press conferences were planned across the country for February 20. We invited every chapter and group to participate by staging some event, but we had especially targeted New Hampshire, Illinois, Georgia, Pennsylvania, Tennessee, Kansas, Ohio, Nebraska, Oregon, and California. We needed to make our point with lawmakers from those states through their own constituents.

Our public affairs people were working on the D.C. press to set up interviews for me and to let them know we would be interested in responding to the President's announcement. We planned nationwide press advisories over the wire services and a 90-second video newsfeed, via satellite, that would be available to 750 TV stations. An op ed article, framed over my signature as a letter to President Bush, had been sent to each local club. Local leaders were asked to cosign it and hand carry it to local papers. Boilerplate press statements and fact sheets had been supplied in the field and two staffers were detailed to keep those up to date, especially with regard to analyses of the Johnston-Wallop Bill. A response to the President's official statement, in my name, would be honed after we heard his actual words, then it would be wired or faxed to 1,000 media outlets. I looked over the plan and smiled to myself. Not bad, I thought, indeed pretty sophisticated, for a bunch of tree-huggers.

In Washington, February 20 began with a joint press conference at 9:00 a.m. in a congressional meeting room, with the Sierra Club and Rep. Barbara Boxer (D-CA) announcing her ocean sanctuaries bill and denouncing the NES. About thirty media reps showed up, including all of the biggies. At 1:00 p.m. Bush was scheduled to make his official announcement. I would be on hand the rest of the day to do media reaction, while staffers phoned editorial writers across the country offering our thoughts.

Two days later, a three-page, single-spaced e-mail message from our public affairs people listed dozens of media successes, not the least of which was that all three networks, ABC, NBC, and CBS, had downloaded our video news release and included it in energy packages they were sending via satellite to all of their local affiliates. We were receiving calls from stations all over the country asking how to find local Sierra Club spokespeople. The e-mail message concluded: "We should all remember that these are just kickoff events. This is the start of a major national campaign that will be unfolding in the weeks to come. The public is ready to hear our message and the first day was a great success."

Having finished my D.C. chores, I took the train to New York City, changed to the Long Island Railroad, and rode out to Norwich, where I stayed at the same motel I had used in September for the trustees meeting.

In the morning I gave a breakfast speech at C. W. Post College. They sponsor visiting speakers and invite the community to hear them over coffee and danish. I gave what had now become my stump speech, part historical, part Blue Planet, then got back on the train to Penn Station, changed to Amtrak, and headed home. I felt very proud of myself. I had gone up and down the seaboard, including some tricky maneuvering in New York City, all on public transportation.

I came home to find the land war in Iraq had begun. I prayed for the safety of our soldiers, but also for the protection of that fragile desert ecosystem where they would be fighting. After all, I knew what already had been done to the waters of the Persian Gulf.

On February 23, I flew back to San Francisco for four days of work, including a meeting with the Board's Executive Committee, and an evaluation of Michael Fischer. It was a mixed-up kind of time. We had all been energized by the energy campaign (this time the pun is intended); now we had to transfer that energy to the Club's other affairs. Marianne Briscoe had resigned as paid staff for the Centennial Campaign. I could have spent the entire week just telling people to "think positively." We were planning our March Board meeting, which was to be held in Washington, D.C. What the Atlantic Chapter referred to as a "compromise co-document" was in the works. I had been invited to give a speech in Albany in March. Troubles in the Adirondacks just might serve to unite us all. Our efforts had helped gain another postponement of the construction at James Bay. Even better, a major French Canadian political party, which had viewed James Bay as a symbol of their nationalism, had made a dramatic reversal and asked for a moratorium on construction. Dan Weiss and Doris Cellarius had authored a draft platform for a waste campaign that needed to be carefully evaluated. Shirley Taylor, our chief water policy activist, had discovered a clean water bill that seemed to be, one, dangerous, and two, moving on a very fast track. She needed emergency help.

The list could go on and on. In addition, we had to focus on our projected revenue shortfall. Michael had informed us that things looked worse than ever, that the projected deficit — without spending cuts — could now go as high as $1.4 million. We could wait no longer. All the cuts we had put off had to go into effect at once.

As I have said, the Sierra Club is first and foremost a volunteer organization. In many similar organizations the staff, on the scene day in and day out, gradually takes over. Not so at

Sierra! Although it is the job of our Executive Director to evaluate the staff under him, the Board's Executive Committee very carefully reviews the work of its chief of staff annually.

Personnel interviews are, of course, confidential, but I guess I can reveal that one suggestion made to Michael was: "Stay home and take charge. You travel more than is absolutely necessary." In discussing all this, it came out that he was planning to leave on the 27th to tour the Pacific Northwest with the Rev. Jesse Jackson. Oh no, my fellow Board members said, you don't need to do that. Sue can go in your place.

Huh?

Yes, Sue, they said. Go to the woods with the Rainbow Coalition!

I thought for a minute. What the heck, it was only an additional four days away from home. If Arthur hadn't divorced me yet this month (I had been home a total of six days), he probably wouldn't for four more days.

OK, I said.

The Carpenters Union had invited Jackson to tour the Northwest. They wanted to publicize the plight of forest industry workers. Jackson, whose political savvy is always on target, decided to include an environmental perspective. He called Michael and offered to let us cosponsor the trip. Michael, who knows an important opportunity when it is placed before him, said yes. It was then that the Executive Committee asked me to go instead. In retrospect, I think it appeared to be more in the Rainbow spirit that the Club was represented by a woman.

We had no way of knowing what was expected of us. Ostensibly, we were supposed to search for common ground with the carpenters. Whether that would entail negotiations, or press conferences, or prayers, I had no idea. Bill Arthur, our northwest field director, accompanied me and we agreed we would try to be ready for anything.

The most difficult dynamic of the trip was that the carpenters made it clear they didn't want us there, right from the start. I suppose they thought we were stealing their thunder. Never at any time during the several days we were with him did the carpenters' representative, Mike Draper, give any sign that he was in the least interested in exploring opportunities for consensus.

It also seemed that Jackson felt he had fulfilled his obligation to the environmental perspective just by having us there. He clearly felt more comfortable with Draper and spent more time with him. For example, Draper was invited to sit with him on the plane to Seattle and to travel with his entourage from place to place. We just kept showing up — much to Draper's chagrin!

The trip got off to a rocky start when the carpenters refused to let us go along on a side trip to Roseburg, a timber town in Oregon. They had orchestrated a big rally of mill workers there, and they insisted there was no room on the plane for us.

We huffed and puffed and then demanded that, if Jackson was going off alone with the carpenters, he later go off alone with us to see the trees. Actually, Roseburg was probably no place for enviros. I don't think the carpenters could have guaranteed our personal safety — nor did they want to.

My first contact with the Rev. Jackson came in Portland where we, along with a contingent from the union and the Rainbow Coalition, met his plane. I was asked to stand on one side of him and Draper on the other during a brief press conference. There was no opportunity for either me or Draper to speak then or at two subsequent press conferences. The people had come to hear Jesse Jackson — and he expected us to understand that.

Jackson was whisked away to Roseburg by the carpenters; Bill Arthur and I went to a regional Sierra meeting in Portland. The next morning we arrived at a little airport north of the city at the crack of dawn. We were meeting Jackson's plane, but, alas, it was fogged in at Roseburg. Andy Kerr, of the Oregon Natural Resources Council, had put together a "walkabout" among the big trees meant to impress Jackson with the main points on our side. When the plane was delayed, we established a logistical headquarters at the Burns Brothers truck stop near the airport. Andy had a cellular phone and went to work reorganizing the walkabout as time slipped away.

Since we were all expected at a Rainbow Coalition lunch in a church basement in Portland, we switched our time with Jackson to the afternoon and made plans to take him to a state park rather than the mountains.

At that luncheon — and, later, at a church breakfast, a high school gym, and a businessman's lunch in Seattle — Jackson gave a stirring speech. He touched on a broad range of issues, including the needs of poor people, District of Columbia statehood, and the environment. He said that environmentalists and union people were not natural enemies, that we should unite and work together against the timber industry.

Although he said he wanted to help us find common ground, there were never any provisions made for us to sit and talk with the carpenters. We were both along for the ride. That afternoon, as we set out for our walkabout, Jackson insisted on bringing Mike Draper too. Draper then tried to rebut everything that Andy Kerr or Bill Arthur said. On points, though, we were the winners. We had knowledge on our side.

Jesse Jackson was most impressed by the Native Americans, who spoke of the loss of their fisheries due to forest practices. An elderly Indian gentleman spoke and then sang a native song. At this point, Jackson called on us (as he did several times during the trip) to hold hands and pray. I took some delight in the fact that Mike Draper was standing next to me and had to hold my hand.

It was impossible to know what Jackson thought of the points we were making during our tour. He did counsel me and Bill to be more patient with the union people. He said that he knew we had "the science" on our side, but that these people were scared for their jobs. He also said that the environmental movement needs to be more ethnically and socioeconomically diverse, and more female. (I tried to look as female as I could, under the circumstances.)

During the rest of the trip, we were asked to appear on the podium or at the head table at every stop, but only Jackson spoke. At one point I turned to Draper and said, "So, do you think we can find some common ground? Do you have faith that this process will help?" He answered, "Not as long as you people put trees before jobs." I'm sorry to say that was as good as it got.

After the final press conference, Jackson took me and Draper aside and asked if we would be willing to continue the dialogue in Washington. We both agreed, but I have few hopes for such a dialogue unless the carpenters become more enthusiastic.

There are two conditions necessary for a successful dialogue. First, both sides have to think there is something in it for them. Second, each side must understand and respect the concerns of the other — and want to find a way to address those concerns while pursuing their own. The Sierra Club has an established record of wanting to deal with the jobs issue. The carpenters are not ready to admit any merit in our desire to preserve ancient forest ecosystems. At this point, they'd rather fight with us than with the timber industry. So much for future negotiations.

While we were on the trip, Bill and I often felt like window dressing; we certainly didn't make friends with the carpenters. On the other hand, we neutralized what would have been a major one-sided press hit for the union. Also, it never hurts for a leader of Jackson's stature to stand up in a crowd and say that the environment is important and that we can have both a healthy environment and a healthy economy.

At the very least (or maybe most), we built a bridge to the Rainbow Coalition that we can call on in our efforts to effect ethnic diversity within the Club.

From a personal perspective, it was another pinch-me experience. I heard Jackson give the same speech four times, and I never tired of it. He is a powerful mover of people and it is a treat to watch him work the crowd. As I flew redeye from Seattle to Hartford on March 1, I wondered what was in store for me next.

March 1991

The ground war was soon over. A ceasefire was declared and the people of the United States gathered in the streets to cheer.

In Iraq, Kuwait, Iran, and India, others moved in to assess the environmental damage that had been done and to begin the cleanup. In Kuwait City, where black smoke from burning oil wells so darkened the air that headlights were necessary for cars driving at noontime, Hadi Hospital reported an increase of breathing difficulties, especially among the elderly and young children, for which there was no help.

"We are talking about an unprecedented ecological catastrophe the likes of which the world has never seen," said Abdelrahman al-Awadi, the Kuwaiti Minister of State for Cabinet Affairs. Ahmed Murad, a senior executive of the Kuwait Oil Company, said, "This is no emergency. This is an ongoing earthquake. We can only classify it as a catastrophe. We hope that those who did this will be considered war criminals."

The Governor of Adana state, in Turkey, ordered his people not to use rainwater or let their animals drink it. The soot from 600 burning oil wells was hanging in a soupy cloud over farmland and villages in Turkey and Iran, with plumes stretching as far as northern India. Rain, filled with toxic chemicals, polluted both the air and water. Severe respiratory illness, cancer, and ruined crops, many predicted, would be the war's most lasting legacy. Dr. James Moomaw, Director of the Center for Environmental Management at Tufts University, said, "The level of air pollution from the burning oil wells exceeds by hundreds of times the most polluted areas of the world."

Now the work of cleaning up the three separate oil spills began in earnest. At risk, in addition to scores of sea birds, were 180 species of mollusks, 106 species of fish, 450 species of animals that live in the coral reefs (the oil that could not be removed eventually sank, coating and clogging the reefs), five species of dolphin, and at least three types of whales.

Bad as the pollution in the Persian Gulf was, the war there was not the only cause of oil-related pollution. It was happening all over the world. Early in the month 630,000 gallons of crude oil spilled from a pipeline onto the ground and into a nearby river in Grand Rapids, Minnesota. The Lakehead Pipeline Company had no immediate explanation for the spill.

On March 18, the President of Mexico ordered the closing of Mexico City's largest oil refinery. Although the plant processed 100,000 barrels of oil a day and was important to the country's economy, air pollution levels had reached nearly four times maximum limits set by the World Health Organization. Hospitalizations for respiratory disease had increased by 20 percent. In announcing his decision, President Carlos Salinas de Gortari said that the 430 acres taken up by the plant would be used for public parks and green spaces. "Let's plant trees where today there is nothing but pipelines," he said.

On March 12, the Exxon Corporation, perpetrators of the world's previously best-known oil spill, agreed to pay a $100 million criminal fine in connection with the 1989 Exxon Valdez incident. This would be only part of payments by Exxon expected to total more than a billion dollars over the next decade as a result of state and federal charges. More than 300 private lawsuits against the company were still pending.

One week later, in Newark, New Jersey, Exxon pled guilty to yet another criminal charge connected to a 567,000-gallon oil spill in New York Harbor a year before. In addition, Exxon agreed to pay $10 million to settle civil litigation over damage to natural resources in New York and New Jersey.

At a press conference on the day of the Valdez settlement, Exxon Chairman Lawrence G. Rawl described the company's image as good and insisted the large settlement would not have an impact on Exxon's earnings.

Earlier in March, speaking to a group of energy executives, Rawl had described officials of some environmental groups as "cavalier and arrogant" in their campaign to keep drillers out of the Arctic National Wildlife Refuge. He also called the idea that geothermal, solar, and wind energy might be cheap new sources of power a "myth," expressed doubts about the validity of global warming, and dismissed concerns that acid rain might damage forests and lakes.

Speaking frankly was evidently in vogue. In Denver, at a conference for people interested in developing federal land, T. S. Ary, the head of the U. S. Bureau of Mines, called environmentalists "a bunch of nuts," and said that he did not "believe in endangered species . . . I think the only ones are sitting here in this room." Mr. Ary was appointed by President Reagan and reappointed by President Bush. He heads an agency of 3,500 employees with a budget of $150 million.

Not all businessmen and public officials were so unchastened about the environmental damage they cause. The DuPont Corporation for instance, announced that it was voluntarily working on a process to recycle the nitrous oxide that it emits while making nylon. Nitrous oxide has been implicated both in ozone-layer depletion and in global warming. DuPont said it hoped to cease all such emissions within the next five years.

In Washington, D.C., lawmakers focused on energy bills. The Senate Commerce Committee passed Sen. Richard Bryan's fuel efficiency bill 14-5, and sent it on to the Senate. There, because its opponents planned a filibuster, it would need a minimum of sixty votes to pass.

In response to the Johnston-Wallop Bill and the White House National Energy Strategy, Senator Tim Wirth (D-CO) introduced his own comprehensive energy bill. It called for the same emissions standards as the Bryan Bill, and left coastal and wilderness areas intact. While not perfect by the standards of many environmentalists because it included some incentives for new drilling, it attracted the support of environmentalists as the most viable alternative to Johnston-Wallop.

A bill to protect the coastal plain of Alaska's Arctic National Wildlife Refuge was introduced by Rep. Robert Mrazek (D-NY). Named in honor of Rep. Morris K. Udall, it declared this 1.5-million-acre Arctic coastal plain part of the federal wilderness system. If the bill passed, the plain would be permanently protected from oil drilling.

Oil was not the only controversial form of power. The gigantic hydropower project planned for James Bay in Quebec made headlines in Australia and Norway when newspapers in those countries learned of private contracts between the sponsoring government utility, HydroQuebec, and thirteen magnesium and aluminum companies. The secret contracts allowed the companies to buy electricity at below-cost rates. Such a practice appeared to run counter to claims that the project was needed to help Quebec's economy and to provide electricity to the province. Laval University economist Jean Thomas Bernard *estimated that the contracts could cost the people of Quebec $300 million a year for the next twenty-five years.*

In the United States, a coalition of industrial and development-minded groups calling itself the National Wetlands Coalition appeared to be winning its battle to reduce wetlands protection. Intensive lobbying to change the definition of a wetland resulted, not only in a flurry of bills that would narrow the regulatory definition, but also the resignation of EPA's chief wetlands ecologist. President Bush's campaign slogan — no net decrease in wetlands — would not be violated, cynics noted, since a wetland cannot decrease if it has been redefined out of existence.

Rep. Jim Jontz (D-IN) reintroduced his Ancient Forest Protection Act for woodlands in Washington, Oregon, and California, the habitat of the endangered northern spotted owl. At about the same time, the U.S. Fish and Wildlife Service declared that the Mexican spotted owl, its cousin, is also threatened or endangered. Mexican spotted owls nest in old-growth forests in New Mexico and Arizona, which have been drastically reduced by logging.

&

The Connecticut Chapter of the Sierra Club — my home base — had scheduled a day-long issues and lobbying workshop for March 2, at Hammonasset School on Long Island Sound. I had to be there — even if it meant disentangling myself from the Jesse Jackson tour, catching a midnight plane, waking up in Chicago to change planes, and driving straight from the airport to the meeting.

I was forced to pull off the road for a bit when sleep overwhelmed me, but I made it by lunch when I was scheduled to speak. I talked about the important work done by volunteers and how they could change the world. It came from my heart. I mean, look where volunteering had gotten me: I had been asleep in every state between Washington and Connecticut in the last twelve hours, not to mention being asleep at the wheel of my car.

I was still tired when I got home, but Arthur and Annie were looking forward to a Saturday night movie, our favorite form of family togetherness. How could I refuse? I did get some rest during the next couple of days. I stayed home and tried to catch up on my e-mail. There was one particularly interesting report.

Dan Becker, our Washington lobbyist, had attended a briefing by the Bush-Quayle campaign pollster, Vince Breglio. The Energy Conservation Coalition, of which Sierra is a member, had hired him to conduct a poll for us on energy issues. We purposely chose a Republican firm so that our data would not be considered biased.

This is what he found out from the poll he did for us: George Bush was more popular than any other President in recorded polls. Vince predicted a thirty- to sixty-day spike of popularity, based mostly on the fact that he had brought closure to the wounds left from Vietnam. Breglio found that the public does indeed believe that oil was the real reason for the war, but that people would not act based on that fact. He advised that we not attack Bush or his policies directly. He claimed there was a "halo effect" from Bush that extended to his policies.

Guilt seemed to be a factor in American thinking. People felt they had let the young sacrifice for them. Breglio suggested that we give them something to do to make up for it — buy a fuel-efficient car, write to Congress. "Give people at home something to do so we never have to put our kids in harm's way to protect our oil interests," he said.

The poll found that people did not connect drilling in the Arctic with environmental degradation unless you pointed it out to them. Once the connection was made, however, they were against it. The poll also showed a growing concern about global warming and nuclear power. Breglio stressed that our message had more credibility when we allowed for some increase in oil production as well as enhanced consumer efficiency and renewable resources. This made it even more important for us to stress our support for getting more out of existing wells.

It was fascinating stuff. I wondered how much it reflected the political bias of the pollster. Still, it showed us where we had work to do — connecting the preservation of the last pristine Arctic ecosystem, the Arctic National Wildlife Refuge, with peoples' day-to-day oil consumption habits, for instance.

Annie was on spring break, a far longer vacation than she ever had in public school, so I was able to take her with me when, on March 7, I returned to San Francisco for a Centennial Campaign planning meeting. The Club, which had been using the

Cathedral Hill Hotel for Board meetings, had some free rooms coming, so we checked in there. It's fancier than the Richelieu — chocolates on the pillow, etc. — and we both enjoyed it.

The next day, while I went to meetings with the Centennial Committee (which was still very much up in the air about changing leaders) and the Sierra Club Legal Defense Fund (which was still trading legalisms with us), Annie took the bus by herself across the city to go shopping in Ghirardelli Square. Oh my, I was getting to be such a carefree mother.

On the 9th, after more meetings in the morning, Annie and I headed for the airport. I was supposed to speak to a workshop for chairpersons of Sierra Club membership committees the next morning at the Bamberger Ranch in Texas. Unfortunately, as we checked in at the airport, we were told that the flight was canceled. The next connecting flight would not leave until the next day.

"No, no!" I pleaded, "I gave my word. I must be there." They wanted to help me, but Annie was flying on a "free" ticket (purchased with frequent flyer miles), and they were not very eager to accommodate her. Something inside me snapped. The nice lady everyone knows and loves took on a feral look and began to breathe heavily. The ticket lady looked at me closely and murmured, "I'll be right back." Twenty minutes later she reappeared with tickets on another airline several hours later, as well as vouchers for complimentary food.

That was not the end of it, however. Delays plagued us all day long. In the end we got to San Antonio so late that I decided to check into the airport motel, rent a car, and drive to the ranch the next day at daybreak.

Despite the fact that it was after midnight when we touched down, an extremely nice man from the local chapter, Walt Farmer, met us as we got off the plane, helped us through the routines of baggage collection, car rental, and motel registration — and even gave us a map showing how to get to the Bamberger Ranch.

We slept four hours, then forced ourselves to get up, and hit the road. I had been to the ranch earlier in the year; I was confident I would have no trouble finding it. Wrong. I misread the map, drove twenty miles in the wrong direction, turned around, began to speed in a car that was much more powerful than any I am used to, and — that's right — was soon explaining to a Texas state trooper why he should not give me a ticket.

I must have been persuasive. He gave me a warning and waved me on. We breezed into the ranch with just ten minutes to spare before my speech. By now my adrenals were going so fast that I tore into my speech. These people were special to me because they were all membership chairs in their local groups — and that was my very first volunteer office in the Connecticut Chapter. Membership is, of course, the very heart of the Sierra Club. The membership chairs help recruit the members and, most important, keep them coming back. Members create the Club out of the money they give, the time they volunteer, and, especially, out of their passion for our cause. Without them we would have no political clout and no feedback on how people really feel about the environment. I was happy to tell those assembled how important their work is.

In what seemed like no time at all, I had to get back on the road to make a 1:30 p.m. plane out of San Antonio. I guess this was what you call a "cameo appearance." I felt cheated, and I was embarrassed. My social life that year *was* encounters like these. If I don't get my quota of visiting and chitchatting at places like this, I don't get my quota. Period. Even more, I didn't want anyone in the Sierra Club to think I had turned into the kind of person who flew halfway across the country, dropped by for an hour, then left to fly across the other half — even if it were true.

Freeman Allen, my erstwhile opponent for the presidency, took on the role of helpful friend and drove back to town with us so he could return the rental car while Annie and I raced for the plane. This was my second trip to San Antonio. As I walked through the flight gate, I wondered wryly if I would ever see the Alamo or the famous River Walk.

This was March 10. Since I was due to make another speech in Albany—a plea for acquisition of key parcels of open space in the Adirondacks—on the 11th, there was no time to go home. We flew into Bradley Field in Hartford, but instead of turning south for home we drove north to a motel on the Connecticut/Massachusetts border. After we checked in, Annie zonked out — but I still had to write my next speech. The following morning we got up early again (since we were now in a different time zone, our bodies were all the more confused), picked up a carry-out breakfast, and headed for Albany.

The Atlantic Chapter was having a big conference and lobbying workshop at the state capitol, targeting state legislators on the question of adding land to the Adirondack Park. This is no small matter. The Adirondack Park is less than a day's drive away for 70 million people. Twice the size of Yellowstone and Yosemite combined, it provides wilderness values, wildlife habitat, and dozens of other critical environmental amenities for the most densely populated region of the United States. Forty years ago, there were only about 100 members of the Atlantic Chapter. Today they are 45,000 strong, and if anything holds them together it is pride in the Adirondacks.

Life has not been easy for the Atlantic Chapter. Internal strife had gotten so bad that they were, for a time, under threat of suspension. That had been put on hold and they had voted only the night before to restructure the chapter so that New York City, which had by far the most members, did not dominate the rural groups. Because of all the conflict they had had with the national Board of Directors, I wanted to do what I could to mend fences and keep the focus on conservation, the real reason we are all in this. As I had in my January speech, I reminded them that the Club was a means to an end and that that end—saving our planet—must not ever be lost sight of.

I was one of several speakers at the handsome new legislative office building in the capitol complex. Since Adirondack Park and the Sierra Club will both be a century old next year, I told them they were part of an unbroken line of activists that stretched all the way back to John Muir. I also brought them reassurance from all the other chapters that the importance of the Adirondacks went way beyond New York State.

"We look to you to be leaders in the fight for the northern forests," I said, "to protect the wild places all the way from New York to Maine." I finished with a quote from John Muir: "God has cared for these trees, saved them from drought, disease, avalanches, and a thousand straining, leveling tempests and floods; but he cannot save them from fools — only the government can do that."

Later that day I did some newspaper and radio interviews. Then, instead of at last going home, we drove to Hamden, Connecticut, where I attended a Common Cause board meeting. After all, they were paying me to do their work, and they had already been more tolerant of my travels than I had a right to expect.

On March 12 and 13, I rested. That is, I worked for Common Cause, caught up on laundry, feasted my eyes on my husband and home, and did an interview with the *Hartford Courant*. Funny, I could be on the front page of the *Washington Post* and not be as pleased as I am when the *Courant* runs a small story on page 5. A prophet truly doesn't get much honor at home. It feels good when it comes.

When the *Courant* ran the story, though, the headline said: "Sierra Club head lives on road." I expected to see an illustration by *Far Side* cartoonist Gary Larson of a disembodied head out in front of my house on Haywardville Road.

I had been at home for a total of eight days in March, and I didn't want to get a reputation for loafing, so on the 14th Annie and I hopped on a train. The March Board meeting was about to be held in Washington, D.C.

The Board holds one of its six meetings a year in Washington. After all, we have an office and staff there, and it is the heart of our lobbying effort. The meeting in Washington isn't exactly a circus, but it is a big one, more like an outing or a celebration than "one more meeting in San Francisco" for many of us.

The March 1991 meeting had a special fillip. An entire war had occurred between this and the previous meeting. Sierrans came from various parts of the political spectrum on defense issues, yet we had never discussed face to face how we should have handled the war. I expected some second guessing, and hoped for some constructive insights into our process.

The first event of the March festivities was set for 5:30 p.m. in the foyer of the Rayburn House Office Building. We were holding a reception for Congresspeople, their staffs, and selected other Washingtonians. This is an annual event, started about a dozen years ago when the Club first got into electoral politics. It is, to be blunt, the Sierra Club gently reminding various legislators that we are a political force to be reckoned with and that we are watching them. Another object, of course, is to impress lawmakers with our savoir faire and extensive grassroots power. For that reason we have two working bars, and the fanciest of hot and cold hors d'ouevres (but our invitations are printed on recycled paper).

There is always one built-in problem. Our members, seeing each other for the first time in a couple of months, and enjoying the party atmosphere, do so much hugging and catching up that sometimes they forget to do their share of mingling with our honored guests.

To remedy this, our Washington staffers stand at the entrance, and advise each Board member, as he or she arrives, which Congresspeople to seek out. Throughout the event, the Washington staff circulates, putting people together. As President, it was my job to greet everyone. Reid Wilson, our Political Director, hovered at my elbow, moving me from person to person, making sure no one was ignored.

By 6:30 the event was clearly a success. The Rayburn foyer — which is a sunken area off the main hall of the House Office Building — was jam-packed. With Reid still at my elbow, I climbed up the three steps, so that I could be clearly seen, and called them all to order. I introduced the guests of honor and said a few brief words about how wonderful they were, and about the important work we did. It was vaguely reminiscent of the reception Chris Dodd had given for me only a few months ago. The difference was that now I was in charge— and that this crowd was far more exuberant and three shades noisier.

But maybe I'm just projecting. In fact I had grown more exuberant these past few months, more sure of who I was and what I stood for, more willing to speak out — more willing even, to climb a few steps and shout a pack of Senators and Congresspeople into silence.

As Reid began to steer me to the next group, I had a moment of déjà vu. I was transported to a meeting in Hartford years ago, when I was a younger woman. I forget the purpose of the meeting, or even the name and affiliation of the young activist who spoke, but there in the Rayburn foyer I remembered his passion, and his words, very clearly. "I'm tired of being right," he said. "I want to be feared!" Environmentalists have come a long way, but we still have to work at being feared. I smiled as I extended my hand to the Senator before me.

The locus of the Board meeting was the Hyatt Regency Hotel in Bethesda (D.C. hotels were all booked). On Friday morning, a van picked us up there at 9:00 a.m. and took us back into Washington to the headquarters of the National Aeronautics and Space Administration (NASA) for a briefing, "Mission to Planet Earth."

A group of NASA scientists wanted us to know how much data they were collecting from outer space about the Earth's environment. We saw majestic overhead projections of our Blue Planet, but this wasn't poetry any more; this was pure science from a highly reputable federal agency. Their charts and graphs gave us insights into the extent of global warming and ozone depletion; their voices and faces showed us their personal concern.

I had wondered why they wanted to give us this briefing. As they spoke, however, although it was never explicitly stated, it began to come clear. Sometime ago, one of NASA's senior scientists at the Goddard Space Center, James Hanson, wrote a paper that warned of the extent and rapidity with which the planet's temperature was increasing. I remembered reading about it in all the papers. The Bush administration tried to issue a watered-down version, and it hit the press. Evidently NASA had learned its lesson. If they got their facts to a concerned public on a regular basis, they would be much harder to muzzle.

When the meeting was over, I said to Shelby Telford, our host, "This is all wonderful stuff, and I would like to trumpet your project across the country — but sometimes being linked to the Sierra Club can make your life more difficult. You do, after all, work for the Bush administration. What do you want from us?" He shuffled his shoes, hemmed, and hawed — by which I understood that we had entered into a very low-key but mutually beneficial arrangement.

Back in Bethesda, right after lunch the Board settled down to a working session. We heard a report on the Centennial Celebration. Things seemed to be getting in gear; there appeared to be less ambivalence about what was appropriate in raising funds for our hundredth birthday celebration. We were hiring an outside consultant on a contingency basis to approach those corporations that have been approved by the Gifts Acceptance Committee.

Michael Fischer talked turkey about the budget. He was projecting membership figures down nearly 70,000 by the end of the fiscal year. Since we had been growing by 13 percent a year for some time now, this was truly bad news. He had a plan all worked out for cutting our expenses, but some of our members felt he had made too many decisions before he came to us. There were some crisp moments debating something that I thought had been settled a hundred years ago, the relationship between volunteer directors and paid staff—just who's in charge here? I moved them along to a report on how things stood with the Sierra Club Legal Defense Fund. That gave us a common adversary, and brought us back to unity, if not total amity.

Also on the agenda that day were our ethnic diversity hiring practices, discussion of a redesign of *Sierra* magazine, and an "open-mike" session on the Persian Gulf War. As I said earlier, the Sierra Club is much concerned about the elitist label that attaches itself to the entire environmental movement, and, with some justification, to the Club itself. We need a more diverse membership, we need a more diverse staff, and we need current staff members to mix comfortably with people who are not exactly like themselves, if we are going to remain relevant.

We discussed a formal diversity-awareness training program for staff and launched an apprenticeship program for recent college graduates, targeted at disabled and minority students. At the end of a ten-month, minimum-wage assignment, apprentices would be given preference for any jobs Sierra Club had open, and would be introduced to other environmental groups with openings.

We also decided to beef up our internship recruiting by searching outside our usual circles and by paying more per semester, so that we could attract students who were working their way through college.

One of the places where we generally could absorb people from those two programs was *Sierra,* a bimonthly, glossy, full-color magazine that goes to every member and is also sold on newstands. *Sierra* brings in a good deal of money from advertisers. The good news at the March meeting came from Carole Pisarczyk, our Publisher, who reported that advertiser interest had perked up considerably as soon as a ceasefire was declared in the Gulf.

Sierra was undergoing a complete reorganization, and we spent some time rethinking exactly what we wanted from this relatively expensive membership perk. It is a wonderful thing to be able to reach out to educate, persuade, and motivate reliably, in a vehicle that readers respect and enjoy. I was very proud of the fact that we had *Sierra*, and of the professionalism of its staff as they explained their plans to us.

As a matter of fact, we were all so pleasantly occupied describing the magazine of our dreams that we ran out of time for the open-mike session on the war. It was probably too soon at that time, but a debate still needs to take place on the appropriate role for organizations like ours in times of national crisis.

The first item on Saturday's agenda was a breakfast meeting with the Honors and Awards Committee. This time I was the lobbyist. My year as President would end in May with our big annual banquet, which includes giving out the John Muir Award. I'm not a full-time, fire-breathing feminist — but I do find that sometimes the women who do all the work get passed over when it comes time to give out plaudits. There is an old expression in my family: the rooster may crow, but it's the hen that lays the eggs. I was determined that the Muir Award would go to a woman at my banquet — and I had two particular women in mind.

Ginny Woods and Celia Hunter discovered Alaska way back in the 1940s. Both good pilots, they enlisted in the Women's Air Force (WAFs) during World War II but were not allowed combat duty. Instead they were assigned to flying in Alaska, where roads were few and the airplane critical to wartime transport.

When the war ended, they homesteaded just outside of Fairbanks. They worked together to establish Camp Denali. Located near Wonder Lake, with a beautiful view of the highest mountain in Alaska (once known as Mount McKinley but now called by its Indian name, Denali), their land became an inholding (totally surrounded by public land) in 1980 when Congress expanded Denali National Park. Camp Denali became a haven for visitors who were willing to spend some time learning something about their surroundings, rather than just passing through. At the same time, Ginny and Celia became expert naturalists, teachers, and cooks.

The two women were founding members of the Alaska Conservation Society. Under that rubric, they stopped a plan to detonate a nuclear bomb so as to create a port in western Alaska; and they stopped a dam proposed for the Yukon River, which would have inundated nearly all of Yukon Flats, an important waterfowl breeding area that is now a wildlife refuge. In the late 1950s, they played a pivotal role in the establishment of the Arctic Refuge.

Retired now, Ginny still guides hikes and raft trips. Celia was for a time Executive Director of the Wilderness Society. Both write magazine and newspaper articles and continue to lobby for their lifelong goal, the preservation of wild Alaska.

By the time I had presented the good works of these two women, the committee was convinced. I left for the Board of Directors meeting at 9:00 a.m. with a small victory already under my belt.

The Board of Directors meeting lasted from 9:00 a.m. to 5:00 p.m. and covered many items, but the most emotion-charged was certainly President Bush's National Energy Strategy. One of our Washington lobbyists, Melanie Griffin, was sparkplugging the "Kick the oil habit campaign." She had the rest of us, volunteers and staff, organized so that the word was going out through op ed articles, paid advertising, letters to editors, public service announcements, the works. She even had people contacting top columnists and whispering in their ears.

The Chevron Company aroused her ire when they announced they were trying to protect grizzly bear habitat. "Not while you're planning to drill in Bridger-Teton," Melanie retorted, and launched a mailing to selected editorial boards across the country.

She also reported that Joanne Hurley, our Public Affairs Director, had made a suggestion which was backed by Carl Pope. They wanted to start a campaign demanding that automakers be forced to label their ads, just as cigarette companies do. Nothing much ever came of our "truth in labeling" initiative, but I shall always treasure the wording they wanted to insert in every automobile advertisement: "WARNING. Driving a 45 mpg car uses half as much oil, creates half as much air pollution, contributes half as many global-warming gases, helps preserve the Arctic National Wildlife Refuge and our nation's coastlines, and greatly lessens the chances that your children will go to war in the Persian Gulf."

On a more serious note, the "Kick the oil habit" petition campaign was coming along quickly. Several other groups had joined us and there was a growing competition among us to see who could bring in the most signatures.

We were also working with the Union of Concerned Scientists (UCS) on a series of regional hearings that would provide citizens with a chance to say what they really thought of the National Energy Strategy. Warren Leon, from UCS, felt such hearings were needed as an antidote to the Watkins hearings, preceding the National Energy Strategy, which had been tightly controlled.

Melanie also told us that the Bush energy policy had just been introduced in Congress, and that a series of hearings on the Johnston-Wallop Bill had begun. She said that Senator Johnston wanted to start the actual markup of his bill on April 9 and was pushing for floor action in May. This meant we had to rush the Bryan Bill or risk eating the good Senator's dust.

The hearing on the Bryan Bill had already been held and went very well. There was a delicious moment, according to Melanie, when a General Motors official said that the low-emissions cars would all have to be about the size of Geo Metros, and that everyone would die on the road.

"Are you saying that Geo Metros are not safe?" Bryan demanded. Hemming and hawing issued from GM. Persistent demands by the Senator, "Are Geos safe cars?" eventually led, of course, to a General Motors endorsement for the safety of small cars.

Senate Majority Leader George Mitchell had appointed a task force of Democrats to work on energy policy. The environmental groups were attempting to talk to each member of the task force to be certain they understood that they must come up with legislation that countered Bush's plan.

At the first meeting, Senator Johnston's representative said, in effect, "Let's just list what we can agree on and call that our package; we can ignore the rest." We couldn't let them get away with that.

There is a term that comes up over and over again in discussing energy policy and air pollution — CAFE — which definitely is not related to any form of entertainment. It stands for Corporate Average Fuel Economy, and refers to the federally mandated number of miles per gallon of gasoline used in highway driving that a given automakers' entire fleet of cars must average. Thus, if in 1991 Ford makes 100,000 Escorts that are proved to average 30 mpg on the highway, and 50,000 LTDs that average 15 mpg, Ford's 1991 CAFE would be 25. If the federal government mandates a CAFE of 30 mpg for 1991, Ford must either make more Escorts compared to LTDs or improve the fuel efficiency of all its models. By law, all American fleets must now average 27.5 mpg. This is called the CAFE standard. If a car gets more miles per gallon, then it will give out fewer air-polluting emissions, contribute less to global warming, and save its driver money by getting farther on every gallon burned. The bigger the CAFE number, the more savings.

Senator Richard Bryan's bill raised the CAFE standard from 27.5 to 40. Representative Barbara Boxer's bill, in the House of Representatives was much the same, but set a CAFE goal of 45.

People who breathe air and drive cars could obviously be big winners if the CAFE standards were raised. People who manufacture automobiles would have some hustling to do to produce a more efficient car. Perhaps it would be expensive hustling. However, most experts believe it could be done, and we had recently seen some signs that the United Auto Workers were beginning to understand our side. They hear their management say that building a 45 mpg car can't be done, but they know those same managers said the same thing in 1974 and were wrong. They also know that, if the original CAFE law had not passed, the more efficient Japanese cars would have completely taken over. From there, it isn't much of a jump to wonder if Japanese automakers won't continue to improve their cars while American manufacturers wring their hands, until American workers are standing around idle.

The big monetary losers, as CAFE numbers increase, are the people who drill, sell, refine, transport, or in any way have anything to do with oil. The Sierra Club has pointed out repeatedly that a higher CAFE standard — 40 or 45 — would result in savings in oil consumption that would exceed our total prewar imports from Kuwait and Iraq combined. We keep urging that our energy future be secured "through gas tanks instead of war tanks," but nobody in the current or previous administration has seemed to hear.

As a matter of fact, the Secretary of Transportation actually rolled back CAFE standards during the Reagan administration.

The Bush strategy would actively weaken federal laws that promote auto fuel economy.

Environmentalists vehemently support increasing the CAFE standards, and we have won the attention of some of the ablest legislators. We felt we were on the verge of winning and so we were much encouraged by some gossip being spread at the March meeting — that Rep. John Dingell, from Detroit, had been telling his auto friends back home to get ready because "CAFE is coming, one way or another."

Congressman Morris Udall is a living legend. The tall, craggy-faced Democrat from Arizona — once a Presidential candidate — is a hero to environmentalists. He recognized the threats to our natural world long before they were widely understood, and he took on what was then the often lonely job of saving the resources so many of his fellow legislators were destroying. One of his many good works was the Alaska Lands Bill, the landmark 1980 law that gave permanent protection to many of Alaska's special wild places, but left the Arctic Wildlife Refuge in limbo—open to possible oil drilling. Therefore, when Representative Robert Mrazek (D-NY) announced that, after the Easter break, he would introduce the Morris K. Udall Arctic Wilderness Bill, many heartstrings were tugged. Melanie had no problem getting the Board's endorsement.

We also instructed staff to support a bill being introduced by Senator Timothy E. Wirth (D-CO), but gingerly. Overall, Wirth's package was great: no Arctic drilling and twenty times better on energy efficiency than Johnston-Wallop. Its only problem was encouragement for new drilling, which we simply could not condone.

Meanwhile, back at the Hyatt Regency in Bethesda, our Centennial Celebration kick-off event was about to have its world premiere. At 5:30 Saturday night, a children's musical called "Celebrating Nature," was to be presented.

The entire show — story, music, lyrics, costumes, staging — was the product of elementary-level children and their very talented teacher, Jean Lutterman, from the Norwood School in Bethesda. It was presented at the Hyatt in a room that held a stage and a couple of hundred people. The children were charming. Their storyline dealt with an evil corporate polluter who is visited by his environmentally-oriented niece. After talking to her, he goes to bed and dreams of his boyhood. His former good friend, Mother Nature, comes to remind him of all the marvels in her world. Needless to say, he wakes up and achieves his own salvation by reforming his company.

The parents of the children, many of them important Washingtonians, all came to see the show. We hoped they were impressed — and we hoped the show would be given many bookings. It may have been oversimplified, but it made a strong point.

There was a reception after the musical; then the Board of Directors and senior staff adjourned to the home of Maxine and Mike McClosky in Bethesda, Maryland, for dinner. Mike, a former Executive Director of the Sierra Club, is part of the fabric of Sierra. When, after sixteen years or so at the helm he felt he should move on, we created a position for him and gave him the title of Chairman, so that we could have the benefit of his unique talents and experience. He now devotes himself to the big picture, to planning and trend analysis—all the things that an Executive Director, constantly fighting fires, never gets around to. It was Mike, for instance, who was instrumental in leading us to NASA, and Mike who conceived of and brought to fruition a worldwide data base on what remains of the world's wilderness areas. It is Mike who guides us in international affairs.

The McCloskey home is exactly what it should be, a brick townhouse filled with books and art objects the family has acquired while traveling around the world. In the family room downstairs, where we gathered, an exquisite collection of American Northwestern basketry was displayed, not far removed from a wall full of hats collected on Mike's travels. It felt like coming home to be there. It was the perfect ending to our Washington meeting.

Annie went back to school on March 18 while I worked in Hartford. The next day I took a train to New York City for a luncheon in honor of James Bay, and of David Brower, who is always referred to as the Archdruid of the Sierra Club (he was the subject of a book by John McPhee entitled *Encounters with the Archdruid*). David is a former Sierra Club Executive Director who went on to found Friends of the Earth, and then Earth Island Institute. He remains our guru, one of the most visionary and articulate environmentalists it has been my pleasure to meet. The luncheon was hosted by the Native American community, but I had the honor of introducing first David and then Matthew Coon-Come, grand chief of the Cree, and my host when I traveled in his territory.

I was seated next to Charles Alexander, the science editor for *Time* magazine, and one of those people who are both totally brilliant and totally affable. We had met a couple of years previously when he was the speaker at a Sierra Club convention in Michigan, so it was easy to share some gossip with him. The story I told him was about the secret sweetheart deals that HydroQuebec had made to sell electricity below what it cost to produce it. I said I hoped he would check it out. (Note: *Time* ran the story, properly verified, a few weeks later.)

I was especially pleased to be going to Concord, New Hampshire, the next day for the grand opening of the new Monadnock Group office there. The Club was sharing space with another respected organization, the Society for the Protection of New Hampshire Forests, and there was a real feeling of new ground being broken in a state not noted for its progressive environmental attitudes.

I did press interviews all afternoon. The *Concord Monitor* ran my picture two columns wide, and quoted me as expressing "grave disappointment" over the National Energy Strategy, adding, "That's the kindest way to put it." My dad arrived, acting very proud of his outspoken daughter. I went home with him, and stayed overnight for a visit.

March 22 was the second anniversary of the *Exxon Valdez* oil disaster. It seemed an appropriate day for us to announce our support for the Morris K. Udall Wilderness Bill of 1991. David Gardiner, our Legislative Director, did the honors in Washington. He faced the TV cameras with a sample of the still-oily sands of Prince William Sound in his hands, and showed his viewers that the oil had not vanished as the oil companies said it would.

"It is still there," Gardiner said, "being uncovered and churned by waves and tides, re-entering the food chain time and time again." He closed by saying that the Bryan Bill could save more oil than the Arctic could produce, "without disrupting a single tundra wildflower." David was still using crutches because of the effects of his August accident, but he looked mighty good to us.

I did not go to Washington for that press hit. For the last couple of weeks I had been working at turning some minor sniffles into The Cold from Hell. I felt absolutely miserable, blue, worthless, angry. I went home instead and stayed there for three days. I fully expected Arthur to scold me (my mother would have) about running myself ragged, and poor eating habits, and "now see where you've gotten yourself." But no, he was a lamb. My friends tell me he is straight out of the Nyquil commercial, but since I don't have TV I can't vouch for that. I just know he was very sweet while I was very miserable.

I had promised to discuss open space and parks on a cable television talk show out of Norwalk, Connecticut, on the 25th and so I pulled myself together and drove down. It was the kind of program that has a series of "interesting guests." I was sandwiched between a chef demonstrating how to cook shrimp scampi and a woman who had written a book entitled *Your Body Believes Every Word You Say.* It sounded logical to me until she explained that the source of her dandruff was that, deep down, she considered herself flaky. She actually said this with a straight face.

No matter. You get the word out however and whenever you can. Later that spring, I was invited back to appear on a show devoted entirely to energy matters, and that is just what I wanted.

My last official act in March was serving as a panelist at a conference sponsored by the Connecticut Environment Roundtable. This unusual group, run by a board representing environmentalists, industry, government, and academia, seems to me to be going places. They are interested in making our environmental protection processes more efficient and believe that a consensus must be achieved among activists, businessmen and other concerned citizens. The conference that day was on collaborative strategies for solving environmental problems. Surrounded as I was by business executives and liberal activists, I got a laugh when I described the Sierra Club as being "on the cutting edge of the middle of the road."

That was an easy, glib thing to say. The truth, I think, is much more complicated. The Sierra Club is neither extremist (as Earth First! and its tree spikers) nor conservative (as many organizations that seek to preserve a special tax status). However, what we do well—grassroots organizing and using that power to effect change within the system—we do very well indeed.

Earlier in the month, at the meeting of the Board of Directors, I had tried to explain what I felt. The President's speech slot on our agenda was my opportunity to discuss where we were headed.

"The Arctic has become a symbol," I said, "to both sides in the debate. It's an especially useful metaphor for our oil addiction. Rather than confronting our chemical dependency, we're asked to rationalize why we should pawn our last valuables — our grandmother's silverware — for one last fix. The pushers are out there telling the people that it will feel good!

"Well, we're out there too, but with all our other issues, the oil-energy-Arctic message will take all the organizing and persuasion skills we've learned in a hundred years. Our goal must be yellow ribbons around every mailbox for saving the Arctic, for coming clean, getting straight, and kicking the oil habit.

"Jon King said it best in an editorial in the most recent *Sierra.* 'If the United States, acting rationally and with foresight, were to adopt a national energy policy that provided safe and efficient choices, we could curb global warming, protect the Arctic National Wildlife Refuge from drilling, save money by the barrelful, clear the air, and take the oil weapon away from the likes of Saddam Hussein, all without lowering our standard of living by a single Volvo or VCR. In short: we would all win.'

"The President of the Sierra Club is prone to several strange conditions, and among them is a chronic case of the should've-saids. I suppose it's because I find myself talking to reporters or groups of people more often than I ever have before, but I seem to spend a lot of time thinking I should've said this or if only I'd said that, or if I'd just said this it might have touched just the right opinion leader, tipped the balance, and started a movement.

"Last Thursday morning at 7:15, while standing in my kitchen, I was interviewed about the Arctic on a radio talk show — the kind where they bait you and try to make you sound a little silly. I'm not especially good at the sparring stuff, but I was dodging and feinting my way along. Finally the host of the show said, 'I guess you mean we should ignore this chance to become independent of foreign oil — all for the sake of a few caribou in some godforsaken place.' I sputtered for a moment. Then he said, 'I'm sorry, folks. We're out of time. We've been talking to the President of the Sierra Club and, frankly, she hasn't convinced me that we shouldn't drill in the Arctic Wildlife Refuge.'

"I didn't get a chance to say the thing that would have blown away that biggest lie of all. I should've said that this tiny bit of oil is a drop in the bucket. If you think beyond a few years, it can't possibly alter our dependence on foreign oil at all, and what a price to pay for that last fix — the destruction of the last pristine arctic ecosystem on earth.

"Well, of course by the end of the day I had myself convinced that if I'd just said the right thing, it would have turned the whole debate around. I was sure that I'd had a chance to save the Arctic and I'd blown it.

"Then I came to Washington and came to my senses. What I say or don't say is just a blip. It's what you and those you represent say and do that will turn around the whole debate. You are the cure for the should've-saids, because you'll tell the truth in a thousand cities and towns and local papers. You'll speak to their hearts. Maybe we could start with Sierra Club members. Then we could move on to reach out to anyone who signed an Earth Day pledge. Maybe we could organize all those individuals who saw 'Dances with Wolves' and felt anything at all.

"John Muir said (and he was talking about trees, but he wouldn't mind if we substituted a wildlife refuge) 'The wrongs done to trees, wrongs of every sort, are done in the darkness of ignorance and unbelief, for when the light comes, the heart of the people is always right.'

"We will bring the light to the people. Then the Sierra Club will be a giant magnifying glass channeling and focusing the light, aiming it at just the right spots to start fires under the right people. We can do this. It's what we do best. It's how we got to be a hundred years old and better organized to reach people's hearts than any other organization I can think of. And since there's no time to lose, I thank you in advance for all that you'll do. Now let's go get 'em!"

April 1991

A year had passed since Earth Day Twenty. The twenty-first year of the environmental movement was coming to an end. The overwhelming outpouring of concern for natural resource protection and for pollution abatement that had been exhibited a year before now was nowhere in evidence. Polls still showed that people the world over were worried about the health of their planet — and willing to sacrifice for its protection — but a major war, a great political and philosophical shifting within the Soviet Union, and a cynical malaise worldwide seemed to have softened the hard urgency of the demand.

Another factor was complacency—the belief that so much had been accomplished already, that environmental mores had become a part of all cultures. In an Earth Day op ed essay published in the New York Times, *Rep. Frank Lautenberg (D-NJ) noted that many products were being marketed with claims that they were somehow environmentally superior. Sophisticated environmentalists, he said, were protesting with their wallets instead of with picket lines, and some manufacturers responding to this marketplace pressure were going too far, he said, in "pulling the 'green' over our eyes."*

Many businesses however, were honestly trying to improve their environmental records. On April 10 the Ford Motor Company said the use of chlorofluorocarbons (CFCs) in plastic foam for seats would be eliminated from 90 percent of its manufacturing by the end of 1992. Four days later, the McDonald's Corporation, which had already abolished its foam clamshell containers and set up recycling programs at each of its stores, announced that it was taking an additional forty steps to reduce its daily generation of two million pounds of garbage.

The advertising industry in Manhattan celebrated Earth Day by announcing environmental awareness campaigns at four major agencies; the next day Apple Computer, Inc. boasted that it had developed a new technique that would eliminate the use of CFCs in its manufacturing processes.

Even as industry moved to clean up its act, scientists indicted agriculture for its role in the greenhouse effect. An article in the British journal Nature *said that methane and nitrous oxide have risen sharply over the last two decades and together account for about 20 percent of total expected global warming. Their study found that cultivation of grasslands and the use of nitrogen fertilizers were important causal agents.*

Perhaps the worst environmental news of the month came on April 5, when the U.S. Environmental Protection Agency announced that the loss of the ozone layer over the country was proceeding twice as fast as scientists had expected.

EPA administrator William K. Reilly called the news "stunning," and said calculations based on the new measurements indicated that over the next fifty years, some 12 million people will develop skin cancer (of which an estimated 200,000 will die). This was in addition, Reilly said, to the current rate of 8,000 deaths per year.

The data, obtained from the National Aeronautics and Space Administration, also showed that ozone depletion extended farther south and lasted longer than had been believed.

Commenting in his New York Times *column, writer Tom Wicker pointed out that the morbidity and mortality rates were now twenty times higher than we had suspected and that, besides skin cancer, there would be "more eye cataracts, more damage to the human immune system and to crops, plants, and the oceanic food chain." Wicker categorized the Bush administration response — "We need to very carefully scrutinize this and other reports to evaluate the accuracy in a deliberative and comprehensive scientific way" — as "gobbledygook."*

Less than a week later, another prestigious group, the National Academy of Sciences panel on global warming, called on the U.S. to act promptly to reduce the threat of global warming. The study, commissioned by Congress, recommended a number of actions, including raising overall mileage standards for new automobiles to 32.5 miles per gallon, up from 27.5. Both the White House and environmental groups praised the panel's work, which appeared to have attempted a compromise between the two factions.

In both cases, ozone depletion and global warming, "It is the magnitude of impending change, not the underlying theory, that is in dispute," commented Michael Oppenheimer, a senior scientist at the Environmental Defense Fund. Oppenheimer said the ozone debacle could have been avoided if earlier administrations had taken action, and charged that the Bush White House had received the two new reports "as if it were staffed by amnesia victims."

In the Middle East, although peace reigned, the environmental aftereffects of the Gulf War continued. About six million barrels of oil, weighing roughly a million tons (around 10 percent of the world's daily oil ration), were reported to be going up in smoke every day from the 550 oil wells burning in Kuwait. Teams of fire fighters estimated that it would be many months before all the blazes were quelled. In the meantime the wells emitted daily an estimated 50,000 tons of sulfur dioxide — the culprit in acid rain — and 100,000 tons of sooty smoke. The amount of carbon dioxide, admittedly astronomical, was uncounted.

John Horgan, writing in the May issue of Scientific American, reported that Department of Energy officials had clamped down on information about potential environmental damage until long after the war ended. Horgan quoted Richard Small of the Pacific Sierra Research Corporation as saying, "We have never seen a pollution event of this scale," and estimating that damage might be felt over an area extending 1,000 kilometers from Kuwait. Horgan also quoted Joel S. Levine, a NASA biomass burning expert, who said the Kuwaiti well fires were "the most intense burning source, probably, in the history of the world."

In the Gulf itself, clean-up of the oil spill continued. By April the spill was beginning to have an effect on supplies of fish, which were up 15 percent in price in Dhahran, Saudi Arabia. Many shoppers, it was reported, were asking fish mongers to cut the fish open on the spot to see if there was oil in the belly.

No part of the globe was free of environmental drama as Earth Day Twenty-One approached. Just as unbearable air pollution in Mexico City in March forced the Mexican government to take a stronger stand on pollution, so, in April, a chemical leak in South Korea brought a dramatic about-face from leaders there. A caustic and highly toxic form of phenol somehow leaked from Korea's showcase industrial area into the drinking water of 1.7 million people. Hundreds, perhaps thousands, became violently ill. A hurried cabinet meeting in Seoul was followed by an announcement that South Korea's industrialization politics were being rethought.

In the Bay of Genoa, the supertanker Haven caught fire and spilled between a quarter and a half of its 41 million gallon load. Towed to shallow waters, where it would be less of a threat to wildlife — and to beaches along the French and Italian Riviera — it sank about 2,000 yards off the northwest coast of Italy.

In the United States, a sad string of gondola freightcars, dubbed "the dirt train," was attracting media attention. Loaded with 2,400 tons of soil contaminated by acrylic in a chemical spill, the dirt train was refused in Freeland, Michigan; Sumter, South Carolina; and Toledo, Ohio. Like the garbage barge that sailed the high seas for four months in 1987 searching for a place to leave its cargo, the dirt train encountered only protestors wherever it tried to stop. At the end of the month, after hiding out in Nashville for three days, the train was reported en route to Utah.

The principle held so dear by environmentalists — that every community must live within its means when it comes to water supply and waste disposal — was dramatically demonstrated in Boston, when a federal judge declared a moratorium on sewer hookups in connection with the $6-billion-dollar cleanup of Boston Harbor.

The no-new-discharge order meant that empty space in most new commercial and residential buildings could not be occupied. The chilling effect on business start-ups and expansions, new home closings, construction loans, and real estate development generally was said to stymie the Boston economy. However, Rep. Joseph P. Kennedy II, a Democrat who represents several of the communities involved, saw it as an attempt to make politicians take responsibility for the city's problems. "I think this will force a political solution before it causes financial devastation," he said.

The impetus for local solutions to environmental problems seemed to be increasing. Some activists attributed the trend to the Reagan and Bush administrations' do-nothing policies. They spoke of the states "building a floor under the feds," by which they meant setting high standards that could be copied by congressional leaders when framing federal legislation.

Commenting on the trend, New York Times writer John Holusha said that some industries were so worried that they were rushing to Washington to seek uniform rules. They claimed to be fearful of a crazy-quilt pattern of state regulations and of single-shot actions like bans and taxes.

Holusha cited clean air regulations, particularly vehicle emissions, and solid waste (packaging and recycling) as issues prone to regional rather than national decision making.

On April 10 the federal government released a summary of fifty-eight scientific studies done by the National Oceanic and Atmospheric Administration (NOAA) concerning the Exxon Valdez oil spill. The studies had been used as the basis for negotiating the $1.1-billion civil and criminal settlement between Exxon, Alaska, and the United States. They showed that far more wildlife had been killed and that damage would persist much longer than had originally been thought.

Page after page of information documented losses in salmon, pollack and herring, whales, sea grasses, and productive salt marsh habitat. Some 380,000 birds were reported dead. Among the details in the studies: large numbers of herring larvae with eye tumors, pollack with elevated hydrocarbon levels 500 miles from Prince William Sound, and oil-filled clams poisoning the sea otters that ate them.

Two weeks later, in a move that virtually no one expected, Federal Judge H. Russel Holland rejected Exxon's $100 million criminal fine as too low. "The fines," Judge Holland said, "send the wrong message, suggesting that spills are a cost of business that can be absorbed." The judge said that fines should have a deterrent effect.

Requests to reject the settlement had begun pouring into Judge Holland when Exxon Chairman Lawrence G. Rawl said the negotiated agreement "would not have a significant effect on our earnings," and escalated when the NOAA studies summary became public knowledge.

"Mr. Rawl. . . completely failed to acknowledge any culpability or responsibility for the damage that occurred," Hope Babcock, general counsel for the National Audubon Society, pointed out. "There was a total lack of remorse for what happened, and that is a basic tenet of the criminal justice system."

❧

Back when I spoke at the Hewlett-Packard Company, one of their women executives told a story that, I feel, states very succinctly how broad and how deep environmental concern is in our society. I have told it to many groups since then. I call it my "hooker story."

She said she was driving her car through Washington, D. C., and was stopped for a traffic light when the door of the passenger side swung open and a gaudily dressed lady of the evening hopped in.

The intruder demanded to be driven to a destination six blocks away and the executive, scared stiff, complied. She was so nervous, however, that she began to babble.

"Oh," she said, "I thought you were going to rob me. I'm so glad that all you want is a ride. I used to carry Mace to protect myself but the House security people took it away from me last week and. . ."

"Yeah," the hooker interrupted indignantly, "and I'll bet they just threw it in the landfill!"

I have told that story often and generally it gets a good laugh. On April 2, it failed me. I was talking to three combined classes at West Hartford's Hall High and I suspect that the term "lady of the evening" was a bit archaic for them. They were eager and bright-eyed, nice kids, but they didn't have many questions for me. I found myself "barking" for the environment—I felt like a Bedding Barn salesman. They did already have a letter-writing effort going on James Bay. Good for them!

I had lunch with David Sutherland from the Nature Conservancy. It was time to start networking, like so many others who had come to me for advice over the years. I would need a job when the Sierra Club put me out to pasture.

The following day I was the dinner speaker for the Storrs-Willimantic Chapter of the American Association of University Women. They got my hooker joke with no problem. They were also in tune with my message. During the discussion period, one woman said, "We aren't fighting over the good and the bad any more, but what's bad and what's worse." A discouraging insight, but more true than even I like to admit.

The University of New Orleans wanted a speaker for a student council program; they could pay $1,000 plus expenses so the Sierra booking agent offered me. (There were days when I felt like a slave on an auction block. Then I remembered that it was nearly over — and felt even worse.)

I arrived in time to be given a tour of the school and to talk with some professors in environmental studies. I made myself at home in the spartan "visiting dignitaries" room at the student center, and then headed for the auditorium. This is mostly a commuters' school and, I was told, people like to head home once classes are done. There were only about twenty people, scattered through a hall meant to hold ten times that many.

I began with a beautiful video about the Arctic with voiceover by Jimmy Carter that I sometimes use to open talks about energy policy. It was about halfway through when a strident clanging interrupted. Fire alarm! We all trooped outside for twenty minutes. But not all of us came back in when it was over. I finished my remarks, trying not to be discouraged. It was clear I wasn't going to capture many souls here, but the Sierra Club would be a thousand dollars richer.

Later I went to dinner with three students who were on "the committee." I had the feeling they had been more interested in the restaurant meal with "an important speaker" than in the issue itself. Ah, well, they were fun kids, and the Chinese restaurant they chose was first rate.

At 8:30 the next morning I caught a plane to San Francisco, where I tackled my in-box and prepared for a two-day Planning Committee meeting that was about to begin.

Peter Schwartz says he made his fortune selling high-priced garden benches to yuppies. He is on the Board of Smith & Hawken, whose catalog pages I have often thumbed, dreaming of gazebos and arboreal mazes and Monet-inspired picnic lunches at the base of a gnarled apple tree. Mr. Schwartz also runs Global Business Network, a high-powered consulting firm. He had agreed to spend two days with the Sierra Planning Committee, at far below his usual fee, to help us improve our strategic planning.

With Peter Schwartz at the helm, we steered through a process in which you brainstorm about all the forces and trends that are influencing your organization and then try to outline several possible scenarios that you might have to confront.

We forecasted three possibilities. The first, *Divided Society*, assumed a decade of economic malaise with continuing problems of poverty, education, health care, drugs, crime, and racial friction. We saw the slow degradation of environmental concern as state and local deficits mounted. The second, *Sierra Club Preempted*, envisioned the Bush administration turning "green," in response to political pressure, and other environmental groups moving ahead of us. The third, *Green Revival*, held that society as a whole would return to basic values, with the church and quality of life concerns preeminent—and the Sierra Club swamped as super-rapid membership growth built to a worldwide high 10-million strong.

All of these potential futures carried inherent problems for the club. Furthermore, Mr. Schwartz noted, the truth would probably be revealed as some unlikely variation of one or more of them.

Not only is Mr. Schwartz extremely well read and up-to-date on every trend, the members of the Planning Committee number some of Sierra's most artful thinkers (including Mike McCloskey, who lent his usual class to the undertaking). It turned out to be a very stimulating experience — and that was as it should be. Mr. Schwartz explained at the end (although by now we understood it too) that the three scenarios we had arrived at were not the most important product of the two-day session. It was the training we had received in how to think about the future.

There was a special moment for me during a dinner at the Schwartz residence in the Berkeley hills. We were eating trendy pizza (the kind with artichokes and pine nuts on it) and watching the sun set over San Francisco Bay. The conversation was sparkling; the weather mellow; the view perfection — and I was sitting on a Smith & Hawken garden bench!

I flew back to Connecticut Sunday night so that I could be at a Common Cause board meeting in Hamden the next day. I was in the habit of giving a ride to an elderly board member, Tom Dunne, who lives between my town and Hamden, in Meriden, Connecticut. Like all Common Cause board members, Tom is sharp and keeps up with all the news. He is always interested in where I have been. I unwound as we chatted and began to fully appreciate how blessed I am to be able to deal with a Louisiana student one day, Peter Schwartz the next, and Tom Dunne the day after. I may be a tree hugger, but my world would be drab indeed without people.

Rising citizen concern in Connecticut about apparent cancer clusters among neighbors of electrical transformer substations led the state government to set up a Task Force on Electromagnetic Fields. The task force, in turn, set up a citizens advisory committee, and an official of the state health department asked me to be on it. I went to an organizational meeting of that committee in Hartford on Tuesday and to an advisory breakfast at WTNH-TV, Channel 8, in New Haven on Wednesday. Channel 8 was planning a series of one-hour programs on state environmental issues and had the good sense to seek advice from people in the field.

Of all the media, local TV is the least equipped to deal with environmental reporting. First of all, they must explain complex concepts in tiny sound bites. I don't think it is possible to mention the ozone layer, explain that it is good (not the bad ozone that pollutes the air we breathe), and then tell why it is thinning and what will happen to us all if it continues to do so, all in thirty seconds, but they try to do that, and more, every day.

Second, their news budgets are meager. There is no time for reporters to get background briefings so that they can improve their grasp on slippery scientific ideas. The environment "specialist" is apt to be the weatherperson.

Third, unlike the printed word, which can be returned to if it is not clear the first time, TV news is fleeting and evanescent. The viewer gets an impression, but does not necessarily comprehend any facts.

For all these reasons, I spend whatever time I can being as helpful as possible to any TV people who want to learn.

On Thursday I flew back to San Francisco for a meeting of the Centennial Campaign Planning Committee.

Although we continued to struggle with the concept of a large donor capability—and probably would for the rest of the year—a number of things had been accomplished. My two favorites were the *One Hundred Heroes* book (with its video spin-off) and the Center for Environmental Innovation.

Centennial Campaign workers had put together a book featuring the photos and stories of a hundred Sierra volunteers, all grassroots activists, all more than worthy of the title "hero" in terms of their achievements in protecting America's natural resources. Not only was the book charming, it had so captivated one talented video maker that he was now working (for the sheer joy of it, not for our money) on a tape featuring five of the heroes.

The Center for Environmental Innovation was an even loftier goal. The committee reported that it had had considerable success in raising funds for a center that would serve as a think tank, staffed in San Francisco, and tapping into the vast expertise of the Sierra Club membership. In its most mature incarnation, the committee said, it would do original research on environmental issues.

The need for calm, cerebral examination of the issues has become more and more critical as we solve the easy problems and are left to face complex moral, social, economic, and technological realities. If the Sierra Club, by existing for a century, can give birth to a place where this can happen, I think we can be inordinately proud.

Five luxuriously lazy days at home followed. It was springtime in New England. Skunk cabbage was unfurling at the wet edges of our meadow. Delicate white snowdrops had burst into bloom by our front doorstep. Buds on bushes and trees were swollen with promise. Our part of the planet was getting ready for renewal. I felt alive with the knowledge that miracles of birth were happening in the soil and the stone walls and the hollow trees all around me.

Connecticut environmentalists celebrate that feeling by having an auction to raise money to help elect good conservationists to the state legislature. As I had at the ELECT auction last year, in 1991 I donated homemade candy and a truckload of horse manure. I bought hand-painted T-shirts and the use of a friend's vacation home. It was a merry time.

Good thing, too. The next morning I had to be up at 5:00 a.m. to drive to Boston. One of our directors, Vivien Li, had arranged to hold a Finance Committee meeting in the conference rooms of her husband's law firm.

Unfortunately the elegant surroundings could not improve the news. Revenues showed no upswing. Like more and more American companies, our sales (new memberships) were down and our previously dependable repeat business (renewals) was weakening.

Should we cut marketing (direct mail and phone sales)? Or would that jeopardize revenues even further? Clearly we had to stop all hiring; we had budgeted an increase of more than $2 million for personnel services; could we instead persuade staff to accept a one-percent across-the-board salary reduction — if it would prevent selected layoffs? A two-percent increase in dues would raise $325,000, but what would it do to the elasticity of demand?

If we instituted a more stringent purchasing process, would it hold down spending or merely anger our volunteers? How could we decrease health care costs? Can a nationwide organization expect to keep more than 600,000 members informed for less than $918,000 in shipping and postage? Can we beef up the increase from outings without damaging the places we visit? How expensive is the recycled paper on which *Sierra* is printed? And, at least in my mind, the overriding doubt: would John Muir even want us to think like this? Would Mother Nature?

The only good news I heard all day was that the cost of a $330,000 global warming advertisement from the year before could be accounted for without adding it to this year's growing deficit. Yet, even that news, it seemed to me, smacked of a reduction in the quality of our main product: effective, enthusiastic advocacy.

Rain poured down all weekend. I was driving Arthur's tiny car (mine had been deemed inadequate for the long drive to Boston) and at one point, I remember packing six other dripping-wet people into it, for want of a taxicab.

I had promised myself that while I was in Boston, I would fulfill a long-standing desire. We had no TV at home and I had heard so much about "Saturday Night Live" that I really wanted to see it. That meant catching it some Saturday night when I was out of town. I had tried several times on the West Coast, but the time difference is such that I never could stay awake. I settled down at the hotel convinced that my chance had finally come. I snuggled under the warm blankets, my head full of words like "offset" and "shortfall" and "contingency" ... When I woke up three hours later, the TV screen was a vast field of electronic snow. I still have not yet seen "Saturday Night Live."

On Earth Day Twenty-One I flew to Washington, D.C., for three days of marathon lobbying on the Arctic and Bryan bills. I flew because staff had packed so many appointments with Senators and Congresspeople into my schedule that there was no time for the train. Too bad there is no lobbying Olympics. I would have set a record that week: twenty-five visits in three days!

And that included time out to do a video clip to be released via TV news satellite. The Sierra Club office consists of two adjoining townhouses in the southwest area of Washington—a

ten-minute walk to the Capitol. Our communications consultants took me out to a little park across the street and had an actor
interview me as if he were a reporter. We pushed the point that
increased gasoline mileage means big dollar savings for the
driver, as well as decreased air pollution and oil dependency.

Things were moving along at a fast clip on Capitol Hill.

• Markup had started on the Johnston-Wallop Bill. Our
tactic was to delay and complicate until the Bryan Bill could catch
up, but it wasn't working too well. Senators whom we counted
as friends did not want to play that game with relatively simple
sections of the bill. Perhaps our best weapon was Johnston's own
impatience. The National Academy of Sciences had recommended raising the CAFE standard from 27.5 to 32.5 miles per
gallon (still too low to suit us) and Johnston appeared likely to
offer that standard as an amendment to his own bill. Having
made that decision, he felt the Bryan Bill, which came out of the
Commerce Committee, ought to be treated as another, compet-
ing amendment. Senator Bryan, of course, insisted that it be
treated as a bill, not an amendment.That rumpus irritated Committee Chairman Senator Mitchell to no end. Along with Senator
Tower's unfortunate death, it gave us extra time.

• Sierra Club lobbyists had begun referring to increased
fleet mileage as the "oil field under Detroit," a resource so big that
it would be unnecessary to depend on our coasts, the Arctic
Refuge, or even the Middle East for oil. I thought it a lovely
metaphor, but it was by no means on everyone's lips. Instead,
otherwise perfectly rational legislators seemed to believe that
you could compromise: raise the CAFE a little, drill in the Arctic
a little. Ugh!

• The Democratic Task Force on Energy was meeting. The
majority seemed to favor considering the Bryan Bill separately,
but that didn't necessarily guarantee their yes votes.

• Two representatives, Jim Jontz (D-IN), and Bruce Vento
(D-MN), had offered bills protecting the ancient forests and the
critical habitat of the northern spotted owl. The administration
said it would announce new policy on that issue before the end
of the month.

• The Senate Environment Committee had held a hearing
on the Federal Facilities Compliance Act. Department of Energy

facilities, especially those producing weapons such as Rocky Flats in Colorado and Fernauld in Ohio, have a poor record for housekeeping. The problem of nuclear pollution has gotten far out of hand.

• The Sierra Club had recently conducted an international lobby week. Our members called on 80 Senate and 120 House offices asking that the United States take the lead at the G-7 meeting next July in halting all funding that contributes to destruction of primary rainforests.

• The World Bank held public hearings on its forestry plan and many environmentalists testified. We figured if we hung in long enough, eventually they would pay attention.

• Max Baucus (D-MT), Chair of the Senate Environment Committee, was going through maneuvers on the RCRA (Resource Conservation and Recovery Act) Reauthorization Bill that we didn't quite understand. We were meeting with him to discuss our concerns. This bill would keep important federal policies on waste management in place. We wanted some improvements, especially concerning municipal refuse.

The Sierra Club had established a Solid Waste Committee almost a year ago (partially with my discretionary funds). Because we knew this important law would be up for reauthorization, the committee had completed a final draft of a Platform for a Waste Campaign. It was being circulated for comment and was not yet public. However, we wanted to make sure that the Baucus Bill and our platform would be compatible.

Waste disposal, ash residue, toxics, hazardous materials, source reduction — the terms are confusing. Mixed municipal refuse is all of the stuff that is dumped in your town at the local landfill or incinerator or resource recovery plant. It includes food waste, paper, discarded household items, leaves, and, very often, the paper refuse, sweepings, broken objects, and so forth from the stores and small businesses in your area.

If all of this is buried in a landfill, it will take many years to decay. While that process is going on, rainwater will trickle through it, leach out various metals and then trickle on into the groundwater. The fluid, called leachate, that ends up in the groundwater consists of the solubles it has gone through, and thus it varies in content. It can be quite toxic stuff.

Many older landfills were also used as a final resting place for more serious dumping. Barrels of chemicals, wastes from metal finishing processes, construction debris — you name it, it's been found in a landfill.

As population increased and land grew scarcer — and as we realized that we were creating more waste than our winds and rivers could absorb for us — we switched to incinerators, recycling, composting, and source reduction, etc. But the fact remains: there is no easy answer. Waste pollutes, if not as leachate, then as gases released in burning, or as the ash that is the final product of a resources recovery plant. The choices we must make are tough. Even the obvious answer — reduce the quantity of what we throw away — has economic ramifications that fly in the face of modern marketing practices.

The Sierra Club's Waste Platform tries to cover all eventualities. It runs five and one half single-spaced pages, and, as it turned out, is far broader than Senator Baucus' bill. It starts out by asserting that states have the right to enact waste reduction, management, and disposal laws that are more stringent than federal laws (that's getting to be standard practice, since the Reagan and Bush administrations).

Its second general principle is that citizens and workers have the right to obtain comprehensive information on all toxic chemicals used and emitted into the environment from all major sources. No more giant corporations refusing to identify what they've dumped into the town sewer system.

Third, polluters should pay for their wastes.

Fourth, fees from waste generators should be used to fund state waste programs.

Fifth, wastes should be disposed of as close to their source of generation as possible. Now that's a big one. What about low-level radioactive waste, for instance? Many people in Connecticut are saying that even the tiny volume we generate should not be buried in the type of soil we live on — that it belongs out west in a desert somewhere. I think they have, as Jesse Jackson would say, "the science on their side." But the best incentive for reducing waste is to be required to get rid of it nearby.

Sixth, low-income and minority communities should not bear a disproportionate burden of waste disposal/treatment facilities.

After that the platform gets more specific. Perhaps most serious are: a call for a moratorium until 1996 on hazardous waste incinerator construction; a moratorium until the year 2000 on the construction of new municipal solid waste and medical incinerators; a federal mandate that packaging materials be returnable, recyclable, or made of recycled materials.

My home state, being small, densely populated, and affluent (rich people throw away more things), has had a very different solid-waste history than more spacious western states. Also, our long history of industrialization gives us more problems with old toxics. For these reasons, I am not entirely in synch with every one of the Sierra Club's recommendations (i.e. moratoria). However, I was impressed last April as I realized how thorough the committee had been, and I have come to believe it is the best outline of the problems facing the nation as a whole that I have yet seen.

While we fought the good fight in Washington, the Atlantic Chapter, like one of those punching bag toys that won't stay down, resumed its in-fighting. On April 23 my e-mail contained a long memo from Neil Fernbaugh describing the April 6 meeting of our recalcitrant New Yorkers.

Remember that I had been in Albany the day after their March meeting. They had agreed to a restructuring; our threat to suspend the chapter had been withdrawn; all seemed quiet.

"The March meeting," Neil wrote, "was attended by a large number of Board of Governance members representing a cross-section of the Atlantic Chapter. The April meeting, however, had a bare quorum, and was dominated by the New York City group. It was announced . . . that their intention was to have a one-day meeting. But by 6:00 p.m. the only significant thing they had done was to vote to reject the agreement and compromise on the restructuring that had been decided in March."

Neil described himself as shocked, angered, and disappointed. He recommended that we move at once to take over the chapter.

I read the memo almost as soon as I came home from Washington. Two things I had vowed to clean up while I was in office, the Atlantic Chapter problems and the SCLDF negotiations. Now time had run out on the former.

I slept at home on the 24th and set out early the next morning for the Fairfield Exchange Energy Show. Among a number of nuclear power and solar power proponents, I was the only one talking about CAFE standards and the sanctity of the Arctic.

That afternoon I got back on the train and went to New York City, where I was to be the dinner speaker at the Asia Society. They were sponsoring a workshop on environmental issues for people from nongovernment organizations in countries like India, Malaysia, and Thailand. The Sierra Club has a "twinning" program that pairs similarly sized Sierra units with overseas nongovernment organizations. The object is to share expertise and resources — and respect for each other's culture. Incidentally, they got my hooker joke!

Last winter, my name in an alumni magazine had garnered me a trip to Japan. On April 29, it got me to Darien, Connecticut, where, the next day, I was scheduled to speak to an assembly at the high school there. It was arranged by my friend, Lynn Carlson, whom I had not seen in twenty-three years, but who remembered me when she read about me.

Lynn met me at the train and took me to her home where I stayed for the night. We had an orgy of reminiscing; even tracked down another old chum for a phone conversation.

On the program with me the next morning was Terry Backer, the broad-shouldered, articulate, colorful "soundkeeper" — the person who serves as the watchdog of Long Island Sound. The funding for this job came as the settlement of a citizen's lawsuit against industrial polluters. Terry wears long, curly hair under a battered seaman's cap and a tiny gold anchor earring in his ear. I have never seen him dressed in anything but jeans and sneakers.

Terry grew up on an oyster boat and still earns some money by harvesting the natural products of Long Island Sound. In recent years, however, his anger about the pollution there has led him to an activist life. He is one of the most respected environmental lobbyists in the state.

At 9:00 a.m. we walked on stage together. We faced an auditorium full of squirming, barely awake youngsters. Having given up telling my hooker joke to younger audiences, I wondered how I would ever get their attention.

Terry knew how. He walked to the podium and asked, "How many of you here use Long Island Sound?" Only a few hands went up.

"Wrong!" he shouted, pounding on the podium, "You're all using it! You're using it for a toilet!"

Here was someone these kids could relate to. They quieted down and stared at him, fascinated. Happily, when he was finished, they extended the same courtesy to my remarks on energy and fuel efficiency.

I shared juice and cookies with the faculty and a few parents, then took off for the airport shuttle to LaGuardia, San Francisco, and — for one final try — more SCLDF negotiations.

May 1991

※

In a highly atypical move, the National Park Service took an adversarial stance concerning two coal-burning power plants planned for southern Virginia. The Park Service pointed to the smog that has cut viewing distances in Shenandoah National Park from sixty-five miles down to fifteen. The air pollution in this eighty-mile-long Blue Ridge Mountain park has grown so bad that it is damaging trout streams and killing ferns, flowers, and forests, Park Service officials charged. Also of concern: pollution problems in Great Smoky Mountain National Park on the Tennessee/North Carolina line, Acadia National Park in Maine, and the Grand Canyon National Park in Arizona.

"We're poised on the edge of disaster," warned J. William Wade, the Shenandoah Superintendent. "We've even had a couple of days up here when we've had to issue pollution health warnings."

The same kinds of industries and power plants blamed for air pollution in the Blue Ridge Mountains were indicted by maple syrup aficionados in the northeast. Sugar maples from the Appalachians to the Green Mountains, subjected to forty years of acid rain (much of it originating in the Ohio River Valley 500 miles away), were dying sooner and producing less sugar. A study of sugar maples on Camels Hump Mountain in Vermont found they measured a 24 percent decline in average height, width, and general bulk, and a decline of nearly 50 percent in the number of new trees, in the last twenty-five years.

"We think we are looking at the early stages of an epidemic problem," said the Director of the University of Vermont's Proctor Maple Research Center. He added that the threat to the sugar maples, based on the letters and calls he received, seemed to have far-reaching impact."*Sugar maples are like bald eagles and apple pie,*" he said, "*They're American.*"

Mother Nature's creatures were also the subject of assault in Golden, Colorado. When a workman at the Coors Brewery there mistakenly dumped more than 155,000 gallons of beer into a nearby creek, it killed an estimated 3,000 white suckers, bass fry, and trout.

In Indianapolis it was human beings, not fish, who were injured when illegally dumped petroleum wastes exploded. Marathon Oil subsequently paid $900,000 in fines and promised $3 million worth of environmental improvements. An explosion and fire at a house two miles from the plant injured two people and revealed that Marathon Oil had used an unauthorized pipe to bypass required pretreatment of its waste.

Excessive amounts of chrome, lead, ammonia, zinc, oil, and grease dumped into the Ohio River at three Pittsburgh Steel Corporation sites in Wheeling, West Virginia, cost that company a record $6 million civil penalty—pending approval of the settlement by a federal judge.

In Alaska, where a federal judge had refused to approve a complex negotiated settlement among the state, the federal government, and the Exxon Corporation regarding the Exxon Valdez oil spill, resolution of the case appeared to be years away. On May 3 the $1 billion agreement collapsed when Gov. Walter J. Hickel of Alaska and the Exxon Corporation formally withdrew.

"We're getting ready for trial," said Thomas A. Campbell, general counsel of the National Oceanic and Atmospheric Administration and a principal negotiator of the unraveling pact. "It's too complicated a problem to solve. Sometimes there are things that need to be resolved in court."

A lawsuit brought by an environmental group six years previously resulted in a final ruling "that is the most stringent in the world for lead in drinking water," EPA officials said on May 7. The agency directed 79,000 water utilities to test drinking water in homes and begin working toward a new standard two-thirds lower than the current standard of 50 parts of lead per billion parts of water. An estimated 230 million people would be affected, EPA said.

In Texas, it appeared that a multimillion-dollar gamble by Hunter Environmental Services, Inc. would also lead to court. The controversy involved underground salt domes outside Houston (said to be bigger in volume than Mount Everest). The need in America, and especially in

Texas, to provide for the safe disposal of hazardous waste is constantly growing. It was the passionate conviction of environmental consultant Keith Price that salt deposits — which have been known to withstand atomic blasts without leaking radiation — are the ultimate solution to the hazardous waste disposal problem.

Although Oliver A. Kimberly, Hunter's Chair, claimed that "the risk we face is 100 percent political," some environmentalists insisted that not all scientific questions had been answered. "If they [the Texas Water Commission] are going to approve a salt dome, (for hazardous waste storage) we'll take them to court," promised a senior attorney for the Natural Resources Defense Council.

The need for a major hazardous-waste burial ground in Texas was evident later in the month when the U.S. Environmental Protection Agency released its third annual Toxic Release Inventory. Texas released more toxic chemicals into the environment in 1989 than any other state, according to the inventory. Although many polluting industries are exempt, and the inventory depends almost entirely on voluntary reporting of legal emissions and discharges, it is considered the best indication the country has as to the amount of pollution burdening water, air, and land. In 1989, Texas's total came to 792.8 million pounds.

In New York State on May 17, documents were released by a Federal District Court indicating that wastes from the first atomic bomb, as well as an army chemical weapons plant, may have been buried at the infamous Love Canal site near Buffalo. Officials from Occidental Chemical Corporation said that more than 100 confidential memos, many of them dating back into the 1940s, would help prove that the U.S. Army should share responsibility for the toxic waste dump.

New Yorkers and Texans, however, could consider themselves lucky when compared to residents of Mexico City. The situation there was a classic example of what happens when too many people crowd into an area without sufficient water and waste disposal amenities to support their numbers. Population had grown from 5 million to roughly 16 million people in the last forty years, the New York Times *reported on May 12, and now the city had the dubious distinction of having the most polluted air of any major metropolitan area in the world.*

Along with explosive population growth, a combination of unfavorable geography, and (until recently), weak environmental regulations weakly enforced had created a fouled city. Because 30 percent of the people lived without toilets or sewer systems, not only industrial chemicals, but an estimated 600 tons of dried fecal dust became airborne each day.

When President Bush, in an effort to avoid delays in a free-trade pact with Mexico, agreed to include environmental considerations in the negotiations, he received praise from Jay D. Hair, President of the National Wildlife Federation. On the theory that international trade is increasingly "the basic way our planet's natural resources are allocated," Hair called formal international trade pacts "inherently statements of environmental policy." Environmentalists were divided on whether to support Bush in his efforts to "fast track" the agreement with Mexico.

Not only chemicals and municipal refuse were of concern to environmentalists in May of 1991. Waste Management, Inc. reported that in the preceding year more than 350 bills were introduced in thirty-six states to restrict the use of plastics, and 54 laws were enacted. Restrictions on disposal of "durable goods" and "bulky waste" such as appliances and autos were also on the increase. As a result, manufacturers said, they were beginning to incorporate concerns about eventual disposal into the initial design of the product.

Because plastic parts in automobiles make them lighter and hence more fuel efficient, it was not expected that their use would decrease. Rather, fewer kinds of resins, parts clearly marked for recycling, components that come apart more easily, and the avoidance of toxic chemicals were forecast by executives of both the automotive and appliance industries.

&

Automobile fuel efficiency saves money for the car owner, as well as cutting down on pollution. On May 1, 1991, after weeks of furious calculations, the Sierra Club issued a different press release in more than a dozen states. Each release estimated how much money per household might be saved annually if the Bryan Bill passed; named the Senators from that state who would (or would not) vote for the bill; and told how they had voted on the Bryan Bill the previous year.

To arrive at the dollar savings, we used state-by-state gas tax data from the Motor Vehicle Manufacturers Association, as well as projections from the Census Bureau, the Department of Transportation, and the American Council for an Energy Efficient Economy. To allow time for the new low-emission vehicles to be available, our projection was for the year 2010. The savings were impressive, ranging from a low of $422 in New York to a high of $1,443 in Florida.

It was also an impressive public relations coup, since it involved personalizing the press releases and then targeting key media outlets across the country with the appropriate numbers. I hoped that this appeal to the pocketbook combined with concern about clean air would motivate people to contact their Senators. There is no way to measure the results of such an effort, but we received many accolades from local chapters.

While I was working the media, Michael Fischer hit every Senator with a long and serious letter condemning the Johnston-Wallop Bill and singing the praises of the Bryan approach.

We scheduled a major energy brainstorming session for Sierra leaders on May 28, and I experienced the first real shock of knowing that I was not indispensable. By May 28 I would be gone. Not only would we have elected a new President, but (since Club rules call for a year off the Board of Directors after six years on) I also would have lost my seat on the national Board. Although past Presidents are welcomed everywhere, they have no official role. Truth to tell, it hurt more than a little to hear people all around me eagerly discussing our future energy strategy, as if they expected to do just fine without me.

One continuing problem I had hoped to clear away before my term expired was our relationship with the Sierra Club Legal Defense Fund. Hopes for a resolution were dim, however, as I joined the SCLDF team at the beginning of the month.

They wanted a license to use our name. We were proposing a "rolling license" concept, which would involve periodic review and renewal. They wanted more protection than that: termination of the license only for cause, and then only after an elaborate process of notice, mediation, and arbitration.

After a brief opening session, we separated so that our mediator, Dave Pesonen, could talk to each group separately. When he emerged from a rather long session with the lawyers, Dave told us he wanted to put a new proposal into the negotiations. He said he knew it was unusual for a mediator to suggest a solution, but that he thought we might be too close to the trees to be able to get a fix on the forest.

I was amused since forestry issues were actually at the heart of the SCLDF controversy. However, I was impressed by what he suggested.

He said we needed to recognize that we would always want control of our name and that SCLDF would always want more independence. He felt that, ultimately, the most sensible way to resolve the situation was with an orderly move toward a name change for SCLDF.

It was so simple, so obvious; yet nobody before had said it quite that way. I thought to myself that it was like coming to the end of the fossil fuel era. You can ignore the inevitable and run the risk of having to confront it in an atmosphere of catastrophe, or you can acknowledge that it's coming and plan for an orderly transition.

The most important element in an orderly transition, Dave said, would be that it was shared by both organizations. Each would need to take responsibility for the success of the transition. Also, each would have to be clearly committed to the idea that both organizations would emerge at the end not only OK, but perhaps even better and stronger.

Both sides gathered for dinner and, for the first time in months, I felt a sense of shared optimism. We were all still very cautious, and affecting hard-headed exteriors, but we were also talking.

We agreed that the name change idea gave us a starting point for solving some of our other disagreements.

The lawyers said they would still want us to be their premier client. We said that was fine because such an arrangement would force us to finalize an internal comprehensive litigation strategy.

Before the meal was over, we had agreed that Michael Fischer and a SCLDF representative would visit a professional "image consultant" to get some advice on a name change. We had by no means achieved closure, but I felt able to relax a little on this subject, and that made my approaching retirement a bit easier to accept.

The Sierra Club Board of Directors is elected in April via written ballot of the entire membership. In 1991, 73,944 members voted. The new Board holds its first official meeting in May. Just prior to that meeting (this is where you came in), the new Board holds a get-acquainted pre-Board meeting and elects its own officers.

In April 1991, the leaders of the national Sierra Club were surprised by the results of the national election. Of the three incumbents up for reelection, only one made it. Our fifteen-member Board would have four new members during the coming year.

I spent a few moments pondering what had happened. Were our members sending a message of discontent? Or was this a sign of increased grassroots activism? There was no way to read it — and no time. If we were going to bring four novices up to speed on matters as complex as the Centennial and our financial problems before the May meeting, we had a lot of educating to do.

I did take time out, however, to celebrate Annie's birthday. The May Board meeting was being postponed this year for one week because of a Centennial Symposium — so for the first time in a decade I was in Connecticut for my daughter's fourteenth birthday.

She wanted a party, but Loomis day-students are so widely scattered it wasn't feasible. Instead we settled on a restaurant dinner and movie for Annie and three girlfriends. Since my car is so disreputable, we rented a car big enough to accommodate me, Arthur, and the four girls (thank heaven for frequent flyer coupons; you can rent cars with them). At the Great American Cafe in Glastonbury, Connecticut, Arthur and I sat inconspicuously at a side table, as we also did at the Meryl Streep movie ("Defending Your Life"), and, later, while the girls ate ice cream at Friendly's. I dropped the last of our guests off somewhere near the Massachusetts border at 12:15 a.m. and began an hour's trek back home. Annie declared the evening a huge success and, come to think of it, I had a good time too.

For most of those few days in Connecticut, I was on the telephone or at my computer. Time seemed to be running out so swiftly; there were so many loose ends. I wanted to leave the Club with everything in perfect order, but as fast as I unsnarled one situation, another one tangled up.

Arthur and Annie, who had been practicing for sainthood all year, were really put to the test. I suppose they saw the end in sight and were glad that I would finally be staying home. However, the way I was behaving, I don't understand why they wanted me back.

I arrived at the Audubon Canyon Ranch in Bolinas on Wednesday, May 8. I hugged my old friends and did my best to make the newcomers feel welcome. I took a long walk by myself, inhaled the eucalyptus, and trotted out my memories one by one. Then I took a really deep breath and went back to the lodge to watch this year's candidates politick.

We used the scenarios that the Planning Committee had recently devised as a framework in which to explore—for the benefit of the new members—the relationship of the Board with its major committees and the role of the volunteer. In a Club growing ever more complex, we tried to decide how to delegate more effectively and how to keep the lines of responsibility clear.

Each of the outgoing members was asked to give a final speech, to talk about his or her joys, regrets, and hopes for the new Board.

When it was all over—the election, the congratulations, the speeches—I went quietly outside and piled my sleeping bag and other gear into the back of my rental car. Our new President, Phillip Berry, had served as President once before, twenty years ago, and certainly did not need me peering over his shoulder.

The road back to San Francisco winds along the Pacific coast. It was lit by a lovely crescent moon; stars filled the sky; the wind was brisk, but didn't quite drown out the distant sounds of the surf. I was totally alone after a hectic, people-filled year. I found I didn't want to listen to the radio and I didn't want to think. So I looked and I listened and I breathed in the smells of a California night, and I tried to keep my mind a blank.

My destination was the Richelieu where Arthur and Annie would, I knew, be asleep by the time I arrived. I let Annie rest, but I tugged at Arthur. "It's over," I said. "Phil Berry is the new President." Arthur woke up enough to smile and pat my hand. "S'nice," he said before he sank back into sleep.

The next two days were wonderful. I had expected to feel left out. Instead, at the Board meeting I was hugged so many times I began to feel bruised. My right hand was sore from being shaken, but my ego was so swathed in compliments that I was incapable of feeling pain.

They gave my final report a standing ovation, then we seated the Directors, they held their formal election, and it was my duty to pass the gavel — my gavel — to Phillip Berry. I felt numb, mostly. I saw this ceremony as an important and formal tradition. At the same time, I knew that Annie and Arthur had taken Phil's eight-year-old son shopping at Ghiradelli Square. It completed the circle, and had its own importance, this informal tradition.

In the late afternoon I returned to my hotel room, donned a dressy dress I had bought for the Jesse Jackson trip, and went with my friend, former Director Marty Fluharty to pick up our dinner speaker, Dr. Wangari Maathai. I needn't have worried about my appearance. Walking with this stunning Black woman, in her draped African print and braided hair, I was all but invisible.

Our annual dinner was being held at the Sheraton Palace, one of San Francisco's grand hotels, damaged in the recent earthquake and now splendidly refurbished. It was like stepping back into the gilded era. I fancied I saw John Muir himself, striding across the lobby (and probably wishing he could get out of town).

I ushered Wangari to the head table and looked out at the nearly 600 people taking their seats. They were noisy and good natured, most of them in very high spirits. I had learned one trick in this past year. Instead of trying to shout them into attention, I put my mouth close to the microphone and breathed a long, low "ssshhhhh." They quieted down at once.

I introduced myself, then asked the Directors to stand and stay standing. Then, in order, I asked the Trustees, the Council, the Regional Vice-Presidents, the chapter activists, etc., to do the same. When almost the entire group was on its feet, I said, "Now anybody who would like to send a message to George Bush that drilling in the Arctic is NOT a substitute for a rational energy policy, please stand." Everyone seated rose, and the entire room let out a roar of approval. With that, we got down to business.

Dr. Maathai started the Green Belt Movement in Nairobi, Kenya, and led the fight against commercial development in that city's largest public open space. Activism like hers was unheard of in her country at the time, and she has become an international heroine. I had insisted on a woman speaker and I was right. As she told us how she worked to get her government to pay women to plant trees in her semi-arid land, and to pay more for each year that they survived, her eyes shone and her accomplishments glowed like a beacon for the rest of us.

At the conclusion of her speech, the Sierra Club presented Dr. Maathai with our Earth Care Award. A month earlier, she had been a recipient of the prestigious Goldman Environmental Prize. The Goldmans give six large cash awards each year, one for each inhabited continent, for outstanding grassroots environmental efforts. It was good to know that our invitation and award decision had been in the works simultaneously but independently with the Goldman Prize. *

There were other heroes to be honored. The videotape made about five of the grassroots activists chosen from our *One Hundred Heroes* publication was shown on a huge screen. It was visually exciting and deeply moving. I saw a good many handkerchiefs dabbing at tears as the lights came up.

As a shoo-in for the Outgoing President's Award, I wasn't surprised when my turn came. I was delighted, though, by the handsomely framed picture of John Muir with which I was presented. I asked Arthur and Annie to join me at the podium and told the crowd, "For everyone like me who gets to stand here and feel your love, there are people like these who have to bake their own birthday cakes, go off alone to parents nights, and even, in Arthur's case, go out behind the barn and bury a dead horse alone."

Our fellow Sierrans cheered my family enthusiastically. They knew that Arthur and Annie deserved their accolades.

The culmination of the evening was the presentation of the John Muir Award by our beloved former President and still active Director, Edgar Wayburn, to the two women from Alaska whom I had nominated, Ginny Woods and Celia Hunter. They made modest thank-you speeches and mentioned how pleased they were to share the evening with Wangari Maathai. My determination to spotlight women's contributions to the environmental movement had paid off handsomely with three de-

---

*In January 1992, *Time* magazine reported that Wangari Maathai had been arrested and jailed in Kenya for "rumermongering."

serving and delightful individuals in the forefront of our festivities.

That Saturday morning when I called to order the last Board meeting I would chair. The President's Report — my swan song — came early on the agenda. I told them this:

"Every Sierra Club President probably thinks that his or her time in office must surely have come at one of the most important times in environmental history. I'm no different. I believe that, when they write the books, this past year will be considered a watershed time for the environment.

"Looking back just one year, I remember what we had going for us last May. We had the euphoria of Earth Day; we had politicians lining up to see who could out-green the other; we had corporations rushing to market their wares to the new green consumer. I clearly remember thinking that we organized environmentalists were in the driver's seat. We would write the agenda for the new era.

"Something rather momentous happened, however, on August 2 when Iraq invaded Kuwait. Suddenly the resources and attention of the world were refocused, and energy issues and all the implications of their importance to the environment took center stage. Global warming, with all its related issues, the Arctic National Wildlife Refuge, and conservation had long been on our agenda, but they came together abruptly in a way that challenges all we know about the public policy process.

"Our energy future — our willingness to take charge, as a society, of whether or not we will live securely in a world where our last pristine wild places and the atmosphere and climate we depend on will be sacrificed to shortsightedness and greed — hangs in the balance right now, in an epic battle in Washington. I believe that we will be judged both as an organization and as a society on how well we respond.

"I believe that the history books will say that we came to the brink and that either we passed the Bryan Bill and protected the Arctic or that we went over the edge. We have a lot of work to do, my friends. I know we often use rhetoric like, 'This is the fight of our lives,' but, by golly, if this isn't something very like that fight, I don't know what is.

"We're here this weekend also to begin the celebration of one hundred years of Sierra Club history. History is useful for lots of reasons, but it has proved most useful to me lately as a source of comfort. The Club has confronted staggering issues before, and we're still here, stronger and better than ever. When they write the book about the next hundred years, I feel sure that they will say that we met the challenges and made the world better.

"Your President gets to see the Club, in all its wonderful variety, as no one else does. I have seen how the Sierra Club turns itself to a huge issue, all the way from the halls of Congress to local group meetings. I have seen the pieces all come together — thirteen simultaneous press conferences around the country; Congressmen who say, 'Enough with the letters already. You've got my vote'; and I'm here to tell you that it's impressive. I never get over the thrill of it.

"I'm also here to tell you that there is something like a special force field that holds us together and makes it all work. I don't know if it's electric or magnetic or what, but it's bigger than any of the individuals that make it up and it binds us together in wonderful ways.

"It will hum in this room today; you'll feel it at the annual dinner tonight; it sometimes sings in the e-mail wires; it has to do with why, wherever you may go, you will feel at home in a room full of Sierra Club people; it's why, when I travelled to some remote spot and didn't know who would be there or where I would sleep that night, it always turned out just fine; it has to do with why, if Polk Street yawned open one day and swallowed up the Club office, even with all the Directors in it, the Club would keep right on going, reinventing itself.

"Amuse yourself sometime by thinking about how long it would take to stamp out all the traces of the Sierra Club. Those traces twinkle in the eyes of the Presidents whose pictures are lined up on the wall in the office watching the current President do his or her work.

"So maybe we're not always nimble. Maybe we lumber a bit now and then because we have a large and complicated organization, but, by God, there's something magical about how, when it really needs to come together around here, it does. It has to do just this in the next few years, and I know it will.

"To have been swept up and danced around with you in this force field will be a treasured memory for me. As a matter of fact, I thought about coming here today dressed up in all my souvenirs from the past year. I would have had my press credential that identified me with *Sierra* magazine from our visit to the G-7 summit, a picture taken with Jesse Jackson in the ancient forest, my Costa Rican T-shirt, a bracelet put on my

wrist by a Penan tribesman who came to Washington to publicize the plight of his people in a vanishing rainforest, the
snowshoes presented to us by the Cree and Inuit Indians on the
shores of James Bay in Great Whale.

"When I got to the cast-iron dragon from Japan, I realized
that visual souvenirs weren't the most practical ones to carry.
The best souvenirs are the ones you carry in your mind. I have
a long list of pinch-me experiences — the ones where you say
to yourself, 'How did I ever get here?' The best souvenir of all,
though, is the memory of your love and commitment to our
little fragile planet. Thank you for a wonderful year."

Late Sunday morning, when Arthur and Annie boarded
the plane for home, I was at long last able to go with them. I have
worked for the environment all of my adult life, but this past year
had been very special. I had put family and home and even some
of my most personal needs in the background. Out of my forty-
plus years of existence, I had given one for the earth.

I leaned my head on Arthur's shoulder, sleepy, a little
proud, and totally content.

Epilogue

&

In May of 1991, after one frenetic year as its President, six busy years on its Board, and almost twenty years in the trenches, the Sierra Club sent me home to rest up. It's not an easy thing to live and breathe an organization's people and problems and then abruptly find oneself put out to pasture.

A former President once said, "It's like the postman has forgotten where you live and the phone's been disconnected."

It takes a while to adjust to the fact that, if things run amok, it's not your responsibility. It takes even longer to disengage from the day-to-day lives of your colleagues. The Sierra Club works hard to keep its past Presidents involved and informed. It's just not the same, though, as having all those bucks—for better or for worse—stop at your desk.

It is not, however, altogether disagreeable to be washed up into the arms of your family, to be back home in Connecticut in mid-May. The lilacs were just coming into bloom when I came home from that last Board meeting. The daffodils had gone, but the azaleas were in full flower, and the rhododendrons promised me that if I stayed home long enough they would give me a dazzling show.

For the first few days I busied myself with getting the farrier and the horse vet to come and ready our barnyard citizens for the summer: trimmed-up hooves, shots, worm medicine, the works. I began to dream of long-postponed house renovations, of some fresh paint here and new curtains there.

Then I set about the process of writing a resume and searching for a dream job — the one that would be as challenging as the Sierra Club presidency and pay enough to fulfill my promise to Arthur. He had hung in there through a year of craziness; now I would make it all worthwhile. I determined to take my time, to chart a course slowly and deliberately, and for once in my life to make conscious, rational choices. Hitherto I had been more likely to be drawn into some vacuum — without much of a fight — than to follow a careful plan. No more, I vowed.

Opportunities are funny, though. They defy planning; they offer themselves without warning. If you are open, willing to allow an opportunity to grab you and twirl you around, you can have some wonderful adventures.

On an otherwise unremarkable June day, an old friend casually mentioned that the position of chief elected official of East Haddam would be open in the next election.

The incumbent had chosen not to run again, my friend said, and the Democrats (of which I am one) were looking for a candidate. Maybe, he suggested, I could just come down and talk to the party leaders. No obligation, or anything like that. I felt the familiar pull of the vacuum, of an opportunity inviting me to dance.

Five months later — after knocking on a thousand doors, mailing many thousands of brochures, attending caucuses and forums and any venue for a speech that I could find — I became the First Selectman (equivalent to a mayor) of the town of East Haddam. The needs of 6,700 people residing within 57 square miles, the maintenance of a hundred miles of town roads, all the challenges of sewage, garbage, potholes, contract negotiations, school buses, state funding, and property taxes are now the meat and potatoes of my daily life. The subject matter is a little different from the Sierra Club agenda, but the demands are surprisingly similar.

One night, just a few days before the election, I was out knocking on doors. In this country town, you must drive from door to door if you ever hope to get anywhere. On the car radio came the news that the Johnston-Wallop Bill had been dealt a resounding defeat in the U. S. Senate.

Defeat of that bill — which embodied the Bush energy policy— had become the focus of the Sierra Club's energy strategy. All the threads of that victory had been spun during my presidency. I whooped a cheer and startled my running mate in the seat next to me. He had no way of knowing how proud I was of that victory and of the organization that pulled it off.

Yes, I know, many organizations worked together to defeat the Johnston-Wallop Bill, but this was the Sierra Club's specialty: the long, slow building of a grassroots effort; the painstakingly targeted clout; the endless pressure, endlessly applied.

I wished that I could be at the Sierra victory party, but just at that moment I was determined to create my own victory party. Small-town government, it seemed to me, really would put to the test that bumper sticker philosophy, "Think globally, act locally."

As for Annie and Arthur, ever supportive, they worked hard on the campaign and they cheered as loudly as anyone when we won. Now they have a mom who sleeps at home every night, but who is greatly distracted much of the time.

I sometimes catch glimpses of what it must be like for Arthur and Annie to find themselves so often second place in my life, behind some organization, behind other people's needs, while I pursue my dreams in the big world. One moment, especially, caught me off guard and hit me hard.

In the early part of the election campaign, I put Annie on a plane for Buffalo, for her annual summer visit with her grandparents. The airport in Hartford is nearly as familiar to me as my own backyard, but this time I was checking the gates and boarding passes for someone else. I sat with Annie in the waiting area, and when it was time for her to go through the door and onto the plane I hugged her hard and wished her godspeed.

I watched the plane back away from the gate, taxi across the tarmac, and disappear behind the terminal. I knew that it would soon come roaring back up the runway and lift off into the distance toward the west. And so it did, that plane carrying my beautiful child, and I lifted it up safely into the sky with my heart.

I turned away from the airport window when the plane was a speck in the sky. I felt very sad. I was already lonesome for Annie, but there was something else: a feeling that the wrong person had gone flying, a transient envy because it was not me up there in the blue. I began to think of the times—in the hundreds, I suppose — when my family lifted me up with their hearts and sent me into the sky. "It's something she has to do," I imagined them saying.

It may seem maudlin now to describe my feelings that day as I walked back up the airport concourse, but I was learning something. The gift of a chance to soar off into one's dream— to be allowed to dance with a shining opportunity— is not something to take for granted. I hope, and expect, to go on dancing the rest of my life, though I doubt there will ever be another year like the one I gave for the Earth.